THROUGH
BLOOD AND
SWEAT

A REMEMBRANCE TREK
ACROSS SICILY'S
WORLD WAR II BATTLEGROUNDS

MARK ZUEHLKE

THROUGH
BLOOD AND
SWEAT

Douglas & McIntyre

DOUGLAS AND MCINTYRE (2013) LTD.
P.O. Box 219, Madeira Park, BC, V0N 2H0
www.douglas-mcintyre.com

Edited by Kathy Vanderlinden
Dustjacket typeset by Shed Simas
Text design by Mary White
Front cover photographs:
ollirg/Veer photo (top); Terry Rowe photo, LAC PA-132779 (bottom)
Maps by C. Stuart Daniel
Author photo by Laura Sawchuk
Printed and bound in Canada
Printed on 100% PCW

Douglas and McIntyre (2013) Ltd. acknowledges the support of the Canada Council for the Arts, which last year invested $157 million to bring the arts to Canadians throughout the country. We also gratefully acknowledge financial support from the Government of Canada through the Canada Book Fund and from the Province of British Columbia through the BC Arts Council and the Book Publishing Tax Credit.

Cataloguing data available from Library and Archives Canada
ISBN 978-1-77162-009-3 (cloth)
ISBN 978-1-77162-010-9 (ebook)

[CONTENTS]

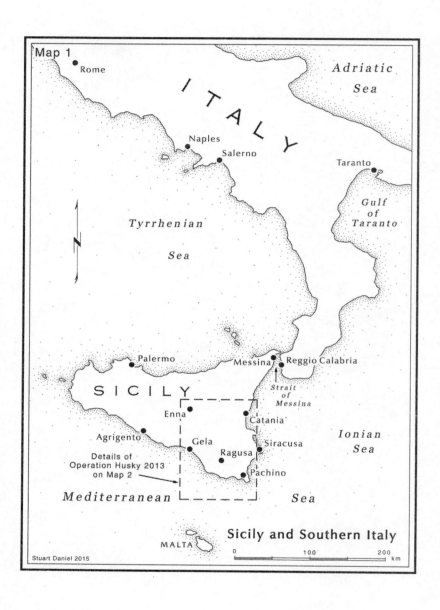

Map 1

Rome

I T A L Y

Naples

Salerno

Taranto

Adriatic

Sea

Tyrrhenian

Sea

Gulf
of
Taranto

N

Palermo

Messina

Reggio Calabria

S I C I L Y

Strait
of
Messina

Enna

Catania

Ionian
Sea

Agrigento

Gela

Siracusa

Ragusa

Details of
Operation Husky 2013
on Map 2 →

Pachino

Mediterranean

Sea

MALTA

Sicily and Southern Italy

0   100   200
                        km

Stuart Daniel 2015

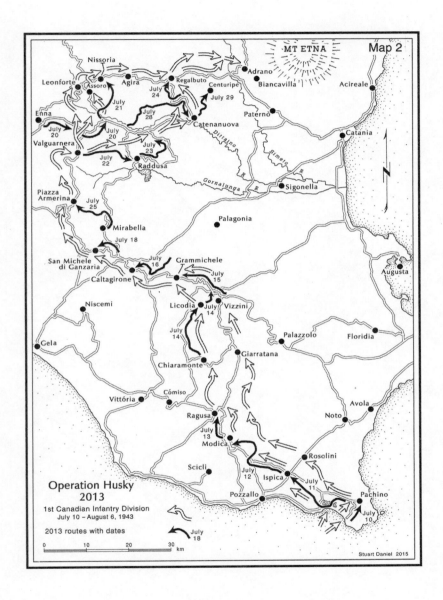

I Will Bring Others

ON AUGUST 2, 2006, Steve Gregory, a Montreal businessman, stands under a blazing sun before a tall stone cross at the centre of the Canadian War Cemetery in Agira, Sicily. He wears baggy khaki shorts, a red T-shirt with "CANADA" emblazoned across it in large white letters, and wraparound sunglasses. Set at the summit of a gentle hill, the cross has a long, bronze, downward-pointing sword mounted on either side of its face and seems to guard the orderly rows of pale marble headstones that extend from its base down either slope. Sixteen rows, eight to each side, containing 504 graves, 490 of which hold the remains of Canadians killed in World War II, and the rest from other Commonwealth countries. Thirteen are airmen who died serving in the Royal Canadian Air Force; the others are army. All died between July 10 and August 6, 1943, during the Allied invasion of Sicily, known as Operation Husky.

This is Steve's first visit to a Commonwealth War Cemetery. He has been drawn to this small, isolated one to find the graves of two men he has read about, Lieutenant Colonel Bruce Sutcliffe and Captain Maurice Herbert Battle Cockin. He has come to pay his respects.

Locating the two graves takes twenty minutes. Each headstone, like those of all the Canadians, features a maple leaf set inside a circle. An inscription below provides the rank, name, and citations won. Both men had served with the Hastings and Prince Edward Regiment of Ontario, familiarly known as the Hasty Ps. Steve knows they suffered mortal wounds in the same moment on July 20. Sutcliffe had died instantly, but Cockin lingered until the next morning, so the dates given are one day apart. Sutcliffe's family had provided no inscription for the headstone. The one on Cockin's reads: "Here my beloved England lives. Go tell the English why I died." Cockin had been born in Mortlake, Surrey, and educated at Cambridge before immigrating to Canada.

After photographing both headstones and spending a few minutes of silence before them, Steve wanders back toward the entrance. On his way out, he glances at the headstone of another soldier, a private. The man's name and regiment mean nothing to him; just another soldier killed in Sicily. Yet a small inner voice suddenly insists, "Hey, why don't you say thanks to this guy?" His eyes move to the adjacent headstone. "Or this guy? When was the last time someone said thanks to these guys? You can't just stand there." The voice is rebuking him!

Approaching the private's grave, Steve rests a hand on the cool marble and offers what he considers a genuine thank you. Later, he would recount: "Then I moved to the next. Each time, I read the headstone and said a variation of a thank you. I tried to do this slowly, so that each man received a genuine thank you. I didn't get through three graves before tears were streaming down my face. About three hours later, I left the cemetery, but before I did, I went to the spot where they have a guest book. There were very few names. I moved to the gate and stood for a moment. As I dried my face, I said aloud, 'I will be back and I will bring others. You will not be forgotten. Canadians will know.'"

Shaken by his unexpectedly strong response to this visit, Steve continues on his journey to honour the memories of Sutcliffe and Cockin. He drives to nearby Monte Assoro. It was this mountain that Lieutenant Colonel Sutcliffe and Captain Cockin, the Hasty Ps' intelligence officer, had been discussing when they were hit and fatally wounded that day in July 1943. They had been planning how to wrest its summit from the Germans.

The two officers had died, but their plan survived, and its execution by the Hasty Ps that night had yielded a legendary victory. The Hasty Ps had scaled the slope, driven the surprised German defenders from the summit, and then held it until relieved two days later.

Having driven to Monte Assoro's summit, Steve finds a plaque that recounts the tale. Standing beside the plaque, he looks over the cliff edge and realizes that it was *right here* that the Hasty Ps had swarmed onto the summit. This place where Canadians and Germans had both died was, he decides, as sacred as the cemetery. So he must bring people here as well. How he will do this, Steve has no idea. But the pledge had been made back at the Agira cemetery, and he reaffirms it now. And he will stake his honour on fulfilling it.

WHEN THE PHONE rang, I was looking out into our backyard from the kitchen window and not caring for the view. It was a dark, dreary day. The temperature hovered near freezing with little prospect of warming. A stiff westerly wind blew, and forecasters were warning that it might even snow. For Victoria, snowfall warnings are serious. A couple of centimetres can bring the city to a standstill because it's always slippery, icy stuff. Cars spin out, drivers skid into intersections against the lights because they allow insufficient room to stop, and one accident follows another. It was December 13, 2008, and a Saturday. Christmas shoppers would be out in hordes. I had just decided it was a good day to stay home, maybe do some housecleaning. Keep clear of the chaos soon to reign. The ring interrupted those thoughts. I don't like taking calls on weekends, but this time I picked up.

A man identified himself as Steve Gregory from Montreal. He had just finished reading my book *Operation Husky* and praised it mightily. Said it was a great read, a huge contribution to Canada's historical memory. More than that, it was a personal godsend. With an enthusiasm I soon came to know well, Steve described his ambition to organize and execute a major act of remembrance in Sicily to coincide with the seventieth anniversary of Canada's participation in Operation Husky. At best, he planned to have hundreds of Canadians marching across Sicily in the footsteps of those soldiers who had done the same in 1943. At worst, he would walk alone. One way or the other, Operation Husky 2013 would happen.

And my book was heaven-sent, he said, because it gave him—as no other source to date had—the full story, one that would enable him to put flesh on his vision. *Operation Husky* had hit bookstore shelves little more than a month earlier. It was the first book dedicated to telling the story of the Canadian army's experience in the Allied invasion of Sicily.

Not only was Steve extremely thankful for the book, he was keen to get me involved in his plan to turn Operation Husky 2013 into a reality. He promised an explanatory email later that day. After he rang off, I went back to looking out at the cold, grey day as I wondered what to make of the conversation.

"Who was that?" my partner, Frances, asked.

I muttered a little grumpily what Steve had said about himself and the project. A Montreal businessman with a crazy scheme that he wanted to involve me in. Was he legitimate? Damned if I knew. Usually, when I get calls from people with bizarre schemes, I find it fairly easy to put them off or humour them, and in short order they disappear of their own accord. Recently, for example, an alleged film-maker boarding a flight from New York to Los Angeles had rapidly and breathlessly declared that he loved my *Ortona* and wanted to make it into a feature movie. He promised to call once he landed in LA or a few days later when he was to arrive in Vancouver. I was hardly surprised to never hear from him again. It seems there are hordes of people who are trying to broker deals and are possessed of a hummingbird's attention span.

Such people usually promise follow-up emails, which do not materialize, and I consider that a good thing. Life is busy enough without getting immersed in schemes that require investing time that is never paid for despite fulsome assurances. I had learned this the hard way over years of writing for a living. I was beyond healthy skepticism. My fallback position was to just not get involved, invoke the "too-busy" mantra, and sever the connection.

But my sense of Steve Gregory and his project was that neither he nor it was going to go away. It might be something worthwhile or something I would regret ever hearing about. But my instinct was that I was running a fairly high risk of entanglement. The challenge would be to ensure that I was the one controlling the nature and degree of it.

About five hours later, I was reading Steve's email. "What a beautiful piece of work you have delivered. I will buy cases of your books for distribution to my friends and associates." I was surprised to see that this thing already had some legs. In a ninety-second YouTube clip of surprisingly high production standards, Steve described the essence of the plan. He and a group of people he had recruited were seeking to bring together five hundred Canadians to spend thirty-three days retracing by foot the "exact path" that Canada's soldiers had taken on those same days. Every day, at 11:00 a.m., the marchers would pause for what amounted to a quasi–Remembrance Day ceremony, which included reading out the names of the men killed on that particular day. In the evening, he hoped that a nearby parish would hold a mass to honour the Sicilians who had also perished in the fighting. Canadian high school students would be enlisted to individually research the background of each of the 490 soldiers who fell in Sicily, and the students would be taken there in 2013 as part of the project. The final act would take place in Agira Canadian War Cemetery, where Steve planned to bring together enough Canadians to answer a roll call, one by one, for every buried soldier. That was the plan, the dream.

My book, he said in the email, had cut their research requirements by 75 per cent. "If you considered joining us in any way, we would be honoured," he wrote. Since starting the campaign to launch Op Husky, Steve had founded the 3rd Battery of Montreal Artillery (Field), a volunteer organization that supported the veterans and cadets associated with the city's 2nd Field Regiment, Royal Canadian Artillery. He had also become the president of the Montreal chapter of Canada Company, a non-partisan charity that supports Canadian Forces personnel and armed forces veterans. Steve wanted to hire me to provide some historical expertise.

"My project in 2013 has become an obsession," the email continued. "Honouring the souls of those who fell in Sicily has been my

mission since my visit to Agira in 2006. Your work will catapult forward the possibility that the souls of these men will be remembered
by all Canadians."

Remembered by all Canadians. That was a resonating theme, one
that Steve had voiced in his YouTube video. And I had written basically the same thing in the epilogue to *Operation Husky*: "Canada's
participation in the Sicily invasion is not well remembered. Even
those who are aware that Canadians fought in Italy are often oblivious to the Sicilian part of the story. Twenty-eight days of grinding
combat have been easily forgotten." The book had been my attempt
to rectify this situation. Now here was a man—and despite his
recruited group of Canadians, I sensed this remained largely a one-
man operation—who sought to do the same in a totally unique way. I
thought it over. Maybe, just maybe, this could work. I would cautiously maintain contact and see where things went. That evening, I
emailed Steve an invitation to further discussion. In the back of my
mind I was thinking, hell, maybe I'd even become one of the marchers. Walking across Sicily in the heat of summer was an appealing
idea on that December day when by evening, light snow carried on a
bitter wind swirled around the backyard.

WHY HAD STEVE Gregory gone to Agira cemetery—the event that
had led to his obsession—in the first place? Why such a deep fascina-
tion with those two officers and the Canadian assault on Monte
Assoro? I soon learned that it all led back to 2004 and a chance
encounter with a Sicilian campaign veteran that Steve invited to dinner. On a spring evening, former Bombardier Charles Hunter sat at
the Gregory family's dining table in their home in Westmount, Quebec, spinning tales of war. In 1943, Hunter had been a
twenty-three-year-old artilleryman in the 7th Battery of 2nd Field
Regiment.

A grainy black-and-white photo shows him in Sicily, sitting on a
small metal seat at a 25-pounder's gunsight. He is lanky and terribly
thin. He wears a woollen cap, short-sleeved shirt, and knee-length
shorts held up by a wide leather belt. As an artilleryman, Hunter had
not scaled Monte Assoro. But his gun, along with the other

twenty-five of 2nd Regiment, had provided almost continuous fire support after the Hasty Ps seized the summit. Hunter, like the other gunners, had stripped to his shorts and still sweated in the terrific heat as the heavy shells were loaded and the firing lanyards pulled.

His grey hair and eyebrows still thick, eyes bright and alert, the now eighty-four-year-old Hunter was a gifted storyteller possessed of an excellent memory. As he described the amazing feat of the infantrymen who took that mountain, eleven-year-old Erik Gregory's eyes had widened in awe. After the dinner, Erik—who had been looking for a subject for a Grade 6 history project—declared that he would write and direct a brief interview with Hunter, create a model 25-pounder under the veteran's direction, and construct a diorama of Monte Assoro and surrounding terrain in which it could be placed. Presentation boards featuring maps and explanatory text in French would follow.

As Steve watched Erik pour his heart into the project, he too became completely engrossed in the Canadian campaign in Sicily. Steve had never been a soldier, never studied military history, and knew little of what Canadians had done in World War II. In university he had studied law and political science. His career path had taken him into management consulting focused on organizational development, training, and group facilitation. He had founded a company, IsaiX Technologies Inc., in 1989 and had been at its helm ever since.

Steve knew his knowledge of war was scant, but it was easy to recognize the incredible courage displayed by the men who ascended that mountain on a moonlit night. And reading what he could about the campaign, Steve saw the extent of bravery, endurance, and personal sacrifice the soldiers had shown during the entire course of those twenty-eight days of action. So why, he wondered, was the Canadian campaign in Sicily apparently forgotten? In the spring of 2004, there had been a great outpouring of media and public attention focused on Canada's participation in the Normandy invasion, which had begun on June 6, 1944, with troops landing on Juno Beach. That year, marking the sixtieth anniversary of the great event, a large interpretive centre had been opened on the western flank of the Normandy beach itself. The Juno Beach Centre was a worthy cooperative venture of private organizations and government intended to honour Canada's significant contribution in World War 11. Yet in all the media stories that year and since, Steve had seen nothing about Canadians in Sicily. It was troubling, but he never considered personally trying to do anything about it.

Instead, he watched with a father's pride as Erik's project was voted by his classmates best of their class, went on to be presented at a regional history fair in Quebec City, and was then selected as one of 160 projects for the 2006 National Historica Fair held in Halifax.

That might have been the story's end, except that in the summer of 2006, Steve took the family on a trip to Italy. One day, while they were in Sicily, Steve spontaneously decided to visit the Canadian cemetery and Monte Assoro. He invited Erik to come along, but by this time the boy was weary of the project and didn't go. So Steve went alone. There amid the headstones, Steve had his epiphany. What had seemed a glorious triumph when viewed through the prism of his son's project was now revealed as a tremendous sacrifice by young men, many only eighteen or nineteen, who had fought horrific battles and then been forgotten. They would be remembered, and the act of remembrance would occur in 2013 to accord with the seventieth anniversary of the campaign code-named Operation Husky. Steve would bring others to Agira Canadian War Cemetery— others who he hoped would experience the same emotional transformation he had.

IF HE HAD to, Steve would walk across Sicily alone, and he needed me to map out the route. That was one possibility he advanced in a note two days after his initial contact. But in his more optimistic missives, which outnumbered the pessimistic ones by factors in the double or triple digits, Steve anticipated that so many people would come to Sicily that a small group could walk each of the various routes our soldiers had taken through the interior. In that case, he needed me to map all these routes and determine points of convergence that accorded with those where all units of 1st Canadian Infantry Division reunited. He also needed a list of the men who

died each day, along with each soldier's regiment and a rough indica-
tion of where he fell.

"I wish to have a different Canadian recite a small paragraph honouring a soldier on the day he fell 70 years before," he wrote. "This
means that, for instance, on 16 of July 2013, I may need 65 Canadians
gathered. My vision is that at 11:00 a.m., the honours would be read
and the pipes played in a location along the route they followed. This
vision is complicated by the fact that many times the 1st Canadian
Division was in many places. If the group we can assemble is large
enough, we would separate such that one group would be in Assoro,
another in Valguarnera, etc..."

Steve wanted to contract me to provide this information. He was
also willing to try to subsidize the expenses of as many of the
Canadians who participated as possible. "So far, Operation
Husky 2013 gets its funding directly from me," he told me, but he
was working to secure other public and private funding.

I wondered how deep Steve's pockets could go. What he was pro-
posing sounded very expensive. My work to develop the routes for
him and the lists of the fallen would take considerable time and cost
him considerable money, too. How any single person could subsidize
the expenses of that many people on a lengthy trip to Sicily was hard
to imagine. But one thing that came through clearly was that this
was a very determined man—a man, as he admitted, obsessed.

A LINGERING QUESTION that Steve soon answered regarded his
determination to follow the route taken by the Canadians on foot.
Lots of individuals and tours trace various routes of Allied troops
across Europe. They do so in rental cars, vans, and coach buses,
unloading at a historic battlefield or before a war monument or
cemetery. Not many walk the routes—especially in the middle of a
Sicilian July when the heat routinely cracks 40 degrees Celsius, and
roads are narrow and wind through extremely rugged terrain. But
even before he happened upon Operation Husky, Steve had
unearthed a historical anomaly that in his mind determined that
any retracing of the Canadian route had to be conducted by
marchers marching.

Normally, World War II armies marched as little as possible. They tried to ride in trucks and troop carriers. They unloaded just short of where the fighting would occur and then marched to the sound of the guns, straight into combat.

But in Sicily, the Canadians had been handicapped by a lack of transport that made this approach impossible. Out of the 125 transport ships that carried the Canadians from Britain to the Mediterranean, three were sunk by U-boat torpedoes over a three-day period. The ships were *St. Essylt, City of Venice,* and *Devis.* Losses to U-boats had been expected. The 1st Division commander, Major General Guy Simonds, and his general staff officer, Lieutenant Colonel George Kitching, had even made a game of it. Pick three chits out of a hat, and if those were the ships sunk, what would be the ramifications? What equipment and supplies would have to be replaced from other sources? What troops would need to be redesignated to fill in for those lost at sea? Dozens of outcomes had to be considered and a plan developed to make the Canadian invasion force able to overcome each unique challenge. For the Canadians sailed from Britain, bringing with them their entire kit. There was nothing waiting for them in Sicily or nearby North Africa. It would be days, weeks even, before the division was slotted into the British Eighth Army supply chain in which they were to serve. So what was the worst-case scenario? The unthinkable scenario?

That *St. Essylt, City of Venice,* and *Devis* would be sunk. That was worst for the simple reason that they carried the majority of the division's transport—its jeeps, trucks, Bren carriers, larger vehicles mounted with long-range and powerful radio sets, and the ambulances to return the wounded to rear-area hospitals. Most of these had been loaded into the holds of these three ships. When the torpedoes struck, fifty-six Canadian soldiers on board perished, and another four were injured. Simonds and Kitching barely noticed this loss of life. More important to the invasion were the 562 vehicles that ended up on the sea bottom, lost forever. Along with the vehicles went the majority of the division's communication equipment and much of its engineering and medical stores. The Canadians were left hamstrung.

Instead of riding in trucks and personnel carriers to the point of battle, they would be like soldiers of another era—marching over hill and dale "on shank's mare," as they described it, and in oppressive heat. Marching inland from the invasion beach, they covered mouths with handkerchiefs to ward off the dust. The steel helmets began to bake their brains, and another handkerchief turned into a bonnet reduced the heat. Draped loosely, the handkerchiefs also served to protect exposed necks from sunburn. Handkerchiefs became essential kit. So intense was the glaring sun that some men closed their eyes for six steps, blinked them open for a brief, orienting glance, and then shut them again.

And this was not just for the invasion's first day. It was routine for the entire long march that the Canadians made into Sicily's harsh mountainous interior.

Steve had known this. And my book reinforced his understanding of the hardships the Canadians had faced. Out of this knowledge came a determination that whatever group of Canadians joined him for Operation Husky 2013 and pledged to be marchers must march as the troops had. They would just not be required to carry all the accoutrements required to make war. The marchers of 2013 could wear and carry what they wanted. They would walk from the beach where the Canadians landed on July 10 to the last town they liberated in Sicily's heartland on August 7. It would be a long, harsh trek of at least two hundred kilometres. A trek punctuated by remembrance ceremonies each day and by evening masses. A trek that would ultimately end at the Agira Canadian War Cemetery with those marchers and other Canadians gathering to remember the dead with a roll of honour.

I was only a few weeks into providing technical and historical support to Steve for a fee when the realization struck me. Although it was almost five years away, I knew with utter clarity that I would be a marcher. I could shake my head all I liked. I could try to explain this away as some fantasy that must surely never come to pass. I tried that approach often. But each time, there was Steve brainstorming ways to carry it forward and repeatedly asserting that he would do it alone if necessary. At other times, he daydreamed over the phone about the two of us after a long day's march sitting under a sky filled with stars, bottle of wine at hand, and knowing those were the same stars young soldiers had gazed toward on a hot July 1943 night. Knowing also that we had together brought Operation Husky 2013 to fruition. And I finally quit denying the fact that there was no damn way I was not going to walk. I was in.

PART ONE

Marchons!

FOUR AND A half years after that phone call from Steve Gregory, Operation Husky 2013 gets under way on July 10—precisely seventy years to the date and time that Canadian soldiers waded ashore in Sicily. An ever-growing crowd of participants and onlookers is assembled on a rocky point just east of the Canadian beach, which was code-named Bark West. Seventy years on, it's hard to visualize the beach as an invasion site. The Mediterranean has risen since then and now almost laps against the sheer limestone cliffs that in 1943 stood twenty-five to forty-five metres back from the waterline. What little sand remains is heavily blanketed with seaweed. So we gather instead on the point. This is one of the first of what will become a series of divergences from strict duplication of the past. It only takes a glance along the length of present-day Bark West to realize that a dogmatic attempt to replicate the experience of the soldiers is not only infeasible but at times would be ridiculous. What really counts is the act of remembrance itself.

Over the years, this remembrance initiative has evolved through multiple setbacks, windfalls, and divergences from Steve's original vision. Yet today, it unfurls in a way that adheres surprisingly closely to his intention. Present is a group of marchers who have dedicated themselves to retracing the route followed by the Canadian soldiers. Each day, a Sicilian village or town through which the marchers will pass has pledged to host ceremonies of remembrance—generally in the central square or wherever the memorial to their World Wars I and II war dead is situated. In addition to the marchers, a large number of other Canadians have committed to participating at specific dates that are of personal significance, and many more plan to attend the final ceremony on July 30, which will honour the fallen buried at Agira Canadian War Cemetery.

Steve's hope that several hundred Canadians, including a large assembly of Canadian Forces personnel, would march the route withered early on. But he won't march alone. Including Steve, we number ten. It's an eclectic group: two women, two militia regiment honorary lieutenant colonels, a militia regiment padre, three men who had fathers who fought in Sicily, Steve, and me. Four of us are from British Columbia, three from Ontario, and the remainder from Quebec. Nobody from the Prairie or Maritime provinces. This is not for lack of trying on Steve's part. Over the years he has crisscrossed Canada many times, holding fundraisers and information sessions in order to recruit as many Canadians as possible.

Padre Don Aitchison is in his early forties, so the youngest. The two women—Frances Backhouse and Jean Miso—Steve, three other marchers, and I are all in our fifties. The honorary lieutenant colonels are in their sixties, and the oldest of us, Philip Bury, turned seventy in January. Compared to most of those 1943 soldiers, we are old. The plan calls for us to march an average of twenty to twenty-five kilometres a day. There is only one rest day. Some marches are expected to be as long as thirty-five kilometres.

Such distances would be challenging even in the best circumstances. The conditions we face here in Sicily promise to be much harsher. First, there's the intense summer heat—daily temperatures in the high thirties and low forties are guaranteed. In an attempt to dodge the worst of the heat and also allow us to get to the host towns in time for remembrance ceremonies at 11:00 a.m. each day, the plan is for us to start walking most mornings around dawn. Not being an early-morning person at the best of times, I look upon this idea with a sense of resigned dread.

In addition to these challenges, there is Sicily's terrain. Here on the coast, things are not bad, as there is a narrow plain between the sea and the interior hills. But we will have only a couple of days of marching on it. Thereafter, we advance—as did our soldiers—into the hills and mountains that spider out from the western flank of Mount Etna to create a labyrinth of narrow valleys walled by steep hills, ridges, and mountains.

To speed travel through this rugged and fragmented countryside, a largely level highway network passes over most of the land on raised platforms held up by concrete pillars. But trying to walk along these would be suicidal. Instead, we will walk as often as possible on secondary roads. These generally follow the grain of the land, snaking up the sides of a mountain from one narrow valley down into the one beyond.

Given these conditions and our ages, each of us knows that we have signed on for a serious test of stamina and personal resolve.

Fortunately, we will not march unsupported. Steve has amassed a small logistical support team centred on four key personnel, all former soldiers. Gilles Pelletier and Gilles Aubé, who are so similar in height, weight, age, and appearance that we have dubbed them Les Gilles, are in charge of a motorhome. This will follow us or, when the roads are too narrow or winding, will take another route to rendezvous with us for scheduled breaks. The motorhome is to be loaded with water and food and will provide a convenient pit-stop facility. On most days, the motorhome will also serve as the transport vehicle for another supporting group—the volunteer pipe band, which consists of four bagpipers and two drummers. Four of these are young men from St. Andrew's College near Toronto, and two of the pipers are older.

The plan is for them to join us each day a short distance outside of the town and then pipe us through to the location of the remembrance ceremony. Bob Stewart, our pipe major, has held that position with the Hastings and Prince Edward Regiment Pipe Band since its formation in 1980. Since then, he's survived a heart attack and a series of heart bypasses. He is almost a stereotype of the gruff, grizzled Scottish pipe major. No questioning the grit there, nor his watchful concern for the youngsters in his band. Also keeping a careful eye on the younger members is Iain MacLeod, who plays the pipes beautifully as well. His son, Dave MacLeod, has been working closely with Steve for several years under contract—overseeing the website, organizing fundraisers, and otherwise helping to bring together all the little pieces in what grew into a complex puzzle. Dave was to have been our eleventh marcher, but on this first day, he will commit to a more demanding duty.

André Durand and Richard Vincent are the other two key logistics personnel. Their primary role is to finalize the route plans and ensure each day that everyone is where they need to be. This is an unenviable job, because it is not just the marchers and pipe band members who need to be organized. There are also four officer cadets from Royal Military College Saint-Jean, who on this July 10 are dressed in 1943 uniforms and whose job is to serve as a kind of honour guard to remembrance.

An addition to the original plan is an utterly experimental undertaking led by Steve's son, Erik, and his best friend, Christopher-Denny Matte. Along the way—and nobody afterwards can say when the idea first emerged—it was decided that the death of each soldier, on the day he fell, should be meaningfully commemorated. The means would be to plant in the Sicilian soil, preferably close to where the soldier fell, a simple white-painted marker with his name on it and two small flags, Canadian and Italian. The markers are three-foot-long pieces of one-by-four-inch lumber. In recent months, about half the markers have been prepared by Canadian high school students and the other half by students in Sicily. The Canadian school was Montreal's Vincent Massey Collegiate high school. In Sicily, the students attended a private English-language school in Pachino. Each student has inscribed a message of remembrance on the marker he or she produced.

Today, nine markers are being installed on the rocky beach. Using shovels, Erik and Chris have managed to dig down sufficiently to place five right next to the waterline. These commemorate soldiers who died at sea or while getting ashore during the initial landing. Another four stand between two flagpoles that have been erected on the beach. Three are in memory of those soldiers and merchant marine personnel who perished when the ships were sunk on July 4 and 5, and the fourth recognizes the Italian civilians and soldiers killed that day seventy years ago. The plan to dig these markers into the soil is quickly foiled by the rocky ground, so a number of us scour the beach for loose rocks large enough to create cairns around each marker to secure it in place. July 10 was a day of few fatal casualties. As we move inland, the numbers per day will grow exponentially. Realizing that finding where to place the markers and getting permissions from property owners or civil authorities will be a daunting challenge, Dave MacLeod reluctantly steps aside as a marcher and agrees to join what we henceforth call the marker team.

Also milling about the beach this day and often getting unintentionally in the way is a host of documentary filmmakers—at least three different teams. One is officially attached to, and contracted by, Op Husky. It consists of five personnel led by Max Fraser, a filmmaker from Whitehorse. Max is a small, compact, serious-minded fellow of about my age. He has a gentle and considerate demeanour. On his left wrist, he wears two watches. One is a modern watch, and the other is the watch his father wore when he waded onto this beach in Sicily seventy years earlier as a soldier in the Hastings and Prince Edward Regiment. Besides Max's team, there is another from the major Italian news network, RAI. Another team from TLN—the Latino network based in Canada—was supposed to be present, but it's been delayed getting on the ground and won't deploy until the following day. Its absence is not notable, as there are so many other media people here because of all the Sicilian- and mainland-based Italian radio and television stations represented. Conspicuously absent, despite many invitations and much goading, is anybody from the Canadian Broadcasting Corporation or any other major Canadian news outlet. The CBC staunchly refused to send its Rome correspondent for reasons never explained.

Op Husky also has its own media relations and promotions team. This is led by Steven MacKinnon, an old friend of Steve's who owns a Mississauga-based advertising firm. When Steve outlined his plan for Op Husky during a dinner in June 2009, MacKinnon was "embarrassed" to have no knowledge of the events of July 1943 and the important role Canadian soldiers played. "Like most people," he tells me, "I wrongly believed our efforts began with D-Day. I signed on that very night. Being in advertising with many media contacts, I believed I could assist with communications, both before and during the event." MacKinnon has an assistant, enlisted three months ago. Brittany Blow is a graduate of Toronto's Humber College Public Relations program. In her twenties, she has the chiselled beauty and figure of a fashion model, a look she reinforces with a keen sense of style. Her wardrobe becomes a source of awe and bemusement for most of us, for not a day goes by that Brittany is not wearing a never-before-seen outfit. The two make a competent team, and at the end of each day the website is updated with new photos and video shorts—the latter shot by MacKinnon using his iPad.

Steve MacKinnon and Brittany have another key role besides making sure Op Husky gets as much media attention back in Canada and in Italy as possible. It's also their job to ensure that present for every ceremony is our star guest, Captain Sheridan "Sherry" Atkinson. In 1943, Sherry was a twenty-one-year-old Royal Canadian Regiment lieutenant. He is the sole veteran of the campaign who will be with us for the duration of Op Husky. Sherry depends on his significantly younger wife, Susan, to do the driving from their guesthouse near Piazza Armerina each day, so that he can speak at and participate in the ceremonies. He is our icon, our touchstone to those soldiers who fought and sometimes died in those murky recesses of the past.

And then there are the Sicilians. Without them, this venture would unfold in a vacuum. We are on their soil. Steve has spent months over the past seven years building personal relationships with key people who can help further the goal of including officials and other citizens of Sicily. Today, the mayor of nearby Pachino is here on the beach, wearing his sash. Local firemen serve as an honour guard. Also present are Carabinieri and local police officers.

Not to be outdone, the Canadian ambassador has come from Rome, accompanied by his military attaché, Colonel Tony Battista. And yet Op Husky is not, as Steve is at pains to repeatedly point out, a government-sponsored undertaking. It remains a civilian project mounted by Steve, his supporters, and Canada Company. And although the plan is for Canadian service personnel to join us for the latter phase and finale at the cemetery, it is Op Husky volunteers who will be coordinating the interaction between this contingent and us citizen volunteers.

IN WHAT WOULD prove commonplace for the ceremonies over the next twenty days, the one on the beach takes a long time to get set up and under way. As we wait, a flat rocky shelf thrusting out into the water from the point draws one marcher after another to it for a moment of solitary contemplation. First, Robert "Bob" Werbiski walks out and stares seaward for a long while. Then Rod Hoffmeister does the same thing. Both had fathers who landed on Bark West seventy years ago today. They are trying to imagine what it would have been like to be in landing craft that morning heading toward the beach and that first experience of combat. After Rod comes back from the shelf, I claim it.

Today, the sky and sea are virtually the same hue of blue and almost featureless, so that there is little definition where they merge at the outer limits of the horizon. This was not the case seventy years ago. I imagine a young *soldato* of Sicily's 206th Coastal Defence Division crouched in a hole close to the edge of the limestone cliff overlooking the beach. Stretching back from a short distance offshore to that limitless horizon, he would have seen a vast armada of ships—the largest in world history to that date. He would have watched the smaller landing craft casting off from the larger troop ships and then chugging remorselessly toward the sand in front of him. Standing farther back, the destroyers, cruisers, and battleships belched fire and smoke as their guns hurled shell after shell down upon the beach and targets inland. Overhead, Allied bombers growled in to hammer the nearby towns and other targets, while small fighters circled protectively. Looking over his shoulder, the young soldier would have seen flames, huge explosions, and dark smoke rising from nearby Pachino and its small airfield. More explosions would have been ripping apart the earth nearby, showering dirt, sand, and rocks down upon him. Amid the deafening explosions, he would also have heard the sounds of men screaming or calling out as they were hit. He was surely terrified, likely unable to control his fearful shaking, occasionally whimpering when the shells fell perilously close.

I picture him—a boy, really. Perhaps before the war he worked alongside his father, who was a mason in the mountain town of Regalbuto, a town standing in the shadow of Mount Etna. Or maybe his was a farm family on the coastal plateau near Ispica, a village being bombarded into a ruin that day. The boy is thin and scrawny, malnourished because the Italian army is entering this battle ill-equipped and ill-supplied. Rations have for months been barely sufficient for basic sustenance. His uniform is ragged and threadbare, his boots falling apart. The rifle is clean, but he has only a few bullets. An officer had spoken bombastically of meeting and slaying the invaders with the bayonet. The boy knows he will not fix the bayonet to his rifle. Perhaps he will fire the bullets, and then he will be done. He and the others in the dugout that shelters them from the falling shells have discussed this during the night when the bombardment made sleep impossible. They will not die for Il Duce. They will not die for Rome.

Sixty-five per cent of this division are Sicilian. Their homeland—this island—has been invaded countless times down through the centuries. Greeks, Romans, Moors, Normans—all have come and conquered, ruled for a time, and been replaced by another conqueror. Now another unstoppable conqueror approaches. The boy and his comrades see no reason to die fighting the inevitable. If they are lucky, they will survive and perhaps soon be allowed to go home or at least be kept safe in a prisoner-of-war camp. If the Sicilians are imprisoned on the island, perhaps their families will be able to visit. Most of the other soldiers are from Reggio Calabria, just across the narrow Strait of Messina on the toe of mainland Italy's imaginary boot. Whether Sicilian or Calabrian, their war will be over, and they can shed these lice-infested, tattered uniforms unwillingly worn since they were conscripted months or years earlier. All they have to do is survive until the Allied soldiers land and can be surrendered to.

That is, I think, what a Sicilian boy soldier would have thought that day seventy years ago.

I turn my back to the sea and walk toward the crowd now arranging itself into some semblance of formation for a ceremony about to begin.

FOR A CIVILIAN initiative, many people today are wearing various uniforms or quasi uniforms. The honorary lieutenant colonels, Rod Hoffmeister and Bill Rodgers, as well as Padre Don Aitchison are in their full regimental dress uniforms. Like Don, Rod's regimental association is to a highland unit, so they wear appropriate regimental kilts and traditional highland Glengarry bonnets. Their pale-green shirts are short-sleeved. Bill Rodgers's uniform doesn't allow for that option. His is what soldiers call a DEU, which correctly stands for "distinctive environmental uniform." As Bill says, this, like many military acronyms, makes no sense, so most soldiers define DEU as "dress uniform with medals." His features a green beret, dark-green dress jacket, the same type of pale-green shirt Bill and Rod wear, and dress pants. Despite the heat, he is not obviously sweating. Tony Battista is also in full dress uniform—blue with service cap and even a tie—and also looks amazingly cool, calm, and collected. Same goes for the Italian police officers in their formal uniforms, and the firemen in heavy shirts and pants. The RMC cadets are in their 1943-period khaki uniforms consisting of peaked cap, shirt with sleeves rolled up and buttoned, knee-length shorts, almost-knee-high wool socks, and boots. A couple of them look very uncomfortable indeed.

Sometime in the past year, Steve hatched a plan for the marchers and members of their support team to wear a form of uniform. This was so we would stand out in a crowd. Having never worn a uniform, not even that of a Boy Scout, I resisted the idea. "I think we'd look pretty sharp," Steve said by phone. "We're going to walk a hell of a long way in stinking heat, Steve," I cautioned. "People will want to wear what they find comfortable." But I also knew by that time that once Steve gets the bit of an idea between his teeth, he is pretty much unstoppable. As the unelected advocate for, at that time, an unknown number of marchers, I negotiated a compromise. Everybody would dress as they wished during most of the march, but wear the Op Husky uniform during the community ceremonies.

So today, we are duly in uniform. For the support team, this consists of a khaki short-sleeved polo shirt with the Op Husky logo on the left breast. The logo consists of a shield holding poppy, maple leaf, and armed forces symbols over a banner bearing the Latin inscription *Nos Memor*, "We remember." The marchers and the pipers wear long-sleeved white shirts unfortunately made from 65 per cent polyester and 35 per cent cotton. The material is thick and doesn't breathe but has a military crispness, an effect to which the two chest pockets with button-down flaps contribute. Having only days earlier come out of plastic wrapping, the shirts are still freshly pressed—a state of affairs that the humid coastal heat will quickly undo. The shirt's right shoulder is adorned with the Op Husky logo, and the left features the logo of Canada Company. It is similar to the Op Husky one with the banner this time reading "Many Ways to Serve."

Canada Company is a charitable, non-partisan organization that seeks to build a bridge between business and community leaders and the Canadian military. Their major aim is to recognize, support, and provide care for both serving and former forces personnel. As Canada Company's Montreal chapter president, Steve is a keen supporter of the organization and has also managed to get it to contribute significantly, both financially and in resources, to Op Husky.

No uniform worthy of the name is complete without some kind of headgear. So we marchers have red ball caps with "OPERATION HUSKY 2013" in white lettering across the back and a fairly large white maple leaf on the front just above the brim. Wearing these shirts and caps, there is no mistaking that We Are Canadian! Because the shirts are so heavy, it has been agreed that only when we get within striking distance of the next community will we, Clark Kent–like, doff our own shirts, don the white ones, stow our own headgear in favour of the red caps, and then advance to the awaiting ceremony. The pipers, meanwhile, riding across the country in the air-conditioned comfort, but also terrifically cramped quarters, of the motorhome spend all of each day in their white shirts and ball caps.

Pachino's marching band, Vincenzo Rizza, is arrayed in three rows and numbers about twenty of its normal full complement of fifty. They wear short-sleeved light-blue shirts, darker blue pants and bright white belts. This is not some high school band. It is a community band, and most of those present today are in their early twenties to late thirties. There are clarinets, saxophones, trumpets, trombones, tubas, a bass drum, snare drum, and cymbals. Also a flugelhorn (the band's name honouring a local and renowned flugelhorn player). Marching bands, we discover, are an important part of Italian community culture, and Sicily abounds with them. There are even standards of instrumentation that most such bands adopt. These were set down by Roman band conductor and teacher Alessandro Vassella back in 1894 and are generally adhered to throughout the country to this day. For us, the existence of these bands is an unexpected but happy discovery. For the next twenty days, almost every town or village we enter has its marching band deployed to greet us. Each is a part of its community's lifeblood and a vital component in local and island-wide festivals, both religious and cultural. Between our pipers and these local marching bands, our journey through the heart of Sicily is to be regularly punctuated by music.

THE BEACH CEREMONY starts with the black-suit-and-tie-wearing bandmaster theatrically raising his right hand to begin conducting. Slowly, sonorously, the band starts playing "O Canada" while drafted-into-service Frances helps Officer Cadet Victor Couture secure the Maple Leaf flag to one pole's lanyard. Victor then raises the flag at a measured pace to ensure that it reaches the top just as the national anthem concludes. Don Aitchison later tells me, "Watching the Canadian flag rise on that crisp July 10 morning was one of the most powerful moments for me. I felt so proud of those who landed and headed into truly unknown danger—as, for so many of them, it was their first operation."

Pausing only a few seconds, the band jumps into "Il canto degli italiani." A rollicking operatic melody accompanied by rousing lyrics, the Italian national anthem contrasts sharply with our anthem's comparatively funereal tempo.

By the time the anthem finishes, two Pachino firemen have raised Italy's flag. A light northerly breeze sets both flags snapping nicely—with symbolic aptness, aimed toward the sea. The anthems are followed by a bugler playing the last post, as Sherry Atkinson and Colonel Battista lay a wreath before the white remembrance markers between the flags. When the moment of silence ends, Steve Gregory speaks. It is the first of what will be many addresses to ever-larger crowds. He holds a small scrap of paper containing scribbled notes and is noticeably nervous, but his voice carries clear and strong. "Today, seventy years ago, off these waters, landed an armada—the largest in history to date—and 25,000 Canadian soldiers walked upon these beaches. On the way here, on the 4th and 5th of July, three ships represented by these markers were sunk off the coast of your beautiful island. The *Venice* was the first to sink. Eleven men, including the captain, were lost at sea." He names the other two ships sunk and casualties suffered. Steve ends by announcing sharply, "We are going to march!"

MARCH WE DO. Our pipers and drummers lead, with us marchers close on their heels. All around us and forming a long trail behind follow at least two hundred people. Most are Italians. The original plan had called for the marchers to have time to collect whatever gear they required to cover the ten kilometres to Pachino. But Les Gilles jumped into the motorhome the moment the ceremony concluded and roared off as if they were driving a NASCAR racer rather than a motorhome that spanned the narrow road running from the beach inland to Pachino. Steve says they rushed to get ahead of the crowd because they need to be set up in Pachino before we get there.

Inside the motorhome is another piece of Op Husky's travelling remembrance roadshow—an easily assembled and dismantled display that relates in English, French, and Italian the history of what we are doing on a series of panels. This has largely been the work of

Andrew Gregory, Steve's brother. Andrew is the curator of the Canadian Forces Logistics Museum in Montreal. When I met Andrew, I could hardly believe he was Steve's brother. They are opposites, both physically and temperamentally. Andrew is slender and unflappable. For the next twenty days, his station is either inside the motorhome or outside overseeing the display.

For most of us, the motorhome's rapid exit presents no more than a small costume or equipment glitch. Jean Miso, for example, is wearing a multi-coloured dress instead of the white shirt because she had thought there would be time to change in the motorhome. Having suffered a ligament-related injury in my left knee two years earlier, I have trained using a hiking pole for stabilization. The pole disappears with the motorhome. Gone, as well, are our hip belts with water bottles, sunscreen, and other odds and sods we think might prove useful while on the march. My camera is inside my pocket, and that is the only bit of kit I consider vital for the march. The lack of the rest poses no significant problems. We won't, though, store any kit in the motorhome or other vehicles from now on, I tell Frances.

For Rod Hoffmeister, however, the motorhome's disappearance will have enduring consequences. Lost for the day are the hiking shoes and socks he had planned to change into after the beach ceremony. His uniform dress shoes and wool socks start scouring away at feet and ankles like so much sandpaper. Occasionally he grimaces, but his pace never falters. I am—and likely the rest are as well—largely oblivious to the extent of his suffering. The next day, the resulting blisters look gruesome. A few days later, the big toenails turn blue and subsequently fall off. This is an injury that will plague him for the rest of our marches. Although he bandages his feet each morning, this scarcely helps. But despite being in obvious pain, he will soldier on without complaint. Rod explains that he was athletic in university, particularly as part of the University of British Columbia rowing team. From that experience, Rod knows he has the strength and endurance needed to carry on regardless.

Our pace is measured but reasonably brisk. The pipe band plays a few tunes and then rests. After a short distance, many of the Italians break off, but they are soon replaced by a long convoy of cars. The one immediately to our rear is an ambulance van with blue lights flashing. It carries a large team of paramedics whose members regularly jump out to trot up and down the line of marchers, dispensing plastic water bottles and encouragement to drink all we like. Not having yet realized how inexpensive bottled water is in Sicily—where most water is potable but disdained by the locals for drinking—I am struck by the generosity of whatever local authority is paying for all this. The water is essential, replacing that lost when the motorhome took off with our hip belts.

In 1943, water constituted a critical supply challenge for the Canadians. Lacking trucks to carry additional containers from which to resupply, the soldiers had to eke out what was in their canteens. Unused to the intense heat or combat conditions where adrenaline and fear contributed to dehydration, the soldiers found it a tough challenge not to drain their canteens dry long before there was any chance of refilling. Also at that time, Sicilian water was considered questionable, and orders were to sterilize it. Many a soldier ignored the order, and rampant dysentery raged through the ranks. Thinking of what it must have been like to march even on that first day in the heat while suffering thirst, we marchers of today realize we are on easy street.

A few Sicilians and some of the Canadians who are not officially marchers continue to walk along with us. This includes three Sicilian men sporting World War II khaki uniforms complete with web harness, attached pouches, and battle backpack typical of those the Canadians wore. One man carries a rifle, another a Sten submachine gun, and the other a Thompson submachine gun. Two wear the red berets and shoulder flashes of British airborne troops. Matters not where you are in Europe, it seems most World War II re-enactors like these chaps favour all things airborne—even if such soldiers served nowhere near their homes. The third man is more genuinely attired in terms of uniform and kit. His headgear is the steel overturned-wash-basin–style "Tommy" helmet that our troops wore.

As we advance from the beach, the heat rises and the breeze fades. The re-enactors stick with us, but the one with the Tommy gun is noticeably puffing. We marchers seem fine. Most of us have trained at least somewhat for this. I started in January, walking a couple of times a week for increasing distances along the Galloping Goose Trail—a Greater Victoria mixed-use trail that offers the advantage of markers indicating every kilometre. This made it easy to measure the distance walked. In February, Frances joined me most days—even though she had not yet committed to participating in Op Husky. By early May, our training marches averaged fifteen kilometres, which we walked at a rate of five kilometres per hour. This was the rate set down by the planners. It's a good pace, one the Canadian military often adheres to for training. In the last few weeks before deploying to Sicily, we upped the ante—walking twelve kilometres one way and then retracing our steps to hit a twenty-five-kilometre total completed in just over four hours. This met the expected average daily distance for the march.

One disadvantage of training on the Galloping Goose is that it uses an old railway bed, the trail being named after an early twentieth-century train that trundled along this corridor during a short operational period. Railbeds have very gentle grades, so we were not walking through any rugged terrain. Given Victoria's topography, finding anything remotely resembling Sicily's mountainous interior proved pretty much impossible. We made do in the latter phases of training by walking eighteen kilometres along the city's coastline from the end of the Ogden Point breakwater to where a steep headland leads up to the Victoria Golf Club and descending again to finish at Willows Beach in Oak Bay. Right turn, quick march, and back to Ogden Point—thirty-six kilometres completed in an average of 5.5 hours. We finished the training regimen by repeating that over two consecutive days. According to the "Operation Husky 2013 Playbook," as the schedule issued by the logistics team was called, thirty-five to thirty-six kilometres was the farthest we would march on any given day. But it also called for two such days to fall consecutively.

Given the training we had done, Frances and I were feeling pretty good about our ability to cope. On the first day, this seemed to be true for most of us. Everyone, it appeared, had done a fair bit of training for this, Jean Miso likely more than any other. With a community ski hill near her Toronto home, Jean had started out hiking up and down the slope three to five times a day. By the end of June, she was up to ten laps. On weekdays, she headed out every morning before work for a forty-five-minute walk with 4.5 kilograms on her back. During lunch breaks, she skipped rope or went for a quick dash up the ski hill and back. Evenings were ended with a one-hour fast walk. On the May long weekend, Jean logged treks of thirty-five, thirty, and twenty-five kilometres over three consecutive days. Steve had been insisting that we should do at least one back-to-back march of at least thirty kilometres each day. "Yep, I over-prepared just a tad!" Jean later says.

Later, too, we learn that Steve never met his assigned target. As the launch point of July 10 closed in, just trying to keep up with the organizational details overwhelmed him. He spent more time on the phone than walking, although I once talked with him on the phone for about an hour while he strode along Montreal streets. Despite such efforts and best intentions, Steve's training suffered.

Today, however, the distance and basically level ground make our march little more than a walk in the park for a group of middle-aged Canadians in marginally decent condition. So we chat and sightsee. Most of us have met only a couple of days earlier, and there is a lot of feeling out going on. We are a bunch of strangers who realize that each is going to be stuck with the others for twenty days. Intensely stuck together.

Although there is some semblance of actual marching attempted by the group, everybody tends to be shifting up and down the columns of three that are generally maintained. So at one moment I walk with Phil Bury and Padre Aitchison, and a few minutes later I'm bookended by Bob Werbiski and Terry Dolan. These last two marchers both had fathers who served in Sicily during the war. They are polar opposites. Bob is quiet and seems to carefully measure every sentence before speaking. A small, thin man, he is physically as measured as is his speech. Every movement is economical, efficient. His father was a pharmacist in peacetime, and he performed the same function in an army medical unit, the 4th Field

Ambulance. Terry is a stocky, fairly sloppily turned-out guy who is quick with a joke and loves to talk. His father was an army photographer. "I'm just like my old man," Terry asserts, "always telling bad jokes but good with a camera." Terry carries a digital SLR with a massive telephoto lens slung over one shoulder.

Later, Frances and I walk quite some distance with Jean. She is a slender redhead with brilliant blue eyes. We learn that she is a schoolteacher and intensely committed to remembrance. She has written two slim illustrated books honouring veterans and those who serve in the military and has also composed a number of remembrance-themed songs. Remembrance, she says, has "been in the foreground of my thought since childhood." Her grandfather fought in World War I, serving as a scout, intelligence observer, and sniper. "He won a Military Medal," she says. "He lied about his age to join. He was seventeen. I have a seventeen-year-old son." For her first book, *We'll Never Forget*, she interviewed a number of World War II male and female veterans. She has since made a point of visiting several of them every week, listening intently to their stories many times over. On most visits to veteran Herb Pike, she listens to him describe, as Jean puts it, some of the "horrid actions of war that he experienced." She sees Op Husky as a chance "to immerse herself in a culture" that he had talked about on each of her visits. "In fact," she says, "he was the last person I called before leaving for the airport. I said, 'Herb, I'm going now to walk and remember all your buddies who died.'" He became very emotional, she says, upon hearing that.

AS WE REACH Pachino's outskirts, we are joined by a growing number of walkers. Other people zip back and forth on scooters and motorcycles. People passing in vehicles honk horns and wave out windows. A bunch of workmen high up on scaffolds laying bricks on the façade of a building set down trowels, hammers, and chisels to stare in puzzlement at this marching column. The pipe band leads, blasting out "Scotland the Brave" with great gusto. An old man comes to his door and looks on quietly with an expression devoid of emotion. Seventy years ago, he would have been a young boy, and the building he lives in today was probably newly constructed. Did he stand in that same spot and watch Canadian soldiers march past?

In the lead-up to the invasion, Allied analysts had given thought to how the Sicilians would receive the troops when they landed. In the April 1943 issue of *Foreign Affairs*, published by the American Council on Foreign Relations, Luigi Sturzo wrote in an article entitled "Italy After Mussolini" that there was "not a village, whether it be lost among the mountains of the interior or sprawled along the slopes of Etna, which has not sent whole families to work and live in the United States." A steady correspondence flowed between these immigrants and those still at home. And many of these American Sicilians returned to buy homes and farms. Some towns even had what were called "streets of the Americans." Because of this, Sturzo predicted that "the Sicilian people would understand that they were not coming to Sicily to conquer her...but instead to bring about the liberation of Sicily, as of the whole of Italy, from both Nazi and Fascist domination."

Sturzo's confidence about this was rooted in deep personal experience. Born in Caltagirone in 1871, he had become a priest who was considered a "clerical socialist." From 1905 to 1920, he served as the vice-mayor of his Sicilian hometown, and in the aftermath of World War 1 also founded the national Partito Popolare Italiano (Italian Popular Party), which won 20.6 per cent of the legislative seats in 1919. This was sufficient to ensure that no government could stand without its support. With the rise to power of Benito Mussolini's fascists, Sturzo went into exile in October 1924. From first London and then New York, he actively opposed fascism and worked closely with Allied intelligence agencies as an adviser on all things Italian.

In the main, Sturzo's predictions proved correct. Most Sicilians seemed only too glad to see the arrival of Canadian, American, and British troops. Many photos show the enthusiastic welcome given the soldiers by large crowds of Sicilian civilians, which was only outdone by the joyous rapture displayed by the Dutch when Canadian troops arrived in 1944 and 1945 to liberate their cities and towns. And so it is also today as we enter Pachino.

Describing his reaction to our reception, Bill Rodgers later says, "We walk into this town, and there are all these people. And I thought, 'Well, it's a small Sicilian town and the circus has come, so we'll all go out and see what this noise is about.'" But he soon realized that the turnout was for us. Jamming the sidewalks, spilling out onto the street, are hundreds of school kids. They are waving small flags—upper half the Canadian Maple Leaf, lower half Italy's flag, with the Operation Husky 2013 logo in the lower left-hand corner. They fall in behind us, adults and children alike, unfurling broad banners that proclaim, "We Will Remember."

Much of this is the work of a Pachino dynamo, Rosalba Scifo. She is a fifty-one-year-old university instructor who also owns and runs Pachino's private English-language school. Rosie is a dual national, as her parents immigrated to Canada and settled in Toronto when she was just two years old. Although the family settled in an Italian neighbourhood, they spoke only Sicilian dialect and a little English. She had to learn both Italian and English to integrate. Even today, she says, when upset or angry she reverts to dialect. Rosie considers knowing Sicilian a hindrance because it interferes with her ability to communicate thoroughly with non-Sicilian Italians. And it's the mainland Italians who run the country and are the gatekeepers to virtually every avenue of advancement—economic, educational, whatever.

When Rosie was nineteen, her parents decided to move back to their hometown of Pachino. She and her younger sister, Enza, moved with them. The moment Steve Gregory wandered into her town to chat up his embryonic vision, Rosie enthusiastically embraced Operation Husky and started connecting him with the Sicilian authorities who could help make it happen. She is a short, full-figured woman who has a motherly nature and a huge heart. "It is not easy for Italians to talk about the war," she says. "There are so many facets. There is the Fascism, the soldiers who fought with the Axis powers, the resistance movement, and the question of whether the Allies brought liberation or occupation." Teachers, like herself, struggle with how to teach the history of the war to Italian children. Many think the best approach is just to avoid the subject. This infuriates

Rosie. "I tell them, 'We must teach it and teach all of it. But we do so gently and with humanity.' This is why it is so important for us to remember the sacrifices of the Allied soldiers, the sacrifices of Canadian soldiers." To her mind, Op Husky is going to change how Sicilians remember the war—turning that period from something that often seems shameful into a time of seminal importance in the history of their island and country, a time that should be remembered and integrated fully into their national story.

She is not alone in this belief. There is gathered today in Pachino a whole circle of academic and popular historians from across Italy who would agree with her. Some have been brought in by Steve to share their knowledge, and others have travelled on their own to be here. Also here are a number of other Sicilians from around the island who have dedicated many hours to ensuring that Op Husky succeeds as the greatest act of World War II remembrance Italy has ever seen.

By the time we reach the central square, the crowd has grown to more than a thousand. There is a podium bristling with dignitaries and military representatives. Rod Hoffmeister and Bill Rodgers are hustled over to take their place on it. Pachino's mayor launches into a long speech in Italian. I take away from it only the poignant story of how during the night of July 9–10, 1943, naval shells started falling on the town, and the people "fled into the country in fear, not knowing what was happening." I know the mayor has said this only because Anthony "Tony" Avola and his wife, Dora, are standing next to us and spontaneously step forward to translate. They are from Valguarnera, a town in the mountains through which our troops passed in 1943 after a sharp battle. In a week or so, we will march through Valguarnera as well.

Actually, only Dora is originally from Valguarnera. Tony was born and raised in the small village of Cattolica Eraclea, which is near Agrigento, the town renowned for its classical Greek ruins. When Tony was eighteen, he joined the Carabinieri and, after training in Sardinia, went to serve in northern Italy. This was in 1957, and five years later he left the force to immigrate to Canada, where most of his family had moved. Shortly afterwards, he met Dora, whose parents had immigrated to Canada when she was ten years old. Settling in Toronto, Tony became a hairdresser and opened a salon. By 1980, he had a staff of seventy-five stylists and had opened the Avola College of Hairstyling and Esthetics. He also became much involved in Toronto's Italian community, eventually taking on the presidency of the Ontario Confederation of Sicily and then presidency of the Confederation of Sicilians in North America. It was in this role that Tony was contacted by staff at TLN and told about Steve Gregory's plans for Op Husky.

After meeting Steve and attending a fundraising reception, Tony and Dora decided to travel to Sicily and join the marchers. Dora was attracted to the idea because we were going to Valguarnera. Her mother and father had often talked of the war, and many of their stories were about Valguarnera's liberation by the Canadians.

Tony would like to have joined us as a walker, but recent knee surgery made that idea a non-starter. Instead, he and Dora will drive each day to meet us either along the way or at the town square ceremonies. And they will always bring a bag of fresh figs provided by a cousin from his farm in the interior. Often there are melons and other fruit as well. Both also pitch in as translators and generally help us to understand Sicilian culture and history.

THE PACHINO CEREMONY ends uniquely with the unveiling in the town's main piazza of a large monument that Steve commissioned. Through the earlier part of the ceremony, the monument has been off to one side tightly wrapped in cloth and flanked on either side by two flagpoles. On one side fly a British Union Jack and Canadian Maple Leaf, on the other the Italian Tricolore and American Stars and Stripes. In attendance are representatives from each nation. Standing in for the British is a retired army officer who has been with us since the beach ceremony. There's no shortage of Canadians on hand, but Bob Werbiski and a couple of the officer cadets act as the formal representatives. There is an Italian army officer in formal uniform, as well as several sailors in dress whites from the large American Naval Air Station at nearby Sigonella.

The monument is a large rectangular chunk of pale cream-coloured stone from a local quarry. An embedded Maple Leaf flag takes up much of the back. On the front, facing the open square, are two embedded plaques. One bears the Operation Husky 2013 logo, and the other provides a brief history of the invasion, given in Italian, English, and French. The monument measures 2.5 metres high by 1.5 metres wide and 1.5 metres deep. The metre-high history section dominates the monument. Its text is brief and to the point and achieves precisely what monuments are meant to do. The Latin root of monument is *monēre*, meaning "to remind." The text notes that 23,000 Canadians participated in "the liberation of Sicily. Over 562 gave their lives, another 1,664 were wounded, and 84 were taken prisoners. These young Canadians came from across Canada, in the name of freedom, to help build a better world....During and after the fighting, Canadian soldiers aided the local civilian population by distributing food, restoring water supplies, and helping to rebuild damaged communities."

Steve's original intention was to have this monument erected on the Canadian beach. But the thicket of Sicilian political and land ownership issues that arose over that idea proved impenetrable. So the monument stands now in Pachino with Steve hoping someday to relocate it beachside. I am among those who on July 10 speculate that perhaps its current location is for the best. Here, it is more likely to be seen by Sicilians and Canadians alike and less likely to fall victim to the seemingly careless vandalism common in Sicily. Schools and other public buildings are generally adorned from one end to the other with graffiti, windows are shattered and locks broken. Untouched, however, is the war memorial to be found in every village, town, or city. Inevitably erected after the end of World War 1 and then modified to include the names of the fallen from World War 11, these monuments are always impeccably maintained. As the Operation Husky monument clearly is also dedicated to war remembrance and located near Pachino's war memorial, odds seem good that it will remain intact.

With the monument unveiled and final speeches concluded, the ceremony winds down. Some members of the large crowd linger to chat and take photos of the new monument as the rest disperse. The piazza is opened again to cars and is soon bustling with people heading for the shops and cafés. We Canadians drift off in small groups to the outdoor cafés for what we consider to be a well-earned cold drink. About six of us marchers corral a table and thirstily fall upon large bottles of Peroni or Birra Moretti. We are a sweaty, tired, but mostly contented bunch. Day one is technically behind us—although word has it that we must shortly mount up in an array of vehicles to go off to a formal lunch organized and hosted by the town mayor. We imagine having some of the afternoon free for a nap or, for those of us staying in a hotel at seaside Porto Palo, a final swim in the Mediterranean before we move inland to other accommodation.

But we will soon learn to both welcome and fear these organized lunches. On the one hand, the meals are large and uniformly delectable. On the other, the price is a renewed series of speeches and a protracted event that can grind on for hours with no possibility of escape. This one, held at a local winery, proves exceptionally long. So it is a very well-fed but weary group of marchers and support team members who finally make their way off to various accommodation points. Everybody is hoping to get in a good rest, as tomorrow's march is to start just after dawn and requires covering almost thirty kilometres.

AT THE END of the first official day of Operation Husky 2013, I sit on the veranda of a small casual seaside café called Playa del Sol sipping another Moretti and watching Italian swimmers and sunbathers on the beach below. It's a narrow, very crowded strip of sand. Many large family groups have come here, most likely having driven down from Catania to escape the withering heat of the city. The older people huddle under flimsy umbrellas while the children splash around in the sea and the teenagers push the edges of safety farther out. Off to my left, an isolated rock rises out of the water close to shore. A three- or four-metre-high chimney-shaped brick tower topped by a small Madonna statue has been erected here. This Madonna has a purpose. She watches over the village's fishermen, keeping those at sea safe and blessing the souls of those who over the centuries have been

lost. Such Madonna statues are common in European fishing communities. Often there is also a church dedicated to the fishermen
and other mariners who venture forth from the adjacent port. The
Mediterranean, so still and gentle looking today, is deceptive. It can
be deadly, especially for those who go out in the small boats that
most fishermen here use in their quest for anchovies and various
species of bream, mullet, and bass.

I shake free of thoughts about fishermen and their mortality. The
reason I'm here alone at this café shortly before sunset is to review
today's events. It's not going well. I'm tired from the day, tired from
the days that have preceded it since July 1, when I touched down in
Italy to join Steve in Rome for a small gathering of Italian historians
at the Canadian embassy. The pace since then has been frenetic. I
have come to think that Steve is incapable of any other pace. And
alongside the speed marches spontaneous chaos. We race here and
there. His attention focuses on achieving one goal, only to swiftly flit
off on another trajectory entirely.

July 7 was a case in point. The night before, Steve, Phil Bury, and I
had driven from Porto Palo to Pachino for a small conference of historians speaking about aspects of Italy and World War II. I described
Operation Husky in 1943, and Steve spoke about the current remembrance project. As was often to happen, the event dragged on
interminably, as each Italian historian in turn spoke far past his or her
allotted time. "Never give an Italian a microphone," I muttered to Phil.
As a result, it was well past midnight when we finally returned from
the conference to our hotel. All three of us were exhausted, and it was
agreed that July 7 would be largely a rest day.

By morning, however, Steve had decided that we should race back
to Pachino and help Rosie with the task of cleaning up the winery
that was the site of the previous night's conference. "It'll take at most
an hour," he declared. We drove to the event venue, only to find that
the cleanup was already largely finished. Enza, Rosie's younger sister, who is always direct, said, "We didn't need your help. It was a
wasted trip." We were now, however, caught in the web of Italian
politeness. The winery owner insisted on giving us a private tour
with multiple tastings. Three hours passed. We learned much about

making organic wine and even more about the owner's difficulties in dealing with the bureaucracies in Rome to support its production and marketing. It was past noon when the tour finished, so Rosie and Enza invited us home for lunch. They would be ready to receive us in just a few minutes. Steve seized the moment to race us over to Rosie's language school, where the markers were stored. A good number of them still needed to have their Italian tricolour and red Maple Leaf glued on. This work was being ably performed by Rosie's students and other volunteers.

We set about finding the glue and figuring out with mixed results how to glue flag and Maple Leaf to the wooden markers. After completing about a dozen, Steve announced—rather suggesting it was Phil and I who were holding things up—that we'd better get over to Rosie's for lunch.

Previously, I had always dealt with Steve from a healthy distance. He was in Montreal, I in Victoria—3,720 kilometres of separation. But these past days, I've been crowded into taxis with him in Rome, wedged into a rental car in which we race at harrowing speeds through the Sicilian countryside and repeatedly the heart of Pachino, and shared a hotel room in Porto Palo when it was discovered the agreed-upon room in the inn for me had not been booked. Chaos aside, though, it's impossible not to get swept up in Steve's boundless enthusiasm and dedication to making Op Husky a success. He's also very likeable. Two nights ago, we sat on the patio of the shared hotel room having a drink and watching the small fishing boats ply the waters. Each boat marked itself for other vessels by mounting a little lantern, so the sea seemed to be alive with a scattering of fireflies. We talked of dreams, ambitions, family, and thoughts about remembrance.

Now, on the veranda of Playa del Sol, I occasionally jot a quick note in the spiral-bound pad I'm using for a diary. When marching, I have a bound pad about the size of a pocket wallet stuffed in my hip belt in case I want to record an impression or incident. I also carry a tiny digital recorder.

I ponder this day of remembrance. Before us lie nineteen more days to be dedicated to acts of remembrance—the marching in our soldiers' footsteps, the planting of remembrance markers, the daily ceremony in villages and towns, the finale at the Agira Canadian War Cemetery on July 30, and other acts as yet unknown. But what does it all mean? What, in the end, distinguishes remembrance of those who served in war from remembering a beloved parent or friend who passed away naturally, or even unnaturally? I think the difference is contained in the words service and duty.

I know a woman in Ravenna, Italy, who keeps a photo of the Sicilian judges Giovanni Falcone and Paolo Borsellino on the mantel in her bedroom. Both were murdered in 1992 by the Mafia. She feels their selfless sacrifice is important for all Italians to remember, even as she believes that their deaths ultimately achieved nothing toward making Italy more honest and less riddled with criminal corruption. These judges, she says, knew that by relentlessly pursuing the prosecution of Mafia kingpins they courted assassination. Yet they did not back down despite regular and escalating attempts to intimidate them. They knew what they did was morally right and believed it to be their duty. So they pursued that duty through to death. Yet they did not seek death. They only risked it in an effort to make their country better and safer.

Required in such acts—whether by judges or soldiers—is a conscious decision to choose duty and service over the self when necessary. The fact that this selflessness courts, but does not seek, death is an important distinguishing feature of it. Those who seek martyrdom for whatever purpose are self-serving rather than engaged in true sacrifice. I have yet to meet a World War II veteran or any other Canadian veteran who sought death. The ones I have met and the ones whose letters I have read mostly yearned for nothing more than to return to home and loved ones. But first, they knew there was a job that had to be finished.

This sense of service is something that a growing number of people deem remarkable and worth recognition. And that recognition is demonstrated through acts of remembrance. At its simplest, that could mean attending Remembrance Day services on November 11. Op Husky is, of course, what documentary-maker Max Fraser is calling "an extreme act of remembrance." But there are many other forms of remembrance that people are engaging in. Thousands travel to the war cemeteries and monuments in Europe that are dedicated to those who fought in the two world wars. And Facebook members have set up hundreds of sites dedicated to the remembrance of veterans of various conflicts.

For the past few years, I have begun to think of this growing population as a remembrance culture. These people share beliefs in the importance of remembrance and the manner of its implementation. Many of them reach out to find organizations they can belong to—the Royal Canadian Legion or other less formal ones, such as the Facebook remembrance sites—to help focus their acts of remembrance. Others, like me, tend to operate in a more solitary and informal manner. Involving myself directly in Op Husky runs counter to personal tendency. But in these past few days, being surrounded by others who take the act of remembrance very seriously and have found a variety of ways to express it, I find myself being drawn more and more into this informal community. Mostly I feel comfortable here—comfortable among these people who were before strangers, but in little more than a day have begun to feel like friends, perhaps even family.

HAD IT NOT been for a man named Fabian Ware, how we remember our dead from two world wars would surely be radically different. At forty-five, Ware was too old in 1914 for military service. Determined to be useful, he finagled a posting to command of the civilian Mobile Unit, British Red Cross Society, with the self-appointed mission of collecting wounded men and stragglers from behind the front lines. As Ware and his little collection of amateur medics drove around the battlegrounds, he became increasingly dismayed by how chaotically the British army treated its dead. Every day, the numbers grew. Thousands upon thousands of corpses were strewn across the mud of Flanders and other battlefields.

In previous wars, virtually every European nation after a battle unceremoniously dumped the dead into massive pits for a common and completely unmarked burial. Senior officers might escape such treatment with their bodies being returned home, but not so the common soldier. Now, in the midst of the greatest cataclysm in history, army regulations merely called for clearing away the dead. The biggest concern was that the presence of so many corpses would spread disease and the lingering sight of decomposing bodies would demoralize the surviving troops.

Collecting the dead was assigned to their comrades, who attempted to mark each grave with a rough wooden cross and to register its location. But as no systematic record was being kept and there was no oversight body within the military apparatus, such records tended to get lost. The destructive nature of the war, with its artillery saturations, constant ebb and flow of troops from one place in the front line to another, and appalling weather conditions, meant that wooden crosses quickly were destroyed, rotted, or simply sank into the mud. Disorganized documentation was lost or even thrown away. It is no wonder that of the 1.1 million Commonwealth soldiers killed between 1914 and 1918, 500,000 ended up missing, and that 50 per cent of those with marked graves in Belgium and 40 per cent in France were of unknown identity.

Without Ware, the situation would have been far worse. By October 1914, he was studiously marking grave locations. It also became clear that the lack of concern for the dignity of the dead common in past wars would no longer be tolerated. Even this early in the war, public sentiment demanded that the war dead be properly buried and those graves maintained. On March 2, 1915, Ware's unofficial ragtag unit was officially repurposed as the Graves Registration Commission.

"It is generally recognized," General Douglas Haig, then corps commander and later commander of all British and Commonwealth forces, wrote, "that the work of the organization is of purely sentimental value, and that it does not directly contribute to the successful termination of the war. It has, however, an extraordinary moral value to the troops as well as to the relatives and friends of the dead at home....Further, on the termination of hostilities, the nation will demand an account from the government as to the steps which have been taken to mark and classify the burial places of the dead."

But Ware was not satisfied just to properly bury the dead and correctly register grave locations. At his insistence, in April 1915, orders were issued that established equal treatment on the basis that each soldier had equally sacrificed. No longer were upper-class officers exhumed and repatriated to Britain, whereas lower-class soldiers found only a common grave. Any exhumation for repatriation was forbidden, not only for hygienic reasons but also "on account of the difficulties of treating impartially the claims advanced by persons of different social standing." This order cemented the practice that would govern treatment of Commonwealth war dead in both this first Great War and the one that would follow: no repatriation allowed, and equality of treatment assured for each soldier regardless of military rank or social status.

By this time, the war had spread widely beyond Belgium and France, while also drawing in soldiers from all parts of the Empire. Soldiers of the United Kingdom fought and died alongside troops from Canada, Newfoundland, Australia, New Zealand, South Africa, India, and virtually every other colony. Battles raged in Macedonia, Gallipoli, Mesopotamia, Africa, and elsewhere. Ware's organization expanded accordingly. By May 1916, he was working in London and overseeing some seven hundred staff. Yet the killing only intensified, making the task ever more formidable.

Gaining support from the Prince of Wales, Ware proposed the creation of "an Imperial organization to care for and maintain in perpetuity the graves of those who have fallen in the War, to acquire land for the purpose of cemeteries and to erect permanent memorials in the cemeteries and elsewhere." At the Imperial War Conference of April 1917 in London, Canadian Prime Minister Robert Borden moved a resolution to this effect that was unanimously agreed to. And thus the Imperial War Graves Commission—renamed Commonwealth War Graves Commission in 1960—was born. France had already offered to "undertake the care of the graves of all soldiers of the Empire who were buried within her territory," Borden reported to the House of Commons upon his return to Canada. But at the conference, it was decided "that we should ourselves undertake that sacred duty. So it is to be." Similar concessions of land for cemeteries were to be sought "in Gallipoli, Mesopotamia, Africa, and all other theatres of war."

In July 1917, Ware solicited the services of three of Britain's most eminent architects—Edwin Lutyens, Herbert Baker, and Reginald

Blomfield—to design and construct the cemeteries and memorials. Lutyens was a classicist and responsible for the magnificent plan for the new Indian capital at Delhi undertaken in 1912. Blomfield was renowned for his Edwardian designs. Baker's work, often considered as physical manifestations of the glory of Empire, ranged across South Africa, India, and England.

Originally, each was to design an experimental cemetery from which a template would be constructed. In the event, however, Blomfield created all three, with the one constructed in Forceville, France, considered the most successful. It was a walled cemetery with uniform headstones in a garden setting. It also featured Blomfield's Cross of Sacrifice and a Stone of Remembrance added by Lutyens. These latter features were considered important because the headstones were uniform and deliberately non-denominational in shape. The Cross of Sacrifice recognized that the majority of Commonwealth soldiers were Christian, and the Stone of Remembrance represented those of all faiths and none.

Although each of the three architects was to have designed a Cross of Sacrifice suitable to the cemetery in which it would stand, Blomfield's creation, intended as he said to "keep clear of any of the sentimentalities of Gothic," was considered so brilliant it was universally adopted. It was a simple cross bearing a bronze longsword and was mounted on an octagonal stone base, weighing up to two tonnes. The block itself rested on three steps of widening stone. To indicate that for those who are buried in the cemetery the war is at an end, the sword's point is directed downward. To avoid the cross being too dominant in smaller cemeteries or lacking sufficient gravitas in larger ones, four sizes were authorized, ranging from 5.5 metres to 7.3 metres in height.

The Stone of Remembrance was intended to be a monolith—"a great fair stone of fine proportions," as Lutyens wrote, "12 feet in length, lying raised upon three steps." Each was to be constructed of a single ten-tonne block of stone, but the logistics of moving such a massive stone in some locations were found to be too difficult. Some were therefore created by fitting together less massive stones.

Dimensions were determined for every element of the graves. For example, the headstones were to be 76 centimetres tall, 38 centimetres wide, and 7.6 centimetres thick. Except for the headstones of known atheists or non-Christians, each was inscribed with a cross. Canadian headstones featured a maple leaf, and British ones bore the fallen soldier's regimental crest or service arm insignia. Where known, rank, name, unit, date of death, and age were all inscribed. The families were invited to submit personal dedications of up to four lines, each containing no more than twenty-five letters.

By November 1918, when the guns finally fell silent, the basic plan for all the cemeteries was in place. It was not without controversy, particularly the decisions that there would be only headstones and no crosses as grave markers and no repatriation of any of the fallen. These matters ultimately were debated in the British House of Commons on May 4, 1920. The strongest defenders of the commission's plan were a relatively unknown MP for the City of Westminster, William Burdett-Coutts, and the Minister of War and ex-officio head of the commission, Winston Churchill. Burdett-Coutts passionately championed the commission's stance on equality of treatment and played a strong emotional card by quoting a letter by Rudyard Kipling. "I wish some of the people who are making this trouble realized how much more fortunate they are to have a name on a headstone in a known place," Kipling had written.

The Empire's most famous author, Kipling referred directly to his own personal tragedy. On September 26, 1915, his only son, John, had gone missing during the Battle of Loos. He was last seen staggering through the mud. His face shredded by shrapnel from an exploding shell, the eighteen-year-old was screaming in agony. And then he was gone, no trace of remains to be found. For months, Kipling convinced himself that John had somehow survived and would turn up. But eventually, he came to accept the loss and with it the guilt—for without Kipling's intervention, John would not have been able to go to war. Despite his Coke-bottle glasses, he had failed the eye test and been rejected for military service. So at his son's pleading, Kipling pulled in favours and the boy was accepted—only to die on his first day of battle after arriving as part of a reinforcement contingent of Irish Guards.

Wracked by grief, Kipling had thrown himself into the work of the graves commission, volunteering to serve as its literary adviser on all the inscriptions to be used in cemeteries and on memorials. It was he who selected the inscription for the Stone of Remembrance: "Their Name Liveth for Evermore." He also wrote the inscription for headstones of unknown soldiers: "A soldier of the Great War Known unto God."

When Burdett-Coutts finished, Churchill launched into a long speech characterized by his typical lucidity and rhetorical mastery. "The cemeteries which are going to be erected to the British dead on all the battlefields in all the theatres of war, will be entirely different from the ordinary cemeteries which mark the resting place of those who pass out in the common flow of human fate from year to year....Personally, I believe, from what I have heard, that nearly all who have been to see these cemeteries have been profoundly impressed by their sense of beauty, of repose, and of dignity, and few have come away from them without a feeling of reverence and of comfort. To suggest that there has been any want of religious feeling in those who have undertaken this work, is altogether wrong. A Cross of Sacrifice will be in every cemetery, and the religious feeling of every creed, so far as is humanly possible, has been studied with utmost care." Churchill's speech awed the House, and the opposition withdrew motions intended to hobble the commission's operations.

The task facing it, however, was astonishing. Although by the spring of 1921, all 1,000 cemeteries were opened to visitors, they were by no means complete. Not until late 1937 were the cemeteries in France and Flanders finished—nearly 1,000 of them surrounded by 160 kilometres of fine stone walls and 100 kilometres of hedges. By 1923, the headstone factory in England reached peak production and was shipping out 4,000 Portland stone markers a week. Again it was not until 1937 that all 600,000 headstones were finally in place, anchored by 402 kilometres of buried concrete beams. There were 1,000 Crosses of Sacrifice, 500 Stones of Remembrance, many chapels and shelter buildings. And for those 500,000 soldiers who disappeared without trace, eighteen memorials had been erected. It was "the single biggest bit of work since any of the Pharaohs," Kipling exulted, "and they only worked in their own country."

Yet in less than two years' time, the Commonwealth was once again plunged into a cataclysmic war. Which meant the commission's work was far from complete.

THE SUN HAS not yet risen at 4:45 a.m. on July 11, when Bill Rodgers, Rod Hoffmeister, Frances, and I shoehorn ourselves into a small car driven by Max Fraser. The only one of us who isn't tall is Max, so we're a cozy and cramped group. But everyone is happy and gregarious despite the early hour. We are all grateful that many Sicilians are early risers. When Frances and I came out of the hotel, we spotted a café with its lights on just up the street. Bill, Rod, and Max were already finishing their second cappuccino at an outside table. The other patrons, mostly fishermen, look puzzled at seeing a bunch of tourists up at this hour. While Max went to retrieve his rental car, Frances and I downed a couple of cappuccinos. We were all ready to go when the car arrived, and we set off from Porto Palo toward Pachino for the march to Ispica. Twenty-one kilometres today, with the plan that we will arrive in Ispica's main square just before 11 a.m. for the remembrance ceremony. Along the way, we will swing by a unique monument, informally known as the Colonel Sydney Frost Memorial, for a second ceremony. The plan is to start marching by no later than 6:00 a.m. That allows four hours for marching, most of an hour for the ceremony at the Frost Memorial, and a couple of short rest periods. This all fits well with the allotted walking pace of five kilometres per hour that everybody was to have trained for.

Our understanding is that the marchers are to form in Pachino's main square where the ceremony took place the previous day. Max circles the square. There's no sign of anybody other than a group of what appear to be municipal workers drinking espressos and eating *cornetti*—the ubiquitous croissants generally filled with cream, chocolate, or jam (mostly marmalade). We figure the others are just late, so find a parking spot and hit the café. Another cappuccino and a *cornetto alla marmellata* each for Frances and me. Rod goes for the *cioccolato*. Both types are over the top, gushing out jam or chocolate. Between all the coffee and the chocolate, Rod's not giving any thought to his injured feet and the march ahead. Bill sticks to just coffee, finding it too early to eat anything. I figure there's no way to know when the next food beyond snacks is coming our way, so it's tank up on calories that will likely burn off all too soon.

Max is out by the car, texting on his smartphone. He's a worried filmmaker. His team is supposed to consist of himself, his wife, Arlin McFarlane, and three young fellows who will handle most of the film and sound recording. But an unusual string of violent electrical storms back in Toronto left the last three stranded at Pearson International, and they only arrived last night. While his crew are exhausted from their trip, more worrisome is that most of the film equipment was missing when their luggage came onto the carousel at Catania Airport. Airline authorities are assuring him that it will soon be delivered, but in the meantime they are having to work with scant equipment. However, they have two cars, which is giving them sufficient mobility to be flexible in following the marchers.

Frances and I are especially grateful for the two-car scenario, I in particular. It saved the day on the night of July 7 when Frances arrived to join me. Because she had not known until a few weeks before whether it would be possible to participate, her flight was booked too late for a straightforward flight path. She ended up having to travel by bus and ferry from Victoria to Vancouver International, then Lufthansa to Munich, inter-Europe carriers to Milan, and then on to Catania. This resulted in an arrival time in Catania of about 8:00 p.m., which was supposed to be fine, because André of the logistics team was to have arranged for everybody coming into the airport to be met by transportation to Porto Palo or other quarters in Pachino. At about 5:00 that evening, however, the motorhome and support cars operated by the logistics team all motored into Porto Palo. Walking over, I introduced myself to André and asked what the arrangements were for picking up Frances. "There are no arrangements," he said. "She will have to find her own way." When I reminded him that the plan had called for every person coming into Catania to be met and transported, André simply shrugged. "There are no arrangements. We can't send anybody back there now."

The next half hour passed in a flurry as I tried to find some way of arranging a taxi to bring Frances from the airport. This proved impossible. July 7 was a Sunday. The one driver who did offer transport between Catania and Porto Palo didn't work on Sundays. Neither was there any public transportation between Porto Palo and anywhere at this time of day on a Sunday. There was also the problem that neither Frances nor I possessed a cellphone, technology we were still trying to avoid. But now I was ruing the decision. We had no way to communicate.

In a state of increasing panic and at the same time anger toward André and the whole damned logistics team, I bumped into Arlin. Tiny, funny, often outrageous, and possessed of a fiery temper, Arlin is also endlessly empathetic to those in crisis. She conferred with Max. They had been planning to go either that night or the next day back to Catania to swap one of their two cars for a larger vehicle that could accommodate the missing film-crew members and to change the designated-driver details on the other. Given my situation, they would go that night with both vehicles. And so we were at the airport in time to welcome Frances, whom Max had met previously when she had been visiting Yukon.

It was a happy outcome for what could have been the complete opposite. But it did not endear the logistics folks to any of us. This was even more the case when we learned that Frances was not the only one who'd been left in the lurch. Don Aitchison had arrived about ninety minutes after we retrieved Frances, concluded Max and Arlin's car rental reorganization, and motored away to Porto Palo. He, too, had expected to be met by the logistics team. Of course, nobody showed. After waiting a long time, while trying unsuccessfully to raise somebody on the smartphone that was destined to be almost a fellow marcher on our trek, Don seriously considered booking a flight right back to Canada. Instead, he called around and booked a hotel near the airport. The following morning, he found a cab driver willing to take him to Porto Palo. As a chaplain, Don is a model of Christian charity, forgiveness, and tolerance. But it is also clear that he now harbours a certain lack of faith in the logistics team and their organizational ability and commitment to fully supporting the marchers.

Back in the square at Pachino, having finished our breakfast and still with no sign of any other marchers, we decide that we'd better search them out. Most of the marchers, as well as the officer cadets and pipe band, have either elected to stay or been assigned to stay in public facilities set aside for this purpose. These facilities have been arranged by members of the logistics team during previous visits to Sicily to develop the complete operational plan for Op Husky. The current facility is Pachino's fire hall, where there is a large empty room with bathroom facilities. Everybody sleeps on folding cots.

Frances and I had decided to forego such communal accommodation for the first few nights in Sicily and stay on at the hotel where Steve and the rest of us had been quartered until the full group assembled on July 9. We intended to move to the fire hall after the march to Ispica and then spend most nights in communal accommodation, with a possible break at a hotel or bed and breakfast midway through. In the planning, it had been made clear that participants could opt in and out of communal accommodation as they wished. Alternative contingency accommodation was to have been checked out and a plan put in place that would allow for seamless movement of people between venues. Those opting for alternative accommodation would only have to pay the cost of it; getting to and from it would be taken care of.

Not sure where the fire hall was situated, Max starts trying to bring it up on Google Maps. He's not getting too far, when one of the Italian workers in the café realizes what we are trying to find. Jumping into his car, he guides us to the fire hall, points it out, and then drives away.

We go in to find the room in a state of disorder. People are still getting dressed and trying to eat breakfast. Steve, who moved to the fire hall the night before, is bustling about shouting departure times, which keep passing by and being replaced by another. "Five minutes, everybody," he shouts. People keep milling about, five minutes pass, and then ten minutes. "Five minutes," Steve reiterates. By the time everybody moves out, at least six deadlines have passed unmet, and it's already after 6:00 a.m.

Marchers march. Pipe band and officer cadets are sandwiched into the back of the motorhome. On Pachino's outskirts, we meet a provincial police car with a couple of officers who will provide an escort. Sicilian roads are narrow, and everybody drives as fast as is safe and sometimes faster than that. The police car's flashing lights will offer some protection, or so it is hoped. We all wear neon-green safety vests, save Steve. He has an orange one to distinguish him as the leader.

The sun is still rising as we walk along roads regularly bordered by thick stands of bamboo that reach high above our heads. We are walking along the plateau that forms a narrow shelf snaking out along the coast to the west of Siracusa all the way to Licota, where the main mountain ranges that cover most of Sicily bump up close to the island's southern coastline. Immediately south of us is Cape Passero, Europe's most southerly point and the place where the Canadian and British troops landed in 1943. Like the Canadian soldiers did on July 11, we march northwest out of the peninsula that leads to the cape and toward Ispica. To our left is the Mediterranean, and in the distance to the right rise the gentle slopes of Monti Iblei—known in English as the Hyblaean Mountains. These mountains are separated from the rest of Sicily's rugged heart by the expanse of the Catania Plain to their north and a deep valley that runs along their western flank to the coast. Once we get to Ispica, we will be marching into the centre of this range before crossing the valley at Caltagirone and entering the higher mountains of Sicily's heartland.

We are barely above sea level, the Mediterranean often hidden by overgrown sand dunes. These dunes also separate a number of large salt marshes from the sea. Passing alongside one of the marshes, I look up to see a tightly packed flock of more than a hundred brilliantly coloured pink flamingos overhead. The flock swoops down to land on the marsh close to us. When the birds stand up on delicate legs, the water is so shallow that it scarcely covers their feet. I imagine the heat of summer evaporating away much of the water, just as it draws the sweat ever more as the temperature climbs. Since the moment the sun fully rose, the heat has been increasing dramatically.

Although there are more salt marshes here, they don't dominate the plateau. Mostly it is blanketed by fields of vegetables,
small orchards, the occasional vineyard, and some greenhouse
complexes. There is little traffic. At one point, a horse-drawn
wagon about the size of a sulky goes past with an older man holding the reins. He stares at us curiously and we at him. We pass a
barnyard with some cattle in a small pasture that reeks of manure
and is swarming with black flies. But livestock are not the focus
here. Vegetables and orchards reign supreme. We come upon a
man who has set up a roadside fruit-and-vegetable stand next to a
battered old truck. I try to buy a few of the strangely dough-
nut-shaped white peaches that are so delicious, but the man waves
away the money. One of Les Gilles is buying a bagful of fruit for
everybody and having the same difficulty getting him to take the
money. Instead, he shakes hands with many of us and is delighted
when somebody gives him one of the small Canadian flag pins we
all carry.

We gather around the motorhome next to the stand and eat fruit.
The peaches are so tender they dissolve in an explosion of juice
inside the mouth and drizzle through fingers. Three types of plums
are making the rounds. I drain one of the two-litre water bottles
stuffed in outside pockets of my hip belt and refill it from a large
water container in the motorhome. Piper Iain MacLeod, wearing his
white Op Husky shirt and red ball cap with a red plaid kilt, gets out
of the motorhome and shoulders his bagpipes. He leads off playing,
and we marchers fall in behind. Back on the road.

The police car is out front idling along slowly. Phil moves out
front. During the planning phases, Steve drafted him into serving as
the march's marshal because he's a retired soldier. In the weeks leading up to our departure for Sicily, Phil sent many emails offering
various bits of advice he had gathered on equipment and clothing.
Each note ended with the rallying cry, *"Marchons!"* It is a cry that is
often invoked over the following weeks. One of Phil's duties is to
ensure that the marching pace is kept at or under the five kilometres
an hour stipulated during our training. Iain with his pipes is about
twenty metres behind, and following him are Bob, Don, Frances,

and me. Because the road is narrow, Phil has asked us to keep to a single column as much as possible.

"Dad never described countryside anything like this," Rod says from behind me. No kilt and army dress shoes today. He's wearing a sensible wide-brimmed sun hat, quick-dry, short-sleeved green shirt, khaki shorts, and running shoes. I'm dressed pretty much the same. We all are, in fact, although Don, Bill, and Phil opt for pants and long-sleeved shirts for sun protection. There are at least three Tilley hats—the original white sailcloth style that became famous when the company gave one to every Canadian soldier who deployed to the Persian Gulf in 1990–1991. These hats are ubiquitous among Canadians travelling in hot climates or just about anywhere. Having travelled extensively and regularly in the deserts of the American southwest, I have decided the Tilley is too heavy, and it doesn't breathe. My hat has mesh sides on its crown that lets air pass through.

Some of us use daypacks, some hip belts, and others just pockets for whatever items we choose to carry. Jean Miso has a lovely old oxblood-coloured leather pack. She's the smallest person among us, but her pack is the largest. And the heaviest. What Jean has crammed in there becomes a source of speculation. At one point, Bill offers that perhaps there are rocks dumped in the bottom to slow her down.

Looking around at all the technically sophisticated gear—save Jean's pack—that extends from our boots to the tops of our heads, I think about the soldiers back in 1943. Most landed in Sicily wearing summer-weight khaki long-sleeved shirts and shorts, though some managed to switch to pants, mainly for protection against the swarms of mosquitoes (common then but today much reduced and seldom malarial). Heavy combat boots. Steel helmet that acted like an upside-down frying pan in the sun. Web gear stuffed with ammunition and some rations, and hung about with grenades, clips for the platoon's Bren gun, and a canteen. Small pack generally worn in combat operations and loaded with minimal general-issue equipment and personal items. Carrying either a Lee-Enfield rifle, Thompson submachine gun, Bren gun (the Commonwealth forces' standard light machine gun), PIAT gun (standard infantry-operated anti-tank weapon), light mortar, or radio set. All this gear weighed eighteen to twenty-five kilograms.

Rod's father, as the commander then of the Seaforth Highlanders of Canada, would have been a little better off. Revolver in a holster on his belt, minimal web belt equipment (his batman took care of most of his kit), and a roll of maps stuffed into a tube about the length of an officer's swagger stick. Some officers carried one of those, too, but that was not Bert Hoffmeister's style. Having come up through the ranks, he had little use for pretention. In photos from Sicily, he is tall and strong looking—like his son. I think of the route we are walking and realize that seventy years ago, Rod's father was likely walking the same one, because 2nd Canadian Infantry Brigade was headed in this direction with Ispica as its objective. A little farther inland, 1st Canadian Infantry Brigade marched toward the village of Rosolini. Ispica and Rosolini stand in line with each other, roughly the same distance from Pachino. The fathers of Phil Bury and Max Fraser would have been on that route as members of the Hastings and Prince Edward Regiment. One or the other of them might have served in the company commanded by Lieutenant Farley Mowat. Where Terry Dolan's photographer father or Bob Werbiski's pharmacist father would have been situated seventy years ago today I have no idea. But they had landed and were certainly deployed.

There was no real fighting on July 11. The Italian troops were mostly on the run or trying to surrender. Sicily—or, more precisely, its summer heat—was the enemy. Mowat described it in his memoir *And No Birds Sang.* Unlike today's paved road, the one he marched on was dirt. Dust rose thick to mix with sweat on his face and form a "cracking crust." Brutal heat, no water. The weight of equipment and gear almost intolerable. Cursing the loss of the transport when those three ships were torpedoed and sunk. The Hasty Ps were part of a long, snaking column strung out for several kilometres as the three battalions forming 1st Brigade worked their way into the hills ahead.

"Sicily is a 'big country,'" wrote the British Army's official historian, C.J.C. Molony, in his account of the campaign, "because a height which is nothing to a mountaineer (3,000 feet and somewhat over is a Sicilian mean) is formidable to the loaded infantryman, the gunner, the signaller, and the porter of ammunition, water, and rations. The terrain is varied, and difficult. There are terraced slopes and foot-hills, long swelling slopes and steep jagged ridges, crests large or small and often false, in jumbles or one after another, sharp pitches, corries and spurs. These features do not occur everywhere at once, but in sum they demanded from troops a degree of physical fitness and hardiness different from that required by fairly flat or rolling country. They were, moreover, perplexing to men not bred to hills or mountains."

WHILE THINKING ABOUT all this, I notice that our pace has quickened. Steve is out at the front and marching hard. It's a struggle to keep up. I see Phil is no longer at the head of the group and realize he's fallen behind to near the rear. I can see that he's finding the pace hard, and so is Terry, right back at the rear. Terry's shirt is drenched with sweat. His big camera with a long-barrelled telephoto is riding heavy on his shoulder. His discomfort is plain to see. Iain is standing by the side of the road. He plays his pipes as we pass by and then is picked up by the motorhome. It's trailing in our wake, emergency flashers on, large Canadian flags attached to the sides and back. I close in on Don, who is looking at his phone. "Six kilometres an hour," he reports and gives me a quizzical look. Don's phone is laden with apps. One gives our pace. One monitors caloric consumption. Another charts a profile of altitudes and grades over which we pass. Don is often walking with the phone held in both hands, monitoring it, searching the web for information about something he has just seen or that we are talking about.

Slipping past Don, I catch up to Steve. As if anticipating my question, he says, "We've got to pick up the pace. At this rate we'll be late getting to the town square for the ceremony." I suggest that we can pick up some time if we cut the ceremony at Frost Memorial a little short. Steve says nothing to this. "I want to be in place at the square by 10:30 instead of 11:00. We don't want to keep people waiting."

I drop back and walk just ahead of Frances. We are both doing okay. The pace is too fast, but manageable. We come to a road junction. I have been to the Frost Memorial once before, when I was acting as battlefield historian on an Italian Campaign tour for a group of Canadians. Steve keeps striding straight along the road leading directly to Ispica, rather than taking the turnoff. That road hooks down to the coast, and the road to Ispica goes inland. I'm certain the memorial is on the former.

When I dash forward to warn Steve that we've missed the turn, he says that we are skipping the memorial in order to get to the square on time. "Aren't people supposed to meet us there?" I ask.

Steve says there was nothing formally planned and it won't matter. Not what I understood, but Steve has the bit between his teeth for sure. We go a little farther along, and then the police car stops. The two officers get out and start talking to Steve. He has been studying Italian and actually has a fair grasp of the language. I am pretty sure the officers have been in radio contact with somebody about the route we are taking. A few minutes pass, during which Steve and the policemen rapidly exchange sentences. My Italian is terrible, and they are speaking way too fast for me to follow any of it.

Suddenly, a small convoy of cars arrives. Out of one climbs a short fellow with grey hair who is wearing a suit and has the formal sash of a *sindaco*, Italian for mayor. The sash is worn over one shoulder and crosses the chest to rest against the other hip. Every *sindaco* wears such a sash during formal functions. He and the police officers start talking. Then Steve is drawn in. From another car, Rosie Scifo appears. She says that people are waiting for us at the memorial. More cars have arrived now. Several of them are police cars, from which emerge a number of female police officers in dress uniform. Some have white caps, others white pith helmets. All are wearing shoes with at least two-inch heels. "Obviously, they aren't planning on chasing down any criminals today," Bill says with a mischievous grin.

Marchers start getting bundled into cars. The police officers jump into their vehicles. Frances, Rod, Bill, and I get into Rosie's car. The *sindaco* and a younger man who seems to serve as his assistant climb into the lead car, with Steve in the back like a man taken into custody. And off to the memorial we go.

ALTHOUGH WE HAVE been calling it the Frost Memorial, it is actually a monument erected by the communes of Pachino and Ispica in
1991 to recognize the nearby landing by 1st Canadian Infantry Division on July 10, 1943. We think of it as the Frost Memorial because,
although Pachino and Ispica facilitated and provided funding for the
building of it, the vision for it was entirely that of a retired army
colonel named Charles Sydney Frost. In 1943, he was a twenty-one-
year-old Princess Patricias lieutenant who on July 16 found himself
assigned to serve as Ispica's military mayor. Ispica had been heavily
bombarded prior to the invasion and fell without a fight on July 11.
The town's administration had collapsed. The fascist mayor and his
cronies fled, and a new administration was yet to be created. Working largely alone, Frost organized the community and set about
seeing that food, fuel, and other necessities were made available to
its struggling populace of some thirteen thousand people. By the
time he handed over Ispica's keys to a civil authority on August 3, the
place was functioning pretty much normally. During his sixteen-day
mayoralty, Frost had developed good relations—even friendships—
with a fair number of people there.

In July 1989, he sought to re-establish those relationships during
a pilgrimage of remembrance to Europe that brought him back to
Ispica. Managing to gain the Canadian beach nearby, he was dis-
tressed to find only "a bleak, forlorn area of sand and soil littered
with driftwood, broken bottles, tin cans and other debris thrown up
by the sea." All this garbage on a spot he considered sacred angered
him deeply, Frost wrote in his memoir *Always a Patricia*. "And where
is the memorial marking this place where Canada's soldiers broke
into Fortress Europe? Graves there are aplenty in Sicily and Italy but
their message is one of sacrifice. I knew instantly what I had to do. I
resolved then and there to do everything in my power to erect on this
beach a Memorial to the achievements of the First Canadian
Division. For the next two years I would relentlessly pursue my goal."

Frost was so like Steve with Op Husky—another irrepressible
visionary. Rebuffed by the then minister of Veteran Affairs, who
advised that it was Canadian government policy "not to erect markers and memorials overseas in connection with the Second World

War," Frost finally ended up working with the local administrations of Pachino and Ispica to fund the project. He quietly invested personally to make the monument a reality. Two years after he began writing letters and talking up the idea, the monument was unveiled on the forty-eighth anniversary of the landing.

It does not actually stand on the beach but is about two hundred metres from its westerly flank. The ceremony we held on July 10 had been on the easterly flank, so when we arrive at the monument, we are not far from where we started off marching the previous day. The monument is large and consists of three concrete columns set within a semicircular cement-and-stone surround. The central column is dedicated to 1st Canadian Infantry Division, and the inscription in Italian and English states that on July 10, 1943, "Canada's soldiers of the First Division landed on these shores. From little towns in a faraway land they came in the cause of freedom. Erected to their memory by the citizens of Pachino and Ispica." The other two columns were added later, in 2000, again largely through Frost's efforts. One gives the names of soldiers from Ispica who died in World War II, and the other lists the town's civilians killed in the bombardment.

Frost had been present for the unveiling of the monument in 1991, but by 2000, his failing health prevented him from travelling to Italy. In his later years, Frost had taken to wintering in Victoria and spending the rest of the year in Toronto. I visited him several times at his Victoria apartment, and he was delighted when I was able to tell him that a group of Canadians on a battlefield tour had visited the monument. Soon after that, on August 6, 2009, he passed away. I hold my memories of those visits close as the ceremony begins. And I think of how the vision of a single soul is often required to build symbols of remembrance that bring divergent peoples together. I realize that is happening here at this very moment, as a roughly equivalent number of Sicilians and Canadians gather at the monument. It's a simple ceremony and one mercifully devoid of long speeches. A bugler from Ispica wearing a white uniform with red cap plays the last post. Beside him proudly stands his son of about six, who is dressed in an identical uniform. Iain Macleod pipes the lament. Steve and the *sindaco* place wreaths. Photos are taken. Then we bundle into the cars and head back to continue the march to Ispica.

AS THE CLOCK ticks toward 11:00, making Steve increasingly twitchy, the convoy drives past the place where we had paused our march and finally stops a short distance from where the road climbs steeply up to Ispica. When I grouse about this, several other marchers echo my disappointment. We have come to march in the footsteps of our soldiers and believe that should take precedence over ceremonies. But Steve is adamant that we must be at the square on time. And it's clear that we're going to be in a race to get there even with the cut in distance, which I estimate as having knocked off about five kilometres.

Steve leads off at a cracking pace. Minutes later, we are climbing up SP47. Just wide enough for two cars to pass, this road is a poorly maintained assemblage of asphalt patches that winds up a narrow canyon of yellowish limestone cliffs riddled with caves. We have left the plateau's verdant agricultural fields dramatically behind. A modern, better road gets to Ispica faster and more directly, and our motorhome peels off on it. Because the older route we take has almost no traffic, it's safer for walkers but has switchbacks far too tight for the motorhome to navigate.

Suddenly, we enter a remarkable, almost fantastical, landscape. Lush foliage spills down the sides of the cliffs to surround the cave openings. Although natural, many of the caves have been transformed into small living spaces—apparently second homes for locals. Bricks carved out of limestone have been mortared into some larger cave openings to create solid walls that surround doorways and windows. Stout wooden and steel doors and barred windows decidedly mark these caves as private property. Through the doors and windows that are open we see the trappings of normal domesticity—kitchens, tables and chairs, televisions, paintings on walls. Stuff you find in any southern Italian home. It's just the dwelling itself that is unique. Although most of the caves have been taken over by people, many remain wild, as they have been for millennia.

Large or narrow openings lead into shadowed spaces that extend who knows how far into the depths. There is little level ground in this canyon, and the postage-stamp-sized patches that do exist typically support olive groves. The trees are lightly dusted with limestone, making them duller than normal green. Most of the ground between the two cliff walls, however, is jumbled and rough, with the road snaking up the one side or cutting back and forth across its narrower parts.

All of us are more than a little awed by this unexpected canyon. Later I will learn that it's an offshoot of the thirteen-kilometre-long fissure known as Cava d'Ispica, situated between Ispica and the town of Modica to the north. Like this disconnected stub, Cava d'Ispica is studded with thousands of natural caves and grottoes. Its caves, and likely these here, have been used for human habitation since at least 2000 BC. Neolithic tombs, Christian catacombs, medieval hide-outs, and Byzantine-era churches carved out of rock are all found there.

We are walking through a spectacular, photogenic archaeological and tourist site. But Steve is so focused on getting to the town square that we are left with no time to stop and gaze about in wonder, or to draw cameras for carefully framed photographs. Instead, we snap pictures virtually on the run. It's either that or fall behind and have to sprint to catch up. Because of the pace and the road's grindingly steep grade, we begin to take casualties. First I see Terry stop and hitch a ride in the car André is driving, which is following our ascent. Then Phil climbs in. Rod and I are close behind Steve, who is becoming frantic over the thought of our being late for the ceremony. "If we're going to get there on time, we need to all get in the cars," he announces.

"You can do what you like," I say, "but I'm walking. It won't matter even if we're half an hour late. Just allows more time for people to gather and makes our entry all the more effective. If we all arrive by car, it's not going to make much of an impression." Rod backs me up.

Steve concedes the point and agrees that his insistence that we be in place for the ceremony at least thirty minutes in advance is unreasonable. "But I don't want us being more than ten or fifteen minutes late—ever," he declares. It is not yet 10:30, and we pause, where some woods and brush offer the women a little privacy, and all don our white shirts and red ball caps. Then we continue up the canyon until we turn a corner and are walking through the outskirts of Ispica. The streets are narrow, and unlike yesterday in Pachino, today there are no large cheering crowds to greet us. In fact, the streets we walk along are mostly empty. Few cars, fewer people, and the houses and businesses are mostly closed up as if the siesta has started early. We walk along these eerily deserted streets until we come to a square with a large church. Here we are met by the rest of the Op Husky team, the *sindaco*, other civic representatives, police and military officials, religious authorities, and Ispica's marching band. Looking at my watch, I see that we are a few minutes early. But it takes until 11:15 before the Sicilians have sorted themselves out.

Steve's concern that we would be late has proven groundless, but I'm not feeling smug—I'm worrying about tomorrow. Will Steve be trying to make us ride in vehicles again, if we seem to be running behind? If he does, I decide, it will be without me. Alone, if necessary, I'm walking. It's what we came to do. These ceremonies are fine, but they are not the heart of this venture. The heart is the daily marching.

With our pipe band leading, we advance through ever-widening streets until we reach the expansive Piazza dell'Unità d'Italia. It's a massive square bordered by impressive civic buildings and churches. A reviewing stand is set up near Ispica's war memorial. Speeches are made. Jean, flanked on either side by one of the female police officers we met at the Frost Monument, is called upon to lay a wreath before Ispica's war memorial. A bugler from the town's band plays the last post. One of our pipers follows with the lament. Both national anthems are sung. The vicar offers a prayer.

Unlike the ceremony in Pachino, this one is not well attended by Ispica's citizens. There is a crowd, but it's pretty small. But then, as the *sindaco* pointed out in his speech, Ispica took a hard beating in the Allied invasion. Most of its citizens emerged safely from the very caves we marched past in the canyon, but the town was severely damaged by the naval and air bombardment and required extensive rebuilding. Perhaps many Ispicans have mixed feelings about the need to remember the arrival of the Canadians. Still, those who have attended seem truly respectful and engaged in this act of remembrance.

When the ceremony ends, Frances, Rod, and I find a patch of lawn shaded by a small tree and wait there until it's time to attend an organized lunch. We are all generally happy with the course of the day. Despite the logistical confusion, to which Steve added his share, the march itself went well and took us into some amazing country-side. There was time for the group to get better acquainted, as well as time to think about the soldiers whose footsteps we are following. The ceremony at the Syd Frost Monument was poignant, and the events inside Ispica went well. We look forward to the morrow.

TODAY IS JULY 12. We walk through country that is sectioned by a network of ancient drystone walls. Most are about a metre high, but in places they rise to more than two metres. Where there are signs of relatively recent repairs—say, since World War 11—the stones have been roughly mortared into place. Have the local farmers forgotten the skill of drystone wall making? And why is this area of Sicily divided up by stone walls, and no other? It's a puzzle that we never solve.

The landscape is gently undulating and often provides wide vistas that reveal hundreds more stone walls, all serving to enclose pastures and fields. Most are small, but some could contain a fairly large herd of cattle. On the Internet I find photos of walled fields in which golden grain is growing. But the fields we pass are all barren. In a few, well-spaced olive trees grow. The soil looks poor, more rock than dirt. Perhaps this is the story. To create even a modicum of arable land, all the larger stones had to be removed. With nowhere to put them, the peasants created walls to delineate their claimed patch of earth. I imagine these Sicilians down through the centuries jealously guarding their turf and the sheep, goats, and perhaps cattle that grazed within. This country resembles nothing any of us has seen before—it seems utterly unique to this small part of Ragusa province.

We are headed for Modica, a town liberated twice on July 12, 1943, by different Canadian officers. One of these officers was our Sherry Atkinson. His Royal Canadian Regiment anti-tank platoon was the only part of the battalion that had transport because of the need for Bren carriers—small tracked vehicles with open tops and lightly armoured sides—to pull the anti-tank guns. After he and the platoon got separated from the rest of his unit, they bumped into a roadblock manned by Italians who actually wanted to fight. A short firefight ended with the Italians routed, a few lying dead on the ground and the rest surrendering. Moments later, Modica's mayor turned up in his finery and made it known that he was prepared to surrender the town. Jumping on a motorcycle with his batman behind, Sherry followed the mayor to the main square. Here, several hundred Italian soldiers waited, weapons neatly stacked, to surrender to the first passing Allied officer. Sherry duly took their surrender.

In the late evening of July 11, a Royal Canadian Horse Artillery captain named George Mitchell had cautiously slipped into Modica in company with a couple of Princess Patricias scouts. The small party encountered several civilians, who led them to where another group of hundreds of Italian soldiers were anxious to surrender. Modica, in fact, was teeming with surrender-bent soldiers. Among them was Generale di Brigata Achille d'Havet, who commanded the 206th Italian Coastal Defence Division. After holding out for a few hours for the right to surrender to someone of equal rank, the general finally agreed to allow Sherry to carry out the formality. The young lieutenant let the general keep his pistol. In this manner, Sherry was responsible for taking virtually an entire division bloodlessly out of the war.

As we walk toward Modica, I point out that it is a very good thing that the Italians had scant interest in fighting. All these stone walls could have been transformed into fortified bastions of resistance. A single machine gun firing through a loophole in one wall could have held up a battalion for hours, and killed a lot of soldiers.

The walls in fact presented a problem for us this morning. We were supposed to march twenty-three kilometres, but when we gathered on the outskirts of Ispica to begin our trek, the logistics team announced that for the first eight kilometres, the road was so narrow and tightly bordered by walls as to be dangerous. So we had to accept being moved beyond that stretch by car and motorhome. The result is a fifteen-kilometre walk with none of the urgency to keep a move on that punctuated yesterday's effort.

Not far from Modica, we find the marker team hard at work at a roundabout. Looking hot and more than a little frustrated, they have been carving away at the unyielding earth with a shovel and pick. As we pitch in to help, the roundabout starts getting crowded. Max's film crew—director Matt Pancer, photography director Oliver Glaser, and cameraperson Duncan Vogel—start shooting footage. The motorhome disgorges the pipe band and officer cadets. There are four markers, and I am surprised to see that each bears the name of a soldier killed while serving in the Royal Canadian Corps of Signals. Lacking any historical records, I imagine they were likely killed by a stray artillery or mortar round while working together with one of the larger wireless sets used by brigade or divisional headquarters.

As on the beach, we end up gathering small boulders to anchor the markers in place. While this work is being finished, Jean and I remark on how stark the setting is. A few metres away are several oleander bushes, thick with pink, purple, and white blossoms. Joined by Frances, we harvest some small bouquets and set these at the base of each marker.

To date, our experience with the markers has been clouded by uncertainty. Beyond planting a certain number each day, there has been no further plan. On July 10, the markers played a small part in the Pachino beach ceremony, but they were not integral to it. Yesterday, our paths and that of the marker team barely crossed. Most of the markers were seen only by Dave MacLeod, Erik Gregory, and Christopher-Denny Matte. Except for the ones at the Frost Memorial, we passed only a small cluster by the side of the road outside Ispica and, because of the pace set, whizzed by with barely an acknowledgement. As Don Aitchison later says, this was something "no one felt good about." So today we resolve to do something more meaningful. We try a moment of silence, but this doesn't feel like enough. Then Steve asks Don if he would mind saying a prayer, which the padre obligingly does. It's a simple blessing of the markers, which stand in remembrance of the soldiers who died on this day seventy years ago. Then Iain MacLeod plays the lament. And, suddenly, the markers become an essential part of what we are here to do.

All my skepticism about the markers evaporates. It's true that the remains of most of these soldiers lie buried in Agira Canadian War Cemetery, or at least there are headstones there bearing their names. The markers in no way diminish that fact. Instead, they give us a chance to remember the sacrifice these soldiers made on, or as close as possible to, the day and place they fell. This, we find, is an important distinction. And as the markers are placed along the route we take each day, they will also be visual reminders to Sicilians passing by. For those who stop to look more closely, the markers provide the names and dates of the fallen. But perhaps more important to the Sicilians will be the inscriptions the students have written, mostly in Italian. These connect the past to the present in a very powerful way.

As we leave the roundabout, Modica is directly ahead. Unlike most Sicilian towns, it lies largely in a valley, rather than being crowded onto a hill or mountaintop. The oldest part of the town, however, is perched on a rocky hill to the south, and many buildings seem to cling perilously to sharp cliff faces. This part of the town traces its roots back to 1300 BC and has a long history of violence and slaughter. Romans drove out the Carthaginians in the Punic Wars, Moors conquered the place and then lost it to the Normans. On August 15, 1474, the predominant Christian population went on a rampage to expel the small Jewish community as part of their Assumption Day celebration. After butchering 360 Jews, they marched through the streets chanting in Sicilian dialect, "Hurrah for Mary! Death to the Jews!"

Things settled down after that for more than a hundred years, until Mount Etna shrugged a little harder than normal in 1613, and Modica suffered a devastating earthquake. This was followed in 1693 by another earthquake, which rippled out from beneath Etna to practically level southeastern Sicily's eight main towns—Caltagirone,

Militello in Val di Catania, Catania, Modica, Noto, Palazzolo, Ragusa, and Scicli. All were rebuilt in Baroque style, the predominant architectural form at that time.

Barocco siciliano had a few unique distinctions. Besides the typical curves and flourishes adorning exterior and interior walls, there was a penchant for grinning masks and a flamboyancy greater than anywhere else—not something easily accomplished given the flamboyancy inherent in Baroque architecture. The form was mostly concentrated in the earthquake-ravished area of the Val Noto, where these eight communities are found. Sicily's Baroque era lasted little more than fifty years and was confined primarily to cathedrals, other buildings erected by the Roman Catholic Church, and palaces of the small but extremely powerful Sicilian aristocracy. Although they nominally ruled the island at Spain's behest, these aristocrats held in their collective fists most of the land upon which Sicily's agricultural economy depended. The peasants toiled for the profit of the rich, while living in a poverty that brought them perilously close to starvation.

Some say the fitful pace of construction during this period stemmed from the aristocrats sensing they raced against time. For most of those living in southeastern Sicily, every glance northward bore a reminder of their mortality. There, Etna towered to a height of just over 3,300 metres from a base 140 kilometres in circumference. Sprawling giant-like across 1,190 square kilometres, Etna could not be ignored. When the ground shivered beneath people's feet, they knew Etna was the cause. She was eternal, a goddess who spewed fire, oozed lava, and split the solid earth apart on a whim. In 1669, a river of lava had spilled down her southern slope and slowly, inexorably, flowed toward Catania. The city might have burned had not its surrounding walls diverted the lava into the harbour. Predicting when the mountain would next visit destruction upon them was futile. Sicilians then tended to resign themselves to the possibility that she might at any time destroy them and all they built. Sicilians today feel the same.

Consequently, perhaps, the absurdly wealthy aristocracy indulged in virtually unlimited excess. This taste for extravagance extended to their architecture, where no amount of embellishment was considered too much. Balcony supports, for example, were often hidden by grotesque masks or the chubby little winged male children known as *putti*. In the early years, much of this was so heavy-handed it was simply gauche, but over time the Sicilian architects displayed a greater subtlety. As the designs grew freer, they became even more differentiated from those common in the rest of Italy. The Sicilians began integrating features more rooted in the physical world around them. The grinning masks supporting balconies remained, but the wrought iron of the railings often included depictions of leaves, fish scales, shells, and common sweets.

Following the 1693 earthquake, Modica spread down the slope, and construction extended out onto the valley floor. That is where most of its population lives today. Building here was a dicey decision, though, as in 1833 and 1902, the two rivers running into the valley flooded and caused more extensive destruction. The threat of future floods was addressed soon after the one of 1902 by channelling the rivers underground and rebuilding on top of them. Modica is reputed to have a hundred churches or the ruins thereof. Like the other seven towns rebuilt in *barocco* style, it was declared a UNESCO World Heritage Site in 2002.

After pausing to don our Op Husky white shirts and red ball caps, we meet up with a number of local police, who escort us into the town. It's a busy road, so they have a car out front and several officers walking alongside on foot. Max's film team is also out front in a black car with the hatch open and Matt squeezed in the back with a camera rolling. We soon come upon the pipe band and proceed a short distance to the smallish Piazza Monumento, where the ceremony is held before the war memorial.

Each day, André Durand selects different members of the group to lay the wreath, which is part of the ceremony. Today, Frances and I draw the duty. After the *sindaco* places a large wreath on behalf of the community, we place the Operation Husky 2013 one. After years of watching wreaths being laid during Remembrance Day ceremonies back in Canada, this is a first experience for me. We place it *very* carefully. Backs turned to the memorial and wreath, hats over our hearts, we stand at quasi attention as a local priest gives the prayers.

Today, the crowd is quite large, and Sherry Atkinson's star status asserts itself. He's wearing the Royal Canadian Regiment's association uniform—a dark blue beret with the regimental crest, white shirt with blue epaulets, and dark pants. Sherry is a small man who's turned quite square with age. His hair and moustache are clipped with military precision. He seems much younger than his ninety-one years. When he takes the microphone and starts speaking, he engages the crowd with his dignity and humour.

Sherry tells the story of the day he liberated the town and took the surrender of the Italian soldiers. Enza Scifo, Rosie's sister, is on hand to translate. Sherry asks if there is anybody in the crowd who was alive in 1943 and can verify his story. It's a line he will repeat in each town hereafter. An old fellow I had noticed hanging on the edge of the crowd comes forward and says he was seven then and remembers. This prompts Sherry to relate how he and the other soldiers were so struck by the sight of the many children in Modica who seemed to be starving that they gave away all their rations, and then realized they had no food for themselves. "We didn't regret that," he says, and adds that perhaps he gave some of his food to this fellow. He ends by saying that remembrance is not about glorifying war, but about hoping that such things never happen again. It's a remarkably moving speech and delivered entirely without reference to notes. I find myself tearing up, and notice that others of us are doing the same. Bill Rodgers said earlier that we can measure these days in terms of how many times we are moved to tears. Today, the marker ceremony outside Modica and Sherry's address to the crowd count as two such moments.

When Sherry finishes, he is swarmed by the crowd. Dozens of people jockey to get their photo taken standing beside him, shaking his hand. Women hug and kiss him. Sherry obviously loves the exposure. A few days later, however, after a similar mobbing, he will say to Frances and me: "It's not really about me. I'm just a symbol—a symbol of all of us soldiers who came here and liberated them. It's the symbol they are recognizing." That may be true, but he's a hell of a good representative for all those others who can't be here today.

After the ceremony, we adjourn to a prepared lunch. Among the dishes featured, and one that over the days proves to be a staple at such affairs, is *pasta alla norma*—spaghetti generously sauced with a mixture of fresh ripe tomatoes, eggplant, ricotta salata, garlic, onion, and lots of basil. This is Sicily's classic pasta. Consequently, each restaurant is anxious to offer the *canadesi* its version, which naturally surpasses any other. In nineteenth-century Sicily, this pasta became so wildly popular that people declared its perfection was matched only by the artistry of the hugely successful opera *Norma*, composed by Sicily's beloved Vincenzo Bellini. The essence of this pasta dish, Sicilians will tell you, is the use of ricotta salata rather than the regular sweet ricotta. Whereas normal ricotta is moist and served fresh, the salata is pressed, salted, and then dried. The result is a hard white cheese that has a mildly salty, nutty, and milky flavour. Sicilians are wild about ricotta salata. They grate or shave it into pastas, onto salads, and over vegetable dishes. And they never seem to tire of *pasta alla norma*.

After the meal, I join Sherry's table. I've known Sherry for several years through correspondence as part of my research for *Operation Husky*, but we have not previously met. And this is the first opportunity to talk since we both ended up in Sicily. I'm enjoying a glass of red wine, and Sherry is finishing up a cold beer that fits within his allowable quota. As we chat about Operation Husky today and yesterday, Sherry tells me he had a friend killed in Sicily. "When I go to Agira cemetery," he says, "we have a little chat. One should never get to know others when you're in the infantry." Sherry's voice softens. "I'm an old man. He died at twenty." He shrugs. "That's just life."

For us marchers, our time in Modica turns out very well. After lunch, most of us take up an invitation from the municipal authority to tour the chocolate museum. We discover that *cioccolato modicano* is famous and sustains an unusual cottage industry largely exclusive to the town and not seen outside Ragusa province. It all traces back to Sicily's history as likely one of the world's most conquered places. In the sixteenth century, the Spanish ruled here at the same time as they were busily conquering the south and central Americas. When the Aztecs fell under the heel of the conquistadors, their method of chocolate making was transported back to Sicily and sustained in Modica.

Today, the recipe remains almost identical to that of the Aztecs. It is made straight from the cacao beans with no cocoa butter or soy lecithin added. The beans are ground with a stone rolling pin, then roasted into a mush that never exceeds 40 degrees Celsius. At this temperature, sugar doesn't melt as it is blended in, and the result is the famous grainy texture that makes *cioccolato modicano* distinct. The original added flavourings were vanilla, cinnamon, or hot chili peppers. Today, many other flavours may be mixed in as well—white pepper, citrus, cardamom, sea salt, and nutmeg all being popular. Having such a hard texture makes the chocolate a delight for artistic carving, and the museum includes an extensive display of fanciful designs. The centrepiece is a huge, topographically accurate, dioramic map of Italy. But there are also teddy bears, the Incredible Hulk ripping apart a bunch of what appears to be early Industrial Age machinery, and classical Byzantine busts. At the end of our tour, we are each given a 100-gram bar of the chocolate that the town has packaged with a specially designed wrapper commemorating Operation Husky 2013. The Op Husky logo is superimposed over a photo of Canadian troops marching into Modica on July 12, 1943. Inside is classic *cioccolato modicano*, flavoured only with vanilla and a dash of remembrance!

July 13, and we are on a fifteen-kilometre walk from Modica to Ragusa. Despite a 5:45 a.m. start time for transiting from Pachino quarters to Modica, we are again running late, because as we passed through Ispica, half of the convoy of vehicles bearing marchers and the rest of the Op Husky team got separated from the lead vehicles when a tractor cut through the column right behind the car Frances, Rod, Bill, and I were in. The motorhome was immediately ahead of us when this happened, but despite our flashing headlights and honking the horn to get the driver's attention, Les Gilles motored on oblivious to the fact that we had lost about half our people—people who had no idea where they were going. Eventually, the mishap is revealed. Motorhome and vehicles still with it pull over. Cellphones are deployed, contact eventually established, and a guide sent back to bring the rest forward.

Logistics and communication, Rod, Bill, and I agree, were the two major factors hampering Canadian operations in 1943. Seventy years later, they confound our plans as well. These two elements are causing an increasing amount of griping within the ranks. Steve MacKinnon has been complaining that André and Richard of the logistics team are giving him too little directional guidance to enable him to ensure that Susan and Sherry Atkinson are in the right place at the right time for the ceremonies. Some of the directions he receives prove wrong. Others are impossible to interpret.

We marchers are finding the same thing. According to the original plan, the marching routes were to have all been worked out and finalized well before any of us touched down in Sicily. On paper, this appeared to have been done, but the reality is proving otherwise. What is happening instead is that each day, either André or Richard is out conducting a reconnaissance to determine the route for the following day as we are marching the route for today. It's a seat-of-the-pants tactic that leaves us with little idea of how far we'll be marching the next day or over what terrain.

The logistics team is defensive, some of us perhaps overly critical. Steve is trying to moderate. Tempers fray. But finally the team is reunited, and we marchers are back on the move. It's another brilliantly sunny day. We walk with a pair of Italy's Carabinieri dogging along slowly in our wake. Previously, we had been supported by local municipal or provincial police. But strings have been pulled through the Canadian Embassy in Rome to have the job transferred to the Carabinieri Corps to ensure consistency as we transit from one province to another. This is a little daunting at first because the Carabinieri play a dual role as both police and military. As their website states, they are "ever present in the lives of the citizens [they] protect, from the largest city in Italy to the remotest village." In Sicily, it is the Carabinieri who lead the pursuit of Mafia. They look sharp and tough, and the first ones we have along are obviously bored to tears at being assigned to babysit a group of *canadesi* crazy enough to walk across Sicily. But they are not unfriendly. In a day or so, the Carabinieri begin to take an active role in helping with the route planning—finding roads that are less well travelled, some that only a local would identify as going in the direction we require.

This road isn't one of those. But traffic is light, and the flashing blue lights of the Carabinieri car have the desired effect. Those cars that pass do so slowly and offer a wide berth. We ascend a ridge that borders a long, straight valley. No stone-walled pastures. Instead, the valley is quite thickly forested and interspersed with parched grassy patches and rocky slopes. It reminds me a little of the Thompson Valley country in central British Columbia, where I lived for some years. There are few signs of habitation until we start to close in on Ragusa, which appears as another lovely-looking Baroque town in the distance. On one side stands a large domed cathedral, slightly obscured by the soaring belfry of another.

Because time is tight, this march has been carried out once again at a faster rate than the plan calls for. When we break to resupply with water and have a quick snack, Steve starts giving us shouted warnings of when the march will resume. "Five minutes, marchers!" he shouts. This is to become a refrain we will hear repeatedly in the days ahead. Curiously, often the deadline comes and goes without us starting out, because Steve by this time is talking on his cellphone, or in discussion with the logistics team, or chatting with the Carabinieri. Then it's, "Five minutes, marchers!" with a sense of frustration edging into his voice, as if we are the cause of the delay, rather than a group waiting for our fearless leader. Increasingly, one or more of us will simply address the situation by starting to walk. And as we are supposed to all stick together to accord with the Carabinieri instructions, that soon gets the whole show advancing.

Closing in on Ragusa, we see that the town is divided into two parts by a narrow valley that cuts through it, with the main road following its bottom and splitting to access either flank. Descending from the ridge to the valley floor, we come across several markers planted just off the road on a scrubby patch of ground surrounded by stark modern apartment and office buildings. A concrete wall next to the open ground is slathered in the all-too-common graffiti. The local Lion's Club, however, has planted a tiny tree in the midst of this patch and surrounded it with rocks for protection. Outside the ring, two clusters of apricot-coloured poppies are blooming. The marker team has planted the markers in a semicircle around this feature, which softens the otherwise harsh setting.

Before conducting our short ceremony in front of the markers, everyone takes advantage of the motorhome to change into their white shirts. Reforming before the markers, Padre Don leads us in a remembrance prayer, and one of the younger pipers offers the lament.

We then form up and march into Ragusa with several local police providing a walking escort ahead of the pipe band. We pass along streets crowded with people, many waving and taking photos, and arrive at the main square. Surrounding it are the Baroque churches we had seen during our approach. The square is only starting to fill with people. Prodded along by Steve, we are early. As the Sicilians begin to muster, somebody realizes that in front of the war memorial, there is a flagpole with the Italian flag flying from it stuck into the centre of a large chunk of what appears to be marble stone—but there is no pole for the Canadian flag. There ensues a great deal of running around by police officers and assorted municipal officials. This is accompanied by much shouting and gesturing. A flagpole duly arrives. But there is nowhere to mount it. More running about, shouting, and gesturing leads to somebody turning up with what seems to be a roll of baling wire. Fronting the memorial are two artillery-shell casings linked together by a chain. The flagpole is quickly lashed to one of the shells with the wire. *Voilà, il* flagpole! The Maple Leaf is run up.

Phil Bury comes over to say how impressed he is by this bit of spontaneous ingenuity. The Sicilian ability to adapt what is present to resolve an issue is something he has been repeatedly noting and admiring as each day passes. While all this has been going on, a good-sized crowd has gathered and waits patiently in the blistering heat. We Canadians are all sweating prodigiously, as are a lot of the Sicilians. But others seem blissfully unaware of how hot it is.

Ragusa's mayor proves younger than the norm, probably only in his thirties. His speech is short, but from the little bit I can puzzle out, it is a thoughtful commentary on remembrance of both Canada's and Italy's war dead—soldiers and civilians alike.

The *sindaco* turns the microphone over to Myriam Rochon, one of our young officer cadets. She is wearing a 1943 khaki uniform complete with heavy boots and wool puttees, the prescribed ceremony outfit the four of them are developing a healthy dislike for. Myriam's task is to read out what we are calling the Action of the Day report. I wrote these months ago, and each offers a short description of what our soldiers experienced in or near the place where the ceremony is held. She reads the Action of the Day in stilted Italian tinged with her francophone accent.

Unwittingly, she reveals another glitch on the part of the logistics team. According to the plan, the Action of the Day reports were to have been photocopied ahead of time so they could be given to the marchers each day before we set out. But the copying went undone in Canada and, since arriving in Sicily, the logistics team has had neither time nor much inclination to track down a copier to do the job. In fact, they have been unable even to find on what computer the Action of the Day files are stored. I don't have them either, so we haven't been able to brief our marchers properly. Instead, I have been improvising short general descriptions of what happened in 1943. These, the marchers make clear, are dismal substitutes for the written briefings they had been told to expect.

When Myriam finishes, the Sicilians seem to have found the day's events of serious import, for they look solemn. The Canadians exchange glances that show they are none the wiser. I decide to start griping about this to get the logistics team to come up with some solution.

When the ceremony ends, Frances and I are approached by a young man with a little boy at his side. The man is wearing what I recognize as one of the D-Day Juno Beach T-shirts sold at the Juno Beach Centre next to Courseulles-sur-Mer in Normandy. He says he was just there on June 26 and had driven to Normandy specifically to get that shirt after learning that Op Husky would be coming to

Ragusa today. "I did this because you landed there in the north and also here in the south," he says. "You came to liberate us. It is important to mark this." The man adds that he particularly wanted his son to see both invasion beaches where Canadians landed in Europe, so that the sacrifice our soldiers made would be clear to him.

Meanwhile, a well-dressed man has been circulating among the marchers and pointing them toward a café on one side of the square. The fellow in the Juno Beach shirt says that the man has arranged with the owner for all of us to get out of the sun and have a granita— the grainy frozen mixture of sugar, water, and flavoured liquid that Sicilians adore. Frances and I join most of the other marchers in following the well-dressed man toward the café, only to have Steve come over and say there isn't time because we have to go on to a lunch being organized by the town. To my surprise, Frances puts her foot down firmly at this. Not going to the café, she says, "would be disrespectful of a generous offer being made by a citizen rather than some dignitaries."

Leaving Steve behind, we go into the café and discover why Sicilians love their granitas. When one is hot and thirsty, this light confection is heavenly and surprisingly rehydrating. As we are thanking our generous host, who has paid the granita bill for all those Canadians who followed him to the café, he promises to see us all at the Agira Canadian War Cemetery on July 30, and makes his exit. Another man, who had his group of Sicilians surrender their chairs to us and helped find others so that not a Canadian was left standing, says he will be there as well. As we are finishing up, Steve comes in and somewhat ruefully accepts a granita.

Whatever the rest of the day holds in store, I decide, July 13 and our experience in Ragusa has been excellent. Despite its chaotic start, the ceremony here was a heartfelt demonstration of remembrance. The crowd seemed especially engaged. And we discovered granita!

WE ARE IN the small village of Licodia Eubea and headed for Vizzini, where our July 14 ceremony will take place. Things got off to a slow start this morning, as the entire group was decamping from

Pachino for a move to Caltagirone, where the next shared accommodation has been arranged. As we are starting to move into the mountains, backtracking to Pachino would take too much time. Last night, Frances and I stayed in the shared accommodation. Finding the common room too crowded and stuffy, we moved our cots onto a loading dock outside and slept under the stars. Despite the free accommodation's lack of privacy and barely functioning and often filthy washroom facilities, it is our intention to stay in the one in Caltagirone and the next operational base of Raddusa. For the final leg, where accommodation has been arranged in Regalbuto, we have booked a nearby hotel. We figure by that time we'll appreciate a break from what is far cruder than any hostel accommodation.

The distance between Ragusa, where we ended our march yesterday, and Vizzini is about thirty-five kilometres. A small group of marchers managed to get organized in time to set off by car at 5:00 for Ragusa, but at that hour, most of the marchers—myself included—were still packing and helping break down the cots and other gear in order to facilitate the move. The day before, an additional rental car had been added to the fleet, with Bill Rodgers designated the only authorized driver, since he was the only person present who held an International Driving Permit. Rod, Frances, and I join him for the drive to Licodia Eubea, where we will rendezvous with the more stalwart marchers. It will be mostly the four of us who will use the car. When the car was being rented, Steve warned Bill that he did not want it becoming exclusively "the colonel's car." Of course, as soon as Bill tells us that, the car is officially declared the Colonel's Car, and henceforth that is how it is known.

In Licodia Eubea, perched on a 630-metre hill, we get an expansive view of rolling country to the north and, immediately below, the wide and agriculturally rich Dirillo River valley. We have taken over the outdoor seating area of a small coffee bar in a square. Most of us are having a pre-march coffee and pastry, although some, like Bill, have gone straight to gelato, making great claims for its beneficial energizing character.

But our attention keeps being pulled away from the bucolic vista toward a large building on the other side of the square. There, gazing down upon it, is the face of Benito Mussolini, clearly silhouetted in black lines. He is wearing a helmet. The jutting jaw is unmistakable. Although faded, the image is striking and still dominating. Above the portrait are the faint letters of a slogan, which I later learn reads, *"Tutto il popolo italiano lo sente e tutto il popolo è pronto a scattare come un solo uomo, quando st tratta della Potenza e della Gloria della Patria."* It is a quote from a speech Mussolini gave in Cagliari, Sardinia's capital, on June 8, 1935, to a teeming crowd of cheering civilians and soldiers in the city's Carlo Felice Square. Mussolini had come specifically to Sardinia to muster support for military mobilization, so that Italy could invade Ethiopia that fall. The slogan on the wall translates roughly as: "All the Italian people hear and all the people are ready to shoot as one man. This is the power and the glory of the Motherland." Heady stuff to adorn a wall in a little village in the heart of Sicily. We are unable to find anybody who can, or will, explain when or how this slogan and portrait came to be painted on the wall of this building. It almost seems that the locals no longer see the image—that it has faded into the background in the way that the two small iron-railed balconies on either side of Mussolini's visage are so ordinary as to go unnoticed.

At the same time, Phil Bury comments that the locals here are noticeably less amicable toward us than anywhere we have been so far. A lot of us are wearing white shirts and red caps. The motorhome is adorned with large maple leafs. It's pretty obvious the Canadians have come to town. Expressions on some faces, particularly some of the old men, are downright frosty. What did you do in the war, old boy, I wonder.

This is not the first time the subject of Sicily's fascist experience has come to mind. It is an essential component of that uncomfortable history that Rosie Scifo spoke of back in Pachino. The shady side, the side many of her teacher colleagues feel is best left undiscussed in history classes. Clearly, as is evidenced by Il Duce glowering down from this wall in Lecodia Eubea, fascism managed to put down roots in Sicily. Various scholars have noted that only a minority of Sicilians were card-carrying members of the Partito Nazionale Fascista (National Fascist Party), or PNF. Yet they also report that there was much tacit support for the regime and embracing of its principles. Most communities had their resident *podestà*—akin to the Soviet commissar—who ensured that local politicians and officials stuck to the party line. The *podestà* also kept watch on the citizenry, tracked the whereabouts of local Jews, could order the arrest of a journalist or any other identified or potential troublemaker, and even censored mail—particularly, before the war, any that was being sent out of country. It was the *podestà* who also made sure the children were schooled in accordance with the fascist-dictated curriculum, which included a ban on the teaching of English. Newspapers and the emerging radio media were strictly controlled and censored. In Sicily, as in the rest of Italy, an entire generation was raised within the confines of fascist ideology. There was no alternative view on offer.

By the time World War II began, this indoctrination was well advanced, leading some Italians to claim that sifting out who was or was not a fascist is impossible. "Everybody was involved," some say. Like all such sweeping statements, this one is a gross exaggeration. But it is true that in Sicily, there was no resistance movement. Only after Mussolini was deposed on July 25, 1943, and placed under house arrest, and Italy formally surrendered to the Allies seven weeks later, on September 8, did a true partisan movement in northern Italy emerge to fight the Germans and the puppet government they installed.

In Sicily, after the Allies passed through a village, there was none of the rounding-up of collaborators or fascists by the civilian or resistance movement that occurred in France and the Netherlands, nor was this to be expected. There were simply too many people implicated. The solution was for everybody to avert their eyes. Stuck on an island, the Sicilian fascists could hardly flee to the mainland and run northward to keep ahead of the Allied advance, as did so many elsewhere, until there was eventually nowhere farther to go. All they could do was change colours and declare they had never been true believers, but were only victims of circumstance. Many went on pursuing the same careers they had had as fascists. Some politicians endured a short period of disgrace and then re-emerged with a *sindaco* sash across their chests. When the Italian government issued a general amnesty in 1948, absolving all Italians who might have been accused of war crimes against their fellow citizens or the citizens of subject nations such as Ethiopia and Greece, many considered the subject happily closed.

But the elephant is not so easily chased out of the room. Under fascism, Italy was a place where arrest on trumped-up charges was a norm, where torture and assassinations were commonplace, where racism and harassment of anyone perceived as "other" was rampant, and where censorship was widespread. Italian troops invaded Ethiopia, Libya, Albania, and Greece and also shored up those of Generalissimo Franco in the Spanish Civil War. Despite Mussolini's pronouncements to the contrary, there was no glory in any of this. It was a period of shame. And it is this legacy that Rosie and the other teachers want to address, but in a way that does not make a child look askance at her grandfather sitting and chatting, as is the Sicilian way, each afternoon with the other old fellows in the village square.

"FIVE MINUTES, MARCHERS!" Steve shouts. I abandon this line of contemplation in order to make sure my water bottles are both full. A litre per side, one to which we have added electrolytes. Frances carries two half-litre bottles. So three litres are available, and there's a regular opportunity to refill whenever we meet up with the motorhome for a break. Les Gilles restock the motorhome water supply daily with more than is required. When they can, they buy large containers that hold dozens of litres but often are forced to buy cases of litre or half-litre plastic bottles. Plastic water bottles are a blight in Sicily. Although Sicilian tap water is potable, few drink it. With thousands of plastic water bottles being drained daily, the number that end up pitched out of vehicles to land in the ditches is beyond belief. They are undoubtedly the largest contributor to Sicily's roadside litter problem, which is considerably worse than in other parts of Italy, where it is also problematic.

In past trips here, I had never hesitated to drink tap water. I only drank bottled water in restaurants, where suggesting you would settle for tap water drew a reaction just below outright scorn. This time, however, is different. Our earlier trips to Sicily were in September or early November. Although September was still quite hot, it was nothing like July. And in November, while Frances and I were wearing shorts, the Sicilians were all decked out like Michelin men in heavy quilted winter jackets. At neither time would water consumption exceed about two litres a day. Now, the quantities we consume are breathtaking. Some days I down five to six litres while on the march and then more water over dinner and into the evening. After a few days of drinking that much tap water, we both found that our stomachs were feeling a little queasy. So we've switched to drinking only bottled water.

The greatest threat we marchers face is dehydration or its opposite, hyponatremia. Drink too little water and you'll become dehydrated and experience a drop in blood volume, so that the heart has to work harder to pump that blood through the bloodstream. Muscle cramps, dizziness, fatigue, and even heat exhaustion or heatstroke can follow. Drinking too much water can induce hyponatremia—low sodium concentrations in the blood. Sodium is an electrolyte, and it helps regulate the amount of water in and around body cells. Effectively, overhydration can cause cells to absorb too much water and start swelling. Rings and watches get tighter, and victims look puffy all over. The brain can swell as well within that inflexible skull, so it becomes squished. This can lead to disorientation and, in worst-case scenarios, death.

You are likely to really start chugging water once you have drunk enough to kick in electrolyte depletion. Your body wants more electrolytes, so your brain signals you to drink more water. But water alone can't replace electrolytes, which are essential minerals necessary for a bundle of bodily processes. They are basically particles carrying an electrical charge and are found in blood, plasma, urine, and other bodily fluids. Some common electrolytes are sodium, calcium, chlorine, magnesium, phosphate, and potassium. Normally, we get enough electrolytes in food to easily supply our need for them.

Not the case when you start sweating excessively—which is what we are all doing every day we march. While we are making a point of scarfing down a lot of fruit, there are just not enough electrolytes going in to replace what is being lost. Les Gilles and Steve try to address this situation by buying not only water but also sport drinks. But in preparing for this trip, Frances and I had done some research about electrolyte replacement because we had run into this issue when hiking in the U.S. southwest desert country. As a result, we set about tracking down sugarless electrolyte replacement products that could be dissolved in water. We came away from a sporting supply outlet with about eighteen tubes each containing twelve tablets. One tablet would treat five hundred millilitres of water. We estimated that if every fourth litre of water were treated, electrolyte replacement would be optimal.

By July 14, we have emerged as the electrolyte-replacement guardians. There is always a tube of tablets in one of our hip belts. If we think somebody is not drinking enough water, out come the tablets. Frances was particularly careful to ply Steve, who tended to get distracted by events and clearly not drink as much water as he should. Steve recognized this, pointing out in a note to everyone after Operation Husky 2013 was over that Frances was always there "with water and electrolytes at the ready."

WELL WATERED AND electrolyted, we leave Licodia Eubia and Mussolini behind and head for Vizzini. We descend a steep, winding road to the valley floor. Circling around some hills, we find ourselves looking up toward Licodia Eubia. We pass small fields where grain has recently been cut so that only stubble remains. Much of the country is too rocky and dry for agriculture. Soon we start up a long steep grade that leads into another village. This is confusing, as I am not aware of there being any village or hamlet between Licodia and Vizzini. Where are we?

Only much later, while trying to make sense of our route with the help of Google Maps, do I solve this mystery. I'm looking at one of my photos, showing Frances walking up a steep street leading into the missing village, when, suddenly, there appears on my computer screen a view of Via Roma, a street in Licodia, that is identical to my photo except without Frances. I realize the missing village was actually another part of Licodia.

I virtually walk the Via Roma and come to where the next photo was taken. It is of the relatively plain—by Baroque standards—Chiesa Madre di Santa Margherita. Carrying on, I leave the village, descend a hill, and pass Licodia's cemetery. Here are the same impressive tombs, some adorned with Baroque facings, many featuring domes and spires, that we passed on July 14, 2013. When the Google camera car passed by in 2010, rain had just fallen, so the road is glistening. In 2013, we saw these features on a dry, hot day under a blue sky broken only by a few wispy clouds. Back home more than a year later, it is somewhat disquieting to walk the same route via my computer and to see that I am walking a streetscape photographed three years before we marched through it. My sense of time is jumbled. My sense of reality as well.

In 2013, however, we soon turn a corner in the road and come upon a group of markers. There are four set alongside the road on a narrow verge amid dry wild grass with a rocky wall behind. All four soldiers remembered by these markers died on July 14. Three fell to the same burst of machine-gun fire that caught a cluster of Loyal Edmonton Regiment troops riding on top of a Three Rivers Regiment Sherman tank just outside Vizzini. Differing reports cited the machine-gun crew as either diehard Italian soldiers or fascist civilians. One of the Loyal Eddies was Private Laurence Robinson. He was thirty-seven and married, and had a young daughter, likely never seen. A Sicilian schoolgirl whose extremely cursive signature appears to indicate a first name of Stella, has printed the following with meticulous care: "Have you ever thought that your life could have been different? A long happy life with your wife, your children. But you decided to take part in that mission. You left your family, your friends. You died for your country. You're a hero. Everybody should remember you as a hero. I wish that you'll never be forgotten. Rest in peace."

The non–Loyal Eddie marker is for Private Orville Borden Thompson, who marched with the Hastings and Prince Edward Regiment. Unlike Private Robinson, Private Thompson is a mystery. I can learn nothing about him other than that he died on July 14. But another Sicilian girl whose signature is illegible has written, again very carefully and clearly in English: "You left your country and your home and you came here to fight a war that wasn't yours, a war started by others, a war in which you tried to defend many others and lost yours trying. A real hero isn't determined by his strength but for the goodness of his heart." As I write down the thoughts of these two girls, my vision is blurred by tears.

Before each marker, we place one of the Canadian popsicle-stick flags we carry. Padre Don leads us in a prayer. And one of us in turn says aloud the name of the soldier who is represented by each of the markers. This is new. But in the days to come, we shall always try to read out the name on each marker. Today, the motorhome with band aboard has gone on to Vizzini rather than follow us, so no piper is here to play the lament.

We carry on through increasingly hilly terrain and then ascend a long, winding, and very narrow secondary road that leads into Vizzini. The temperature is blistering by now, and the grade is so severe that all the support vehicles—even the Carabinieri police car—abandon us for an easier route. Any attempt to stay together is lost as each of us sets an individual pace to overcome what is the most difficult distance we have so far had to cover. Don and Jean are way out front, despite having gone the thirty-five-kilometre distance. They are taking this stretch pretty much in stride. Frances and I walk together, heads down, no words, just inhaling and exhaling, until we come to a small square where the vehicles wait and the band is forming for the march into Vizzini's heart.

I learn later that Terry ran out of steam on the way up. Bill Rodgers had sensed this coming and hung back to walk alongside him. Bill suggests the two of them just sit on the side of the road for a bit and take a rest. Terry wants to beat himself up for not having trained enough, but Bill directs the conversation into neutral terri-tory. In time, the two make their way up by stages, arriving a few minutes before we set off on the final leg of this day's journey.

PIPE BAND OUT front, we march in fairly good formation—despite the fact often noted by Rod and Bill that I am utterly unable to stay in step—into Vizzini. At first the streets are empty, but we turn a corner and are met by the town's marching band, its *sindaco*, a good crowd of Sicilians, and a number of Carabinieri. Passing through a large square, we see Sherry and Susan Atkinson, their daughters Mary Lou and Patty, Steven MacKinnon, and Brittany Blow standing with a couple of elderly Sicilians. A few of us wave as we march past and continue out of the plaza and along a street that provides long views over the countryside below Vizzini.

At the end of the day, Susan will note in a blog she is writing that the two Sicilians were veterans—one ninety-four and the other ninety-three. Both had been taken prisoner, likely in North Africa, and ended up interned for three years in a prisoner-of-war camp. "There was much mutual admiration and hugging!" Susan writes. "They did not need words to understand each other."

When the big gaggling procession passes them by, there is a general scramble to cars. With MacKinnon behind one wheel and Susan the other, they slowly pursue us through the streets to where the ceremony is to unfold. The first thing I notice about this square is a large three-storey building that is completely shuttered. On the second storey, painted in large pale-blue block letters between doors that open out onto balconies, are the letters PNF. One letter per walled space, then a balcony, and then the next letter.

A man comes over and tells me that the building became a fascist headquarters in 1929. When the Canadians arrived on July 14, 1943, he says, there was a short fight for its control. Looking more closely, I can see where bullets pockmarked the walls. There is also a part of one balcony where its floor and supporting buttresses seem to have been blown away. I imagine a Three Rivers Sherman rolling into the square and taking some fire from this third-floor balcony. A single blast from its 75-millimetre gun tearing away a great chunk of masonry. Its machine gun spraying the building with short, measured bursts. Then the battle ending as abruptly as it began with a clutch of fascist civilians dead, wounded, or taking to their heels. The building stands abandoned, and the man says the owner refuses to erase the PNF logo. But at the same time, nobody wants to live there or rent any of the ground floor shop space. A bar at one end and a bakery at the other are both shuttered and appear permanently closed, although I am unable to confirm this.

During all previous ceremonies, there has been a police honour guard situated alongside the war memorial. Today, the honour guard is provided by the Carabinieri. The officer commanding the guard comes over and cheerfully gives us various crests and insignia. He hands me an epaulette worn by a senior inspector and a silver Carabinieri cap badge. The latter is described in various literature as a stylized early grenade exploding in a flash of flame. The silver badges are worn by lower ranks, such as the two chaps providing the honour guard. Our friendly officer has a gold wire badge on his cap. He is also wearing an officer's formal black jacket despite the heat, whereas the guards have been allowed to don the summer-weight blue short-sleeved shirt.

Once again, Sherry is the star of the show. After it ends, he patiently and happily is photographed with a swarm of fans. Most of our group heads off together to where another large luncheon is to be served. These luncheons are organized according to a meal plan that the majority have agreed to participate in and pay a daily fee for. Jean, Frances, and I opted out because the idea of a full dinner-sized lunch each day was not appealing. Unfortunately, we find that most of the lunches have been booked at restaurants where there are no nearby cafés or alternative food sources available. In such cases, we can opt back in. Jean volunteers to keep a tally of these times, and at the end of Op Husky, we will all pay Steve. Thankfully, today is one where alternatives are just down the street from the square, so we grab a table at a small outdoor café. Frances and I each order a panino and beer. Jean, meanwhile, tracks down a small grocer and returns with some vegetables and fruit. Raw vegetables, which Jean is used to consuming daily, rarely figure in Sicilian restaurant cooking, so she's content.

After eating, we set off exploring. The other reason we opted out of the meal plan is that these sit-down lunches go on interminably. Often they are drawn out even further by a series of speeches given by attending dignitaries or descriptions of forthcoming events and logistical issues by members of the team. We find it easy to remain in the loop of the planning, which is increasingly chaotic despite all this talk, without having to listen to it all. Today, we know that the lunch will undoubtedly drag on for a couple of hours.

We head over to where an impressive flight of stairs inlaid with tiled mosaics leads up into the heart of the town's old quarter. These stairs are not as long or wide as the famous ones found in Caltagirone, but the workmanship that has gone into making the tiles is excellent. As we start climbing, a stray dog falls in alongside us and is soon leading our ascent. He's a scruffy mixed breed with probably some collie and spaniel in there, whose coat has likely never known a brush or a decent bath. His fur is reddish-blond with a white patch at the scruff of his neck. White forelegs and paws, white-and-black muzzle, and black ears. Regularly, he glances back with a friendly, grinning expression to see if we are keeping pace.

The dog guides us along a winding path through narrow streets, many too tight for any size of car. Most of the buildings are ancient, some with elaborate carvings over windows that have wooden shutters so bleached and dried by the sun they could be centuries old. Whenever we come to a church or other building that is of particular interest to tourist minds, the dog seems to sense this. He pauses, watches us with a self-satisfied smirk. I almost expect him to start pointing out that this or that structure was built in such-and-such neoclassical Baroque style after the manner of so-and-so architect. We finally are brought to a small opening between buildings that affords a view out over the roofs and spires of Vizzini. Then, as if sensing that our time is running out, he briskly retraces our route— taking a couple of shortcuts down shoulder-width staircases—to the top of the mosaic stairs. We descend, with him still out front, and are in time to join the others for the ride to Caltagirone and our new quarters. As the vehicles pull out of the square, I look back. The dog is sitting on his haunches, keenly watching our departure.

AS SOON AS we enter the sports centre that is to serve as quarters during our time in Caltagirone, we encounter a major problem. There is no running water, the toilets are all blocked, the place is filthy, and there are no cots or anything to sleep on. Rod and Bill take one look around and announce that they are bailing out of there. I tell Frances that we are going, too. She offers no argument. Rosie is there. She's a whirlwind of activity, trying to sort out the problems. A cellphone call brings a young local contact of hers. He starts making calls and soon announces that there is a bed and breakfast with two rooms available for us.

Rosie and the young man jump in a car, and we pile into the Colonel's Car and follow, winding up into the splendid heart of the old town. There are Baroque architectural masterpieces around virtually every corner. Jostling for attention are also hundreds of Caltagirone's famed ceramics. They are visible on walls, steps, and the domes of churches and even inlaid as paving stones in plazas. Swirling patterns, vivid colours, and incredible detail are everywhere. Soon we are parked outside a residence on a narrow street. Our cars nearly touch the buildings on either side. A brief negotiation takes place, and the rooms are ours. Rosie and the young man race off to solve more problems. We jumble our luggage in. The rooms are spacious and comfortable looking. A few minutes later, it is decided that Bill and I should take the car back to the sports centre and input the coordinates on a GPS unit that André gave Bill, so that we can easily find it each morning.

After a few wrong turns, we find the gym at the base of the town and have the GPS remember the coordinates. And that is when we realize that neither of us noted the name of the street we're moving to or even the name of the bed and breakfast. We also have no map, and there is no obvious place to get one. It's still siesta time, so most businesses are shuttered, including the tobacconists, which generally have maps available and in my experience are great at giving directions—mostly with some accuracy. So blindly we set off, trying to retrace our path, which proves hopeless because Caltagirone is full of one-way streets. We are soon lost, knowing only that *our* street is near the top of the hill that the town stands on. If we can get to the top, we know there's a parking area at an overlook next to a school. And *our* street is just down the hill from that parking area.

But finding a road that neither peters out nor suddenly turns back around on itself and descends away from the summit proves a daunting challenge. After almost an hour of circling about, I start recognizing many of the places, having passed them several times. "We've been lost here before," I tell Bill. He seems to not find this helpful. And then we take a turn and descend an extremely narrow lane, only to suddenly come to a barrier. Had it not been there, we would have plunged straight down the famed 142 steps of the Scalinata di Santa that connect old Caltagirone with the town's newer part, to erupt—likely after crushing many tourists for whom ascending these stairs is an essential element of their visit—into the town's main square. Luckily, there is a little side lane, and after much shunting back and forth that involves cooking the clutch and brakes, Bill gets the car turned around and we retreat under the watchful, possibly anxious, gaze of two shopkeepers opening their ceramic stores for post-siesta business. We turn up another street and, suddenly, there is the parking area. A few minutes later, Bill and I are at the B & B. In the meantime, Rod and Frances have gone out and got some precious provisions, of which Bill and I agree the most precious is a cold beer. This is possible, as we have access to a little refrigerator in a small, cozy living room that connects our rooms. There is also a large balcony to which we retire, feeling only a little guilty about abandoning the others to the sports centre.

Except for two more nights, on July 19 and 20, the four of us are done with the communal free accommodation. Those last two nights will be spent in another sports centre at Raddusa, where cockroaches swagger without fear, the walls are covered in graffiti and grime, and the bathrooms are equally filthy and barely functional. Outside, a volleyball tournament will carry on until after midnight. Teenage spectators or just plain hooligans will spot Frances making her way alone to a bathroom that has been set aside for her and Jean. They will pound on the glass of the outside door and yell for her to open up and let them in. It will be more than a bit frightening. The next night will prove little better, and the following morning, the four of us will agree it is past time to get out of Dodge. Using Rod's cell, I will call the hotel outside Regalbuto where we're already booked for the last few nights and book a second room for Rod and Bill, as well

as arrange for Frances and me to check in several days early, on
July 21. We will not feel guilty about doing this.

On the balcony of the B & B in Caltagirone, though, on the night
of the 14th, I start thinking about guilt. How can we with the means
justify moving into a relative heaven when others on our team are
stuck in a shared hell? I articulate our excuses, and they are valid. A
major one is that both Rod and I have been posting daily Internet
reports aimed at raising Op Husky's profile back in Canada. A major
point of what we are doing is to raise public, media, and political
awareness of the importance of remembrance. Rod does this through
a blog posted on the Seaforth Highlanders of Canada website. I do so
through my Facebook site dedicated to the Canadian Battle Series,
my personal site, and Twitter feeds. Steve MacKinnon and Brittany
are tying into these as well, especially to share photos that I post on a
daily basis. It is telling that neither the marketing/publicity team nor
any members of the logistics team are staying in the shared accommodation. They are all quartered in hotels or bed and breakfasts
where there is Wi-Fi available. Each night, they leave the marchers,
band, and cadets at the shared accommodation and go to their separate quarters. Rod and I spend a few hours posting our material, as
do Steve MacKinnon and Brittany, while some of the logistics team
are using Google Maps to create a route map for the next day.

So although I feel some guilt about escaping the sports centre, I
remind myself that we are paying the cost out of our own pocket, as
well as doing voluntary work for Op Husky that everyone agrees is
important. As for Bill, he feels no guilt at all. He notes that many
people are on the tour because they have a personal connection to
it—the marchers who had fathers who were veterans, me with my
role as historian and self-appointed chronicler, Steve the organizer,
and Jean and Don with connections to the 48th Highlanders. But
he's not sure why he came. "At the beginning, I wasn't really committed to the trip," he says. "I was quite prepared to get on the bus if
it turned out to be chaotic or less than satisfying. I was going strictly
day to day. But when we got started, I was overwhelmed by what had
been organized. One of the reasons I stuck around was that it
became very, very interesting."

And Frances? Being more of a team player than I am, she feels guiltier. But the Op Husky tour is not one she would have signed on to had it not been for me. Although she has trained hard, is determined to walk as far as possible, and has become friends with many of the people on the team, this is not a cause to which her heart is deeply committed. It is an experience and a vacation of sorts. And although the various acts of remembrance we participate in move her—sometimes very deeply—she feels ambivalent about the lasting importance of what we are doing. Remembrance aside, though, Frances is loving walking the Sicilian countryside and the company we keep while doing so.

What none of us loves, however, are the early mornings. On July 15, we are up earlier than ever, at 3:30 a.m. We grope quietly in the dark from rooms to bathroom in order not to wake the rest of the household. Whispers are exchanged as everyone makes sure their gear is complete. We tiptoe down the stairs, slip quietly into the street. As Bill starts up the car, I turn on the GPS and instruct it to take us to the sports centre. Two hours to get there, it reports, after finding satellites and drawing maps. At most, we should be ten minutes away. Useless GPS unit goes back in glove box. Frances produces the tourist map the B & B owner gave us last evening. We grope slowly down the hill making only a few wrong turns and arrive at the sports centre in good time.

A quick glance inside reveals that most of the worst conditions have been rectified. The toilets work, there is running water, and some mats have been found for sleeping on. Everyone is still getting organized. A lot of bleary-eyed people, young and old, are trying to grab some breakfast and get their kits sorted out for the day. The food on offer, which Les Gilles have brought in, is all strangely Canadian, as if they had somehow happened upon a large grocery chain store from back home. There are brand-name cereals, spongy white bread, processed cheese slices, and other stuff that looks entirely unappealing at 4:00 a.m., or just about anytime. But there is also fruit. I tuck an orange into my hip belt for later.

Realizing we have time to kill, we hop back in the car and drive down the street. And there, just a short distance away, is a café opening up for the day. Bless the Italians. With their siesta tradition comes the need to rise early. How else would anything get done? Many are up and working before sun-up, and after the siesta they work for hours more. This is true of all siesta-oriented cultures. Experience travelling in Italy has shown me that the stereotype of the lazy Latin is simply not true. Given our bizarre sleeping and eating patterns on this tour, we are grateful for these early birds running the café. We stand at their bar drinking cappuccino and eating *cornetti alla marmellata*. Except for Rod, who is fully addicted to the *cioccolato* variety.

Returning to the sports centre, we find everyone starting to move to the vehicles. André comes over and hands me a walkie-talkie. To avoid another foul-up like the one in Ispica, where half the convoy was cut off and ended up lost, the Colonel's Car will play tail-end Charlie. If part of the convoy looks like it might stray from the pack, I'll radio André in the lead car, and they will slow down and as soon as practical pull over to let everybody regroup. After only a couple of slowing-down incidents along the way, we are soon pulling in to the square in Vizzini where the ceremony was held the day before.

AND THERE TO greet us is yesterday's stray dog-cum-tour guide, who wanders about happily on the periphery as everyone prepares to march. When we set off, the dog follows us along the streets through town and straight out into the country. At this point, I had expected him to soon turn around and trot back to familiar streets. Instead, the dog continues to trot along, often diverting off the road to investigate some gully or cluster of woods. But he always returns.

Our descent toward the valley is via a narrow, twisting road curiously bounded by an inordinate amount of rubbish. There are, of course, the ubiquitous water bottles of all shapes and sizes. But there is also an unusually large amount of clothing, particularly brassieres—wired ones, large-cupped ones, see-through ones, lacy and gauzy little nothings. They dangle from tree branches, decorate small bushes like so many Christmas ornaments, and lie discarded and forgotten in the ditches. It's as if a great throng of Sicilian

women of all ages suddenly experienced a return to the 1960s and
'70s, casting aside their inhibitions and the subjugation of freedom
symbolized by a brassiere's restraint.

When we reach the valley floor, however, and start walking
through wide fields sown with grain, all this littering ceases. We
leave the garbage inexplicably behind. And the dog, whom we are
now calling "Husky," is still there, ambling patiently along. At various times Bob, Phil, and Steve have tried unsuccessfully to shoo him
back home. Then, worried that he's going to keel over in the heat, for
it cracks 40 Celsius in the valley, we try giving him water—which he
refuses. Nor does he allow himself to be easily touched. He never
snaps, just sidles away when you come too close.

"Those dogs are territorial," Rod says. "They are not usually fed.
They survive on scraps and garbage, which there's plenty of in any
Sicilian town. For a dog to decide to leave his town and walk sixteen
K with a bunch of marchers who don't have food for him, you have to
ask what motivates him to do that." A few of us, not entirely seriously
but not entirely in gest either, begin to ask whether he's "a stray or
a spirit."

This speculation kicks into high gear when we come to a group of
markers. Right away, Husky goes over to a particular marker, that of
a Royal Canadian Air Force flyer, and lies down next to it. We worry
that he is going to urinate on it, for Husky has been regularly marking bushes, tree stumps, and anything else worthy of a territorial
declaration. Steve and Bob try to get him to move away. But even
when physically dragged off, Husky turns right about and returns to
lie beside the same marker. Finally, Steve says, "Maybe there's
another way to do this. Let's just leave him and see how it goes."
Which we do, and it goes fine. At first, Husky had shied away from
too many people being around him. As the marker ceremony unfolds
here, however, he is dead in the centre of the action. Arlin is right
down at his level filming the dog, the marker, and the piper playing
the lament beyond. He just lies there, mouth open, breathing, obviously hot as hell under that heavy coat. Someone says, "He must feel
the flyer's spirit." Another marcher says, "Or *is* the flyer's spirit."
Nobody dismisses this as paranormal nonsense. "It wasn't as though

that marker was in the shade or differentiated in any way from the others," Rod says afterwards.

And when we march away, Husky follows. He walks with us as we move along a broad plateau forested with low-standing pines and eucalyptus trees. Eventually, the forests thin out, and there on another hill is Grammichele. It had been the Hasty Ps who led the advance to this town, and one of their officers had described how they marched up a long straight road to get there. His road was white because it was dirt; ours is paved. Otherwise, I figure it's the exact same road and likely about the same width as it was seventy years ago. There were cornfields here then, but they're gone now, the country slowly going back to a semi-natural state. Farming here is obviously not as important now as it was then.

Grammichele stands about seventy-eight metres above the plateau. The road we are on runs straight up it and into the town, which is where today's ceremony is to take place. Husky is still there, padding along close to me. And then, as we enter a square, he is just gone. And nobody saw him go. One moment there, the next not. A phantom? If merely a terrestrial stray, I wish him luck in his new hometown. For it is hard to imagine that he would bother retracing his steps back to Vizzini. For one thing, Vizzini's population has been in steady decline since a high point in 1911, when it stood at about 22,000. Today, the town has around 7,200 people. Grammichele has slightly more than 13,000. Sicilians tend not to feed strays, but his odds of finding some sympathy are almost doubled. And there will also be twice the garbage and maybe scraps available.

Waiting in the square for us is a very large throng of people, more than we have seen since the Pachino ceremony. There are the dignitaries, of course—the *sindaco*, several high-ranking Carabinieri officers, and others wearing various signs of notability, such as special ties or full business suits. There is also the almost inevitable town marching band. But most of these people are just citizens of Grammichele. They fall in behind the people of importance, alongside whom Steve is solicited to stand despite his ill-kept dress. At the beginning, Steve had indicated he'd be dressing up for these ceremonies, but he quickly stopped trying to do so. Despite the white shirt and red ball cap, he looks exactly like a man who has walked fifteen kilometres under the searing Sicilian sun. His baggy beige shorts are sweat-stained, his ankle-height brown boots and socks are dusty. Yet the Sicilians recognize that he is the man of the moment. We—even our star, Sherry Atkinson—are only here undertaking this day of remembrance in this town because of Steve Gregory. And the *sindaco* and other officials are eager not only to honour the Canadians who liberated Grammichele but also to recognize Steve, who made the remembrance of that event happen.

As our parade—for that is what it becomes—moves up a long, dead-straight street that leads to the main square, ever more people join in. Many seem unaware that we were coming or that there is a planned event under way. They just get up from where they were having coffee at a café or step out of their doorways and join the advance. There are women in fashionable heels and carrying designer purses. Children vie for the little Canadian flags, and some have identical Italian flags that they wave as they walk. Canada pins are an instant hit with anybody we hand one to. Most of us try not to give too many of those to anyone but children and the elderly. Steve is always cautioning that our supply isn't limitless. And usually after saying that, he immediately races over and gives out a handful to a clutch of people, regardless of the age criteria he has just emphasized.

Off to one side, standing at the entrance to a grubby alley, I see a very old man. He's wearing a stained blue shirt, and his grin reveals few teeth. He is vigorously clapping. When I dash over and press a Canada pin into the palm of his hand, he grasps mine in both of his. "*Grazie, grazie,*" he says softly and repeatedly. Tears spill down his cheeks. When I start to pull away to return to the parade, he continues to cling to my hand. "*Grazie, grazie, canadese,*" he says through tears. I stand, letting him shake my hand, until finally his grip softens. Turning, finding my own cheeks damp, I return to the parade and rush to catch up to the rest of the marchers.

As I do so, I wonder if the old man was here when the Canadians approached Grammichele and met their first real battlefield resistance. For this is where they came up against German troops for the first time. A short firefight ensued in which twenty-five Canadians became casualties, though only one died. That was a tanker, Trooper Ellis James Lloyd. He was twenty and from Verdun, Quebec. I remember his marker was back in the valley, standing alongside the one carefully tended by Husky.

The street we have been on debouches into an enormous square that is quickly filled by the parade. We stand in the literal heart of Grammichele. When the town was rebuilt after the 1693 earthquake, the architects involved gave it a unique spiderweb layout. Grammichele is hexagonally shaped, with six roads radiating outward from this square.

Despite the heat, the crowd is extremely attentive as the ceremony rolls out pro forma. But when it is over, the town band and our pipe band add a twist. Normally, each puts on a short performance during the ceremony. Now, however, they engage in a friendly battle of the bands, with the Grammichele band playing one number, and our pipers and drummers responding. As part of the Canadian performance, piper Charles David Mitchell and his younger brother, drummer William, play a duet that is stunningly good. When the two return from Sicily to Canada, they hope the very next week to win a prize with this tune at the prestigious Glengarry Highland Games in Maxville, Ontario. The competition goes on for some time, until Pipe Major Bob Stewart recognizes that the Sicilians will never concede and will keep playing until somebody—and it definitely won't be one of them—drops from heatstroke. With a wry laugh, he orders the pipe band to stand down and walks over to shake the band leader's hand.

The performance ends just before siesta time, and within minutes the square empties. We are given a short tour of the municipal hall, where there is a large diorama showing the town in relief so that the spiderlike design is evident. From an upper-storey window, I gaze down upon the vast emptiness of the square. There are fewer than ten people visible, and some of them are our people. We soon load up in the vehicles, and driving out of Grammichele is like leaving a ghost town. Yet in a couple of hours, I know the streets will once again teem with life.

THE NEXT DAY has a slightly discordant aspect, in that as part of our quasi retracing of the steps taken by our Canadian soldiers, we are to go from Caltagirone back to Grammichele, which is today's departure point for a march to Caltigirone. In the end, it is not a complete return to Grammichele, as the road leading from it toward Caltagirone has been deemed a deathtrap for walkers. So our convoy stops next to an old water tower, which we are assured is situated in a line directly parallel with Grammichele, in order to walk a safer road that still is fifteen kilometres from Caltagirone.

Before we set out, I am at last able to provide everybody with a brief but thorough description of what happened to our troops this day. Dave MacLeod has solved the problem of the missing Action of the Day reports. Having found the files, he uploaded them to a small tablet, and I can now fill everybody in with the text I wrote for July 16. Don Aitchison, now the padre of the 48th Highlanders of Canada, and Jean Miso, who is also aligned with the regiment because of its base in Toronto, are particularly interested in today's march, as the Highlanders figured heavily in the events of this day in 1943.

Caltagirone, I explain, had a population of thirty thousand at that time, and our intelligence knew that the German Hermann Göring Division was using it for a headquarters. Because of this, the town was subjected to heavy Allied aerial bombing. During their advance from Grammichele to Caltagirone, the leading 48th Highlanders of Canada were greatly slowed because the road was heavily mined. Finally, the troops left the road and marched cross-country, arriving in Caltagirone to find that the Germans had fled. Because of the bombing, Caltagirone was described by official Canadian army historian Lieutenant Colonel G.W.L. Nicholson as "a veritable shambles, with the streets blocked by rubble and many fires burning." Taken by surprise by the bombing, many civilians were killed and far more wounded. With the 48th Highlanders' medical unit quickly overwhelmed, the 4th Field Ambulance raced in and set up in what proved to be an extremely inadequate local hospital run by a handful of nuns. Despite the extent of the crisis, the nuns insisted on serving the Canadians coffee, which turned out to be made from crushed acorns.

In closing, I emphasize that wherever our troops encountered civilian suffering, whether from lack of food, disease, or injuries resulting from the battle, they always stepped forward to provide whatever assistance they could. And that these humanitarian acts distinguished them from the German and even Italian troops, both of whom often abused local people by looting their crops and anything else that might be of value. This fact, I say, is a major reason we are being so enthusiastically received in most of the Sicilian communities.

After the briefing, Steve takes Bob Werbiski aside and, I learn later, asks him to consider speaking about his father and what the 4th Field Ambulance in which he served did in Caltagirone. Bob is a very quiet, seemingly private person, but he readily agrees. "It was to be a long walk that day, so I would have some time to mentally prepare myself and find the words to say. At least I thought I would."

Under a dazzling blue sky, we walk through gently undulating country past large grain fields and orchards. Although I notice Bob is even less talkative than usual and tends to walk alone, I don't yet know the reason for it. Six days in, though, we are all completely comfortable with each other. Rod likens us to the pilgrims in *The Canterbury Tales*. Stories are related, conversations arise and flow easily to a natural ending, and often several of us will walk in amicable silence for an hour or more without any need for talk. We have become comrades. We have become, as Max Fraser puts it, "a bond of strangers," playing on the famous "band of brothers" speech from Shakespeare's *Henry V*. And I think it is on this day that Don finds the play on his smartphone and reads the classic speech by King Henry to his scant band of knights before the Battle of Agincourt in 1415. Don can act, and skilfully reads the passage where King Henry says that those fighting there on Saint Crispin's Day shall always be bound together by that fact. "We few, we happy few, we band of brothers; For he to-day that sheds his blood with me, Shall be my brother."

Bill, Don, and I walk together after that and ponder how wonderfully Shakespeare captured the special bond that seems to exist between veterans of combat. We have all known World War II veterans who never spoke of the war with family or non-veteran friends and how often they seemed to keep themselves more than a little distant from others. But put those veterans together with those alongside whom they served and the conversation would flow, they would become more emotional, and it was clear that here was another family that forever held a special place in their hearts and souls—a band of brothers. Soon I drift back in line to walk beside Frances and Jean. Bob is behind us looking thoughtful. Bill and Don turn, as they often do, to discussing philosophy.

Later, Bill tells me that the walking became the most important part of the trip. "Generally, when we have conversations in a social setting," he said, "they consist of brief banter back and forth without any exploration of topics. There aren't pauses between questions and answers. But on that trip, we would be walking along for three or four hours, and some topic would arise beyond the usual who are you, what are your interests, what's your favourite flavour of ice cream. And you'd ask a question of the person you were walking with, and it might be an hour before you would get a reply. And you were comfortable with that hour of silence. You might not get an answer for a day or two. Later, when you would fall in step beside that person, that person would say, 'Remember when you asked me about something or other? I've been thinking about it.' And so the answer would have some meaning and thought behind it. Most of the marchers were skilled conversationalists. Not all, but most. And that made a difference as well. They understood how to keep a conversation going, understood how to reflect upon a question before answering."

And so we walk and sometimes talk. Today, we do not walk through small-farm country. There are few farmhouses. One gets the feeling that the farmers might live in the towns and commute to their work each day. As we pass by one orchard, a wiry fellow wearing a long-sleeved, blue-striped shirt over a paler blue polo shirt emerges from among the trees and bids us to wait for a moment. He races off in an old car. Another older, somewhat portly fellow comes out of the orchard and stands with us until the wiry guy returns. He pulls from the car a green plastic crate brimming with green-skinned oranges.

Steve sticks one of the small Canadian flags in the man's chest pocket, and the two of them mug for the cameras. Then the two Sicilians flick wide, flat-bladed knives about the size of a jackknife from their pockets and show us how to carve the skin off the oranges in long swirls that they throw carelessly onto the road. We eat, orange juice dribbling down our chins and off our fingertips. To my eye, the oranges had looked green and likely to be sour or stringy. But I have never eaten an orange as delicious. Aware that the logistics team and everybody in the motorhome are missing this opportunity, we accept the man's urging to take as many oranges from the crate as we want. Hip belts, packs, and pockets are all stuffed full when we start walking again. Jean's already formidably heavy leather pack is so loaded she can't close the top.

Despite the heat, the walking is easy on this route—all gentle grades with long straightaways. We walk facing the traffic, but Steve hangs protectively at the back to keep a wary eye open for cars passing others. Straight secondary roads are rare in Sicily, and the Sicilians all transform into Mario Andrettis when they encounter one. "Car!" Steve yells, when a vehicle careens past another one going somewhat slower. We all crowd to the roadside as the car streaks past. Today is unusual, as we lack any police presence, a rip in the protective cocoon that has been in place and is somewhat taken for granted.

Coming to a cluster of markers, we find the motorhome, band, cadets and the rest of the team waiting. Oranges are passed around and prove an instant hit. The setting for these markers is lovely. Not for the ground in which they are placed, but for the panoramic view over the Sicilian countryside. Close by is an olive grove, and then the view just stretches away down a long, gentle slope to a wide series of rolling hills covered with fields and orchards. And always above the landscape that perfectly clear blue sky. Someone produces a Sharpie and we take turns writing short inscriptions of remembrance on the markers. "Thank you for your service and sacrifice," I write on one.

Steve today is oddly relaxed and not forcing the pace. We are all tired, of course, and we pretty much all by now have patches of skin where an uncomfortable rash has broken out. As we walk along, Don trolls the Internet on his phone. "Prickly heat," he declares, "also called miliaria." The rashes are caused by our excessive sweating, which is blocking the sweat glands. Rod and Steve have particularly bad cases of it—large patches of raw, red, and blistered-looking skin on the backs of their legs. Terry's is also bad and again mostly centred on the back of his legs. I have only a little line on my right ankle where the top of the sock contacts skin. Others have slightly worse cases. "How's the rash?" becomes a regular question we ask each other during the ensuing days.

"What's the cure?" Rod asks.

"Keep the affected area cool and dry," Don says. "Avoid excessive heat and humidity." We all laugh. We figure it is probably this problem that has made some marchers' wrists and ankles puff up. Nothing to be done about any of this. Just keep marching. And keep in mind that in 1943, the troops likely barely noticed such discomfitures while coping with dysentery, malaria, lack of water, and the fear that at any moment this lovely landscape you walked through might erupt with gunfire and the explosions of mortar bombs, grenades, or artillery shells. "At least nobody is trying to kill us" becomes a daily observation.

And so, lulled by the beauty of the countryside, nursing and discussing our minor health woes, we walk more slowly and arrive late in Caltagirone. A covey of police riding scooters is waiting on the outskirts. They lead us at a brisk pace, which at times shifts to jogging, on streets that require a police officer to rush ahead and close to oncoming traffic because they are one-way and our advance is in the opposite direction. Soon enough, we reach a narrow square where the town's war memorial stands. Here a large group of dignitaries and more police have been waiting in the blistering sun for our arrival.

There is no shade. Not a single tree. Thankfully, somebody has one of the khaki-coloured umbrellas emblazoned with the Op Husky logo that Steve brought from Canada. One of the officer cadets holds it over Sherry Atkinson. In the middle of the mayor's seemingly interminable speech, a female police officer quietly folds down to the ground in a faint and is carried from the field by some of her colleagues. When Steve finishes saying a few words, he calls Bob forward. Enza Scifo stands at his side and translates.

Bob describes the bombing, the Canadian attack into the town, the destruction and death. "Finally, the task was given to 4th Field Ambulance to help the injured civilians. Apparently, there were many casualties," Bob relates. He tells the crowd that his father was in 4th Field Ambulance and remembered treating the civilians here. He ends by saying, "I'm proud to walk in my father's footsteps." Bob breaks down then, weeps softly, while Enza translates. I look around at the others. We are all choking up.

Bob says later, "It was difficult to deliver that address. Enza would translate in Italian after each sentence so that I could regain some composure. I realized that day that in all the years before, talking with my dad, I had never thanked him for his service, for everything he taught me through the years."

Like most veterans, Bob's dad talked little of the war. His uniform was stowed away in a valise in the attic, where Bob discovered it when he was six or seven. "A battle dress (wool, khaki), sergeant stripes on the sleeves, beret, and parts of his webbing (his belt, haversack, straps, spiked army boots)." His dad let Bob try on the uniform. Although it stayed in the valise, over the years Bob often went up to the attic to look at it.

Then there was the time when he was nine or ten and saw his dad going through the nightstand beside his bed. "I sat on the bed next to him, and as he was going through odd things, I noticed three or four small boxes, maybe three inches by two and not quite half an inch thick. I asked him what was in those boxes, and he opened them. They were his war medals, Italy Star, France, Germany, voluntary service medal and bars. The ribbons were all wrinkled, there was an assortment of pins and two brass cap badges from the Royal Canadian Army Medical Corps, and one had been polished so often it was worn out. He told me they were his medals from the war and what they signified with regard to the campaigns he was in. He told me he had joined the army reserves in 1939 or so as an artilleryman and later joined the active service sometime in 1941. I remember him holding the medals for a few more seconds, not minutes, and then he packed them in the boxes and casually tossed them back in the drawer. His medals are still in the same boxes, a bit tarnished and the ribbons still wrinkled."

Sometime later, Bob asked his father why he never had a gun or went shooting or hunting. "I've seen enough killing in my life," his dad answered. Bob later says, "I don't think I realized all that it meant for a long, long time. Probably 2013 at Caltagirone, Sicily."

It was only when Bob was twenty-one, attending university and serving in the reserves ("medical services like my dad"), that there was any talk of the war beyond the funny anecdotes veterans often use to distract people from prying deeper. "When he did share his thoughts, they meant so much. The pauses he took and the expressions on his face left no doubt that there were difficult memories. He did tell me about what the civilians went through—the bombings, loss of life, starvation, fear. He also told me how grateful the Sicilians, Italians, and Dutch were to the Canadian soldiers.

"My dad passed away in July 1999. On Father's Day, a few weeks before he died, I had brought him to my house. I trimmed his hair, and I dressed him with his battle dress jacket. I wanted his grandchildren to see him with his jacket. My father suffered from Alzheimer's. I brought him in front of a mirror. He looked into the mirror for a few minutes; I can't say what his thoughts were. I said, 'It must bring back a few memories.' He answered, 'Yes, it does.' Those were the only words he spoke that afternoon. Every day, I have a thought about my dad. It might last a second, sometimes more, but it happens."

Two ICONIC CANADIAN army photographs from the Sicily campaign are of the Seaforth Highlanders. One becomes relevant later, as it shows the Seaforth Highlanders pipe band performing in the main square of Agira on July 30. The other is a panoramic shot of the entire regiment strung out in a long line and ascending a steep slope via a switchback track. The men wear helmets, but none are armed. At the head of the column is, unmistakably, Lieutenant Colonel Bert Hoffmeister. He is leading his men to meet General Bernard Montgomery. As part of the British Eighth Army, the

Canadians in Sicily are under Montgomery's command. Montgomery always delighted in opportunities to directly address the troops, and when they were Commonwealth soldiers he liked to refer to them as "my Canadians" or "my Australians." Pick a nationality and he claimed ownership, although I can't say that there is evidence of his ever regaling the Indian divisions as "my Indians," or "my Gurkhas," or "my Sikhs." He was probably too inherently a colonialist to do that.

The photograph was taken by army photographer Terry F. Rowe, who loosely dated it August 1943. And so that is what everybody believed. When I was writing *Operation Husky* in 2008, the plan had been to use this photo as the final image. The date seemed right, for the record shows that Montgomery addressed all ranks of 1st Canadian Infantry Division on August 20, when they were in a rest area on the Catania Plain and awaiting the invasion of mainland Italy. But whenever I looked at the rugged countryside the Seaforths were walking through in that photo, I could not reconcile it with the terrain in the area where the rest camp was based. There were valleys near the camp, and some were quite deep, but they were not likely to have been used as rest areas. And they were too far from the village of Militello, where every day a thirty-six-man guard paraded with the Seaforth pipe band in a changing-of-the-guard ceremony. Surely, this duty would have fallen to one of the other regiments closer to Militello if the Seaforths had been camped in one of those deeper valleys.

And then I remembered that Montgomery had also addressed the regiment earlier—although its official historian, Dr. Reginald Roy, was unaware of this when he wrote the Seaforth history of World War II. That time was on July 13, when 1st Canadian Infantry Division stood down from combat operations on Monty's orders to recover from the rigours of the amphibious landing and following rapid advance by foot. The Seaforths camped then in a valley just north of Ragusa, which they dubbed Happy Valley. This is also what the Seaforths called the different valley where they were encamped in August. Examining the photo repeatedly, I began to wonder if in fact it had been taken when Hoffmeister led his men out of that *first*

Happy Valley to see Monty. There are accounts by Seaforths and members of other regiments that describe the steep, hot walk up to where Montgomery waited. Two different walks, with the troops dressed the same—shorts, shirts with sleeves rolled up, puttees, boots, steel helmets, and web kit. Hoffy leading the way through those dry, stark hills around Ragusa. Terry Rowe might have wrongly dated the negative. I had seen this happen elsewhere. There could be long lags between the time an army photographer shot his film and was able to get it developed. Consequently, I decided not to use the photo, and the mystery remained unresolved.

Segue to the run-up to Op Husky, when Rod Hoffmeister contacted me for help in locating precisely where the photo was taken. He needed to know because the Seaforths had commissioned Max Fraser to make a video focused primarily on the forthcoming concert re-enactment by their pipe band in Agira's main square, on the evening of July 30, which would be Op Husky 2013's final act. But the video was also to include Rod's participation in the marching, and he was hoping we could recreate the photo in a small way (lacking the cast of hundreds who followed his father through the hills).

Since the writing of *Operation Husky*, a new Internet resource had come to light that I realized might help solve the mystery. Fortunately, the Seaforth war diary provided topographical map references for the first Happy Valley near Ragusa. The website is an ingenious "coordinates translator." Plug in a reference from the World War II maps that the Allies used, and you are taken precisely to that point on Google Maps or Mapquest. Using the satellite function, I saw that the country looked right. But we would only know for sure when we got there and could search for the spot.

On July 16, after the Caltagirone ceremony, that is what a group of us sets out to do. We in three cars and Max's film crew in another convoy will converge on the area north of Ragusa that we've identified as the right spot. Certainly, it is close to where the Seaforths were camped. We have five people crammed into the Colonel's Car. Frances has our map book on her lap, but we are following the car driven by Gaetano Catalano, one of Steve's Sicilian helpers. Steve is with him. Before leaving Caltagirone, we discussed the route and where we wanted to end up. Go to Ragusa, coming in on the main road from the south. Hook around the outskirts to get on s194, and a few kilometres north of Ragusa, take a side road off to the right. That is our target. All goes perfectly. We are soon on s194, and the right turn comes up just as expected. And Gaetano punches right on past. We have a walkie-talkie, and so does Steve. "You've missed the turn," I say. Much crackling. "Gaetano says he knows where he's going," Steve comes back. "We need to turn around," I insist. By the time a halt is called, we are practically in Giarratána, which is about fifteen kilometres off track.

But we are also in cellphone contact with Max and discover that his people are parked outside a small hamlet called Balata di Modica, next to the other end of the secondary road we wanted. If we take sp59 out of Giarratána, we can link up and drive in from that side. This is what we do, but by the time we arrive, a good ninety minutes has been lost. And the previously crystal-clear blue sky has been replaced by an ominous bunch of black clouds. The secondary road proves narrow and in poor condition. Our long string of cars rolls past locals who look at us like they have never seen a formation of this size before. There is now lightning flashing and thunder clapping. By the time we are just above where I think the iconic photo was taken, the skies open and a hard rain lashes down.

The road before us snakes downhill. We stop in a decent pullout. About eight of us stand in the pouring rain trying to develop a plan. We have no idea if there is anywhere down the hill where this many vehicles can park. And we also don't really know if the spot we want is down there.

Photography director Oliver Glaser, who is a take-charge kind of guy, announces that he, Duncan Vogel, and I will conduct a reconnaissance and report back. We edge down the switchbacks. The road is flooding, water spilling off the sides. Dangerously slick. So much water is rushing across the windows that it's difficult to see anything. We turn a corner, and suddenly things look right—but also not. I call for a stop. Oliver and I get out. Rain lashes us. Oliver pulls out his phone and brings up the photo. He grins. "This is it. Look." He points to a hill. "There's the hill to the right, there's the draw. It's all right there." I realize he is right. The trail the Seaforths took is barely visible, overgrown now by spiny grass. We are a little lower down—probably no more than twenty metres—from the point where Rowe must have had his camera. In that direction is a steep driveway barred by a large gate. It is swathed in No Trespassing signs and other dire warnings in Italian. No going up there. But there is another driveway to one side and sufficient room on the verge to get all the cars down here and safely off the road. We agree on the logistics of bringing everybody down, and the rain stops as suddenly as it started. Oliver and I are soaking wet, but the heat is such that in just a few minutes, our clothes are dry.

Oliver explains the situation by phone to Max, whose chief concern is safety. Can we get the vehicles safely parked and everybody in place to do the shoot without having somebody run down by a passing car or truck? Oliver assures him it is possible. We direct all the vehicles into various places. Steve announces he has to get to a meeting about the forthcoming days and can't stay. A quick head count reveals that we are too many to fit everybody else into the remaining cars, so Jean says she will go with Gaetano and Steve. That leaves Max's film crew and nine people to re-enact the march.

Rod duly leads, followed by me, Terry Dolan, Bill Rodgers, Bob Werbiski, Andrew Gregory, Frances, Don Aitchison, and Steve MacKinnon. We are being filmed by at least four cameras. All of us are careful to not look sideways as we pass Arlin McFarlane lying down in the tall grass with her camera poking through a gap so that she is out of the frame of the other cameras. We are more spread out than were the Seaforths, but that is the only way to enhance the image we project. Certainly, we are pretty unmilitary looking—just a sweaty bunch of mismatched Canadians treading across a barren Sicilian hillside. But to realize we are reliving an iconic historical moment is still a thrill—especially for Rod. After the shoot, when Max asks him how he feels, he says, "It's almost like a dream. To stand on this spot, I almost feel like my legs are tingling. It's quite emotional, for the first time since we arrived here, to actually be standing on a spot and looking at a place where my dad walked and where he stayed for two evenings. It's extraordinary. I never thought we would have an opportunity to do this in Sicily, and it way, way exceeds any expectations I had for this trip."

On July 18, we set off walking a backcountry road from near Caltagirone toward a small village called San Michele di Ganzaria. The distance is once again about fifteen kilometres. We had left for the starting point just before dawn. Unlike other mornings, it was misty, and Etna, which should have been visible, had wrapped herself in a cloudy cloak. By the time we begin walking, however, the mist has lifted, but the sky remains partly cloudy.

Everybody is in good spirits, still savouring the previous day, which had been one of rest. For the four of us at the B & B, this entailed a delicious sleep late into the morning. Then we did laundry, giving our white Husky shirts in particular a thorough scrubbing. But they are never again going to be pristine. The grungy, sweat-stained collars resisted our best efforts. When our hostess saw us trying to find places to drape underwear, shirts, shorts, and other odds and sods of damp clothing, she quickly got out a drying rack, and soon all was in order. The four Husky shirts were arrayed like marchers in formation on hangers hooked to an eavestrough running along the back of the balcony. Being nicely shaded, the balcony has become a favourite haunt for us all. At one point, all four of us were out on it reading books, and I was struck again by the simple camaraderie we have that demands no conversation.

Using a mix of English and Italian, we were also able to explain to our hostess what we are doing. She understands that our visit is connected to remembrance of *i canadesi* and *la guerra*, but she obviously remains perplexed as to why anybody would want to rise in the predawn hours to spend the day hiking across the Sicilian hillsides.

Laundry done, Frances and I played tourist for a short time and bumped into Dave MacLeod, who was literally jogging up the 142 steps of the Santa Maria del Monte and then back down. When he is not working for Steve on Op Husky, Dave is a personal trainer. Had he been able to march with us as planned rather than signing on with the marker team, Dave would have given Jean a run for her money. We confined ourselves to getting a photo taken standing on the steps and then climbing them in a very leisurely fashion. When we got back to the B & B, Bill and Rod were out exploring. Frances had a siesta, and I spent a couple of hours catching up on sending out Facebook updates about the march.

It is amazing how a single day of rest can put some spring back in the step. I think it was probably that way for the troops as well. Even a few hours of true rest would have rejuvenated them. Relatively sprightly as we now feel, however, we are in fact two days behind on their advance; and henceforth, on most days we will not be walking precisely where they were at that time. This lag is due mostly to the difficulty of sequencing the daily community ceremonies. As the organizing of these fell into place, it evolved that communities that had been liberated on the same day were now vying to participate on that day. As we could not be in two places at once, some towns' liberation had to be celebrated on historically incorrect dates. This is just another of the compromises and deviations from Steve's original scheme that is required by the reality of being on the ground.

We marchers have come to terms with this. We are content to walk in some semblance of the paths the Canadian soldiers walked. There is, I think, a likelihood that we are now walking the route that the Loyal Edmonton Regiment and 'C' Squadron of the Three Rivers tanks took on July 16. The road is much like what is described in the war diaries. Because it is so little trafficked, the two Carabinieri officers who met us in the morning and suggested this route said they did not need to provide close support. They drove off with a promise to be waiting where the road joins the one leading into the village. We encounter not a single vehicle nor a single soul. It is just us, the road, and this part of Sicily's vast expanses. Wide grain fields, all recently harvested, swirl across narrow ridges and hilltops. These rolling hills and fields stretch to the outer reaches of the horizon. They are seemingly endless.

As has been true on most of our marches, we often see abandoned houses and clusters of farm buildings on the hillsides. Many of the farmhouses have two storeys. All are built of the stone so common in this area and match the earth so well they seem part of it rather than fabricated above. "It always seems sad to see an abandoned house," Phil comments. But we agree they are probably "the inevitable consequence of farm mechanization and aggregation." Phil notes that many of the rural towns we have been passing through suffer severe unemployment. We recall how shrunken the populations of Licodia Eubea and Vizzini seemed. There, too, many houses stood abandoned. We imagine families migrating to Palermo or Catania in the hope of finding work. Many others cross to the mainland to seek employment in the northern factories or go farther, to Germany, in search of a livelihood. And, of course, the migration from Sicily to North America continues as well.

I hang back at one point to let the others get well ahead so I can photograph them as they walk in a long line across a stone bridge supported by three elegant arches. It surely dates to well before the war. It is a long jog to catch up, and I rejoin the group just as it enters a strange tunnel cut through a low rise. The moment we enter its dark gloom, the luminescent strips on the backs of our safety vests glisten, the only thing visible in the inky darkness. We emerge from the other end and again see the hills and fields, as well as a narrow, winding gulch choked with bamboo and other green flora following a stream bed in which no water is to be found this time of year.

When we come to the junction and meet the motorhome and Carabinieri escort, I regret the walk ending. I could have happily wandered these hills for the rest of the day. Instead, we put on our white shirts and red ball caps, form up behind the pipe band, and start the ritual march toward the heart of San Michele di Ganzaria. As we come to the village's limits, we see that a large banner with the Canadian flag and "Welcome Canadians" printed on it has been mounted on the village sign, along with two Italian flags. As we advance farther into the town, more Canadian flag banners appear, affixed to various signposts and walls.

When the Loyal Eddies and Three Rivers tankers rolled into this village, they were also greeted in grand fashion. Hundreds of white sheets hung from the balconies, and a crowd of Italian troops had gathered in the village, anxious to surrender. As the Canadians' actual objective was Piazza Armerina, orders were given to press on and leave the Italians to surrender to the regiments behind.

Instead of defeated soldiers, we are greeted by hordes of school-children. The teenagers wear green T-shirts, the younger ones white T-shirts with a little logo that appears to be a stylized map of Sicily. No matter their ages, the kids are all waving small Canadian flags. It soon becomes evident that the teenagers are group leaders in charge of the younger kids. There are also hundreds of adults. Everyone is sweltering in the heat of the day, and the humidity is also high. A digital temperature display outside a pharmacy reads 38 degrees Celsius, but the humidity makes it feel even hotter. I estimate that the crowd in this little village is not appreciably smaller than that of Pachino and am impressed that so many people felt compelled to attend despite the ferocious heat.

Each day, during the ceremony, one of the officer cadets is tasked with calling the roll of honour for those soldiers killed on this date. Although San Michele di Ganzaria was liberated on July 16, the roll call is the one for today, July 18. Twenty-five names are read. It is very sad to hear those names ring out across the village square. Adding to the emotional impact this has on most of us marchers and other Canadians is the painful awareness that the daily fatality toll is only going to rise on every day ahead. Once the Canadians reached Piazza Armerina, their advance was straight into the mountains beyond—excellent terrain for defence and tenaciously held by the elite German formations of the Hermann Göring Division, which were soon joined by the even more formidable 1st Parachute Division. I am thinking about this as the village's *sindaco* thanks us for coming and helping to initiate this remembrance ceremony. By this time, the heat is excruciating, and the group leaders have told the children to all sit down. They do so in orderly lines determined by the ball caps they wear. One row has blue caps, another has green, a third yellow, and a fourth wears Op Husky red caps. The Sicily map logo on their shirts is the same colour as the ball cap they wear. A little girl in the green row sees me taking their photograph and, with an infectious grin, waves her Canadian flag.

Having retrieved a number of the Op Husky umbrellas from the motorhome, we marchers crowd under them. One of the officer cadets is supposed to be shading Sherry Atkinson, but the umbrella stands instead directly over his own head. Frances and Phil Bury are grouped under one together. After Sherry addresses the crowd and the ceremony is beginning to wind down, an adult leader with the children has them all rise and crowd into the shadow cast by a tall building. I am amazed that nobody has collapsed yet. Across the square, an elderly woman is hanging dishtowels on a line running between a couple of two-storey balconies. She hangs six towels in two groups of red, white, and green—forming two Italian tricolours.

Ceremony over, we are happy to learn there is no planned lunch. Instead, we are free to return to Caltagirone. Back at the B & B, I contentedly sleep the afternoon away. Then CBC host Jo-Ann Roberts of the Victoria-based radio show "All Points West" interviews me via Skype. The connection is poor. She can hear me, and the quality is good for taping, but I am unable to hear her. We improvise by having her type questions to which I respond. In this manner, we share one of the rare moments when the national broadcaster provides any coverage of Operation Husky 2013. This is not for lack of trying. Steve MacKinnon has been playing every card he can think of to get major media attention. Because of its reach, the CBC is a particular target. He has been calling every top executive possible, but to no avail. The coverage we are getting is generated by local contacts of some of the marchers. In addition to my interview, Rod and Phil have been able to attract some local attention. But though Steve MacKinnon reports daily that we have been featured on this or that Italian radio station or television channel, or in the country's newspapers or magazines, media attention in Canada remains slight. Phil Bury is moved to send a plea by email to his friends and family back home. Citing the "regrettably scant" coverage in Canada, he reminds them that "the whole point of our being here is to inform and educate Canadians. So far we are failing." He implores them to use any access they may have to attract "public or media attention" and refers them to the Op Husky website, where news of our progress is posted daily.

Phil was only six months old when his father went to war. His parents' wedding photo shows about six of his father's friends, all in uniform, forming an exit arch with their swagger sticks. His father became a Hasty P, landed on July 10 in Sicily, marched through that campaign and on up the Italian boot, until he was badly wounded at the Moro River, just outside Ortona, in December 1943. After a long hospitalization in Britain, Phil's father came home to a little boy whom he knew only from his wife's letters. Of the exuberant, smiling soldiers in the wedding photo, he was the only one to survive the war. "I was privileged to have my father," Phil says.

For as long as he can recall, Phil has faithfully attended Remembrance Day ceremonies. "Since I was a small child," he recalls, "Mom tried to get Dad to wear his medals, and he usually contrived to forget. He wore a tiny red-enamel rectangle pin, and said that was enough." The pin identified soldiers of 1st Canadian Infantry Division, as it symbolized the red identification patch sewn on their uniform shoulders. It was in Sicily that the Germans nicknamed them the "Red Patch Devils," because whereas soldiers in other Allied divisions could be driven to ground by intense mortar and machine-gun fire, the Canadians kept on coming. "I think I have that pin somewhere," Phil says. "But although I nominally was a member of 1 Canadian Infantry Division as a young soldier, I don't think I could ever wear it."

Phil, who was a career soldier until retirement, believed he had always had a good sense of the meaning of remembrance. He attended Remembrance Day ceremonies, regimental ceremonies, funerals of old military comrades, and "in the last few years, some pretty sad ones for young men [who fell in Afghanistan] at Beechwood Cemetery." But, he says later, perhaps he'd gotten "just a bit accustomed to it." Then came Sicily, and the continuous ceremonies there "plus the moments on the road really drove it home, embedded it somehow." He admits to a feeling of having walked on hallowed ground. "I sensed that near where I stood at any moment, Canadians had fought, been wounded and died, and that the fallen included friends of my father, and of regimental old comrades I'd known a little. I told myself that I might be standing on soil once soaked with the blood of a young fellow-countryman. This sounds melodramatic, but I really did think that at the time."

In an email home, Phil writes that "the usual high point of the day is to march behind the pipes and drums, past often significant crowds, cheering and waving. We don't pretend to be soldiers, so we wave back, dart into the crowd to hand out pins and (mostly to kids) miniature flags, and shake the occasional hand....On the other hand, perhaps I might call this a high point, sad as it is: We stand by the side of the road before a row of white markers. We've just planted them....Our chaplain says a prayer, and at each marker one of us will read the name and unit of the young man who fell. Then a piper plays a lament as we bow our heads or stare into space, lost in our thoughts of a young Canadian whose life was cut too short so long ago."

Before the marches began, Phil had spent a day helping to prepare markers. He did so alone at Rosie's school. "I tried to connect with those whose names I was gluing to the markers," he wrote later. "That had given me a chance to read the inscriptions by the school kids who had made up the marker boards, some of them real heartbreakers. Steve's purpose to stamp that bit of our history in the national memory was achieved, at least with some Canadian and Italian kids, who would remember that contribution all their lives. And stamped more firmly in mine, too. As later on I stood in the sun, I recognized some markers I'd done. With those and with all the others, I tried to imagine the young man and the family that awaited at home and then got the telegram with the Minister of National Defence's 'regrets to inform you,' and how all the rich life ahead had disappeared in an instant.

"It's still hard to get my head around it, but I got a lot closer to it then. And I realized that every time my mother, with a newborn baby, read one of my father's letters, she didn't know if he was still alive. In fact, she read once in the *Montreal Gazette* that he was missing, presumed killed, and didn't know any different until she heard from a friend. Perhaps now I understand a bit better what she went through...The remembrance service at each marker site was a significant part of the whole experience, and brought it all home to me perhaps more than any other part. When I called out a man's name, I felt that I knew just a little of him. I saw more grownups cry in those few moments than I have in a long time."

Not long after the 2014 Remembrance Day ceremonies, Phil again wrote in an email: "About two weeks ago I stood again at the village cenotaph with the Scouts and Cubs, who were trying really hard to understand it all, and as I tried to help them understand it, I was still trying to understand it myself. Names on that war memorial are family names of folks I know. Wreaths were laid that day by neighbours: widows, and families of men, some of whom I knew— men who joined up with pals and came home without them; and some who didn't come home at all." He returns to his feeling of privilege at having a father who did come home. "All this I knew, took it seriously, and did my best to bring it within me." After Sicily, he adds, "I think now I know it just a little better."

WHEN THE GUNS fell silent in Sicily, the Canadians killed there were scattered from the beach at Pachino up through the hills to Adrano. All had been buried exactly at, or close to, the places they fell. The padre of each battalion carefully noted the locations to enable eventual exhumation and relocation to a War Graves Commission cemetery. Sometime that September, in 1943, Canadian officers stood on a small hill near Agira. With Agira spilling down the eastern slope of 824-metre-high Monte Teja to the west, Salso valley below, and Mount Etna off on the eastern horizon, the site seemed perfect—picturesque, but in a serene rather than gaudy way. They had 490 dead Canadians to inter, six of whom were never identified.

There would be three Commonwealth War Grave Cemeteries in Sicily—the Canadian one next to Agira and two British, one at Catania and the other, Siracusa. Because commission policy was to bury war dead in the cemetery closest to where their bodies were found, twelve Royal Canadian Air Force personnel and one army lieutenant were ultimately buried at Catania and two in the Syracuse War Cemetery. The bodies of all other Canadians killed in Sicily were interred at Agira. Twenty-eight dead were never found, and they are commemorated along with more than four thousand missing Commonwealth personnel from the Italian Campaign on panels of the Cassino Memorial. Retrieving and relocating the dead took time. The first burials at Agira began on October 9, 1943, and the last one occurred on October 17 of the following year. The cemetery was formally ceded to the care of the Imperial War Graves Commission on March 28, 1945. At that time, the

On July 10, 2013, honorary colonels Rod Hoffmeister and Bill Rodgers stand on the invasion beach next to markers honouring those Canadians lost at sea on the way to the landings in Sicily. PHOTO COURTESY OF BILL RODGERS

On the afternoon of July 10, 1943, troops unload a landing craft, mechanized, with warships protectively offshore at Bark West. FRANK ROYAL PHOTO. LAC PA-141663

Jubilant crowds, young and old, fill the streets of **Pachino** as Op Husky 2013 marchers enter the town on July 10. AUTHOR PHOTO

A large group of local children turn out for the ceremony at San Michele di Ganzaria on July 18. AUTHOR PHOTO

Most Canadian troops had to advance on foot but where possible also commandeered carts, mules, and donkeys to carry supplies. On July 12, 1943, troops of Princess Patricia's Canadian Light Infantry marched out of Ispica toward Modica.
FRANK ROYAL PHOTO. LAC PA–163669

Rod Hoffmeister was watching for contemporary mules to befriend. His chance came on July 23 near Castel di Judica. AUTHOR PHOTO

Frances Backhouse, Bill Rodgers, and Don Aitchison (behind) march toward Ragusa. AUTHOR PHOTO

Marchers are on the road at dawn in the drystone-wall country between Ispica and Ragusa on July 12. BILL RODGERS PHOTO

Members of the team recreate the Seaforth's march at the same spot that the historic photo (shown on the cover) was taken. As his father did before him, Rod Hoffmeister leads.
BRITTANY BLOW PHOTO

Guylaine Tarte kneels at her Uncle Ephrem Tarte's headstone with their mysterious stray dog hovering close.
CHRIS VAUGHAN-JONES PHOTO

Husky I pauses in a spot of shade during the march from Vizzini to Caltagirone on July I5. DON AITCHISON PHOTO

Unshaven and bronzed by the sun, 48th Highlanders Sergeant H.E. Cooper used a mesh cloth to try to protect his neck. Such efforts, however, generally only increased the discomfort caused by the intense heat. JACK H. SMITH PHOTO. LAC PA-I302I5

To avoid the worst of the day's heat, Jean Miso, the author, Frances Backhouse, and Steve Gregory get ready to start marching just after dawn on July 20. André Durand stands in the far background. STEVE MACKINNON PHOTO

Sherry Atkinson (right) hits it off with a Bersaglieri veteran in Raddusa on July 22. SUSAN ATKINSON PHOTO

Frances Backhouse was delighted to meet this elderly lady, who was about eighteen when the village was liberated in 1943. AUTHOR PHOTO

Steve Gregory hams it up with a farmer and his delicious green oranges on July 16. FRANCES BACKHOUSE PHOTO

A section of PPCLI finds cover in a barren field during intense fighting on the outskirts of Valguarnera. FRANK ROYAL PHOTO. LAC PA-I63670

On July I9, Bob Stewart plays the lament on Valguarnera's outskirts next to markers of Canadian soldiers who died liberating the town. AUTHOR PHOTO

Steve Gregory addresses the crowd at the ceremony in Agira Canadian War Cemetery. STEVE MACKINNON PHOTO

With his painful rash visible on the backs of his legs, Steve Gregory takes a phone call during a break in the marching. STEVE MACKINNON PHOTO

On July 18, the Op Husky marchers walked over vast open country from Caltagirone to San Michele di Ganzaria. AUTHOR PHOTO

Every dawn as the marchers gathered, Mount Etna loomed in the distant background spilling a stream of smoke southward. FRANCES BACKHOUSE PHOTO

On a barren hill, Padre Don Aitchison leads the Op Husky team in a prayer over markers. BRITTANY BLOW PHOTO

In this schoolroom, the marker team organized their markers—one for each fallen Canadian—for each day's deployment. BILL RODGERS PHOTO

Frances Backhouse walks beside a row of more than eighty markers at Adrano on July 29. BILL RODGERS PHOTO

Valguarnera's marching band performs on July 19 in the town's sunny memorial square. AUTHOR PHOTO

The Seaforth Highlanders Regimental Pipes and Drums marches into Piazza Armerina on July 26. AUTHOR PHOTO

PPCLI Bren gunner Stephen Wallace rests on a barren slope probably in the frying pan of the Dittaino valley. JACK H. SMITH PHOTO. LAC PA-130217

Marcher meltdown in the Dittaino valley on July 20. Phil Bury begins to succumb to heat exhaustion. In the foreground is Husky II. AUTHOR PHOTO

Veteran Sherry Atkinson was always a hit with the Sicilians, particularly the young women. SUSAN ATKINSON PHOTO

Members of the marker team install markers on a dry hill outside Regalbuto. *Left to right:* Christopher-Denny Matte, Erik Gregory, Chris Vaughan-Jones, Dave MacLeod. BRITTANY BLOW PHOTO

Monte Assoro dominates the Dittaino valley just as it did in 1943. SUSAN ATKINSON PHOTO

The Canadian Forces contingent gathers for a remembrance ceremony on Monte Assoro's summit. DON AITCHISON PHOTO

The entrance to Agira Canadian War Cemetery dramatically frames the rows of headstones and Cross of Sacrifice. SUSAN ATKINSON PHOTO

Crowds gather for the roll call at Agira cemetery on July 30. SUSAN ATKINSON PHOTO

Bob Wigmore stands before his chosen headstone during roll call. Emilie Vaughan-Jones is in the background. LOUIS-PHILLIPE DUBÉ, CANADIAN FORCES PHOTO

Carabinieri photographers captured the roll call ceremony at Agira Cemetery from a helicopter hovering overhead. PHOTO COURTESY OF L'ARMA DEI CARABINIERI CATANIA, VIA THE CANADIAN DEFENCE ATTACHÉ OFFICE, ROME

The Seaforth Highlanders Pipes and Drum Band beats the "Retreat" in Agira's main square on the evening of July 30, 1943. PHOTOGRAPHER UNKNOWN. LAC PA-I93886

Today's Seaforth Highlanders Regimental Pipes and Drums recreates the historic performance on July 30, 2013, in the same Agira square—with Pipe Major Mike Bain leading in the foreground. SUSAN ATKINSON PHOTO

cemetery was primitive, just a chunk of ground with the graves marked by crosses.

As was true for the World War I cemeteries, the commission contracted some of the best architects in Britain as designers. The architect responsible for most cemeteries in Italy, including Agira, was Louis de Soissons. He was born in Montreal in 1890, but his family moved to Britain when he was a child, so he had no particular connection with his birth nation. Following in his father's footsteps, de Soissons trained as an architect, and, in the 1920s, he formed the company Louis de Soissons Partnership. Although influenced by eighteenth-century Italian architecture, the Agira design kept to the simple standard principles for Commonwealth cemeteries. The sole exception is the placement of the Cross of Sacrifice on the very crest of the hill. This makes it unusually dominant in relation to the rest of the cemetery, as the headstones descend the slopes on either side. Standing at the gateway and looking up the slope, visitors see the cross first—particularly on a typical Sicilian day when the blue sky forms a stunning backdrop. The cross, like all those in Italy, is made of Botticino limestone rather than the Portland stone used in northern Europe. The headstones are marble. There is no Stone of Remembrance.

The tender for Agira Cemetery's construction was issued in July 1950, and the ensuing contract signed that September 15. The actual date of completion is unknown, but the commission believes it was sometime in 1951.

The Agira cemetery is one of 559 the commission built following World War II. Once again, the task was massive and only completed in the early 1960s. As World War II had been truly global in scope, there was a need to create cemeteries on every continent save Antarctica. More than 600,000 Commonwealth dead had to be commemorated, and 350,000 headstones were required. Thirty-six new memorials to honour the missing were also constructed. Completed in 1949, the Dieppe Canadian War Cemetery was the first finished. Seven years later, 90 per cent of all 350,000 graves were marked with permanent headstones. That was the same year the last bodies were recovered from along the infamous "Death Railway" in Burma (now Myanmar), built by British prisoners of war and used by the Japanese army to transport troops and supplies.

With the building of cemeteries and memorials completed, the commission's continuing task is maintenance and renovation as needed. Even headstones made of Portland stone or marble deteriorate over time. Over a hundred years, Portland stone erodes one to three millimetres in thickness, depending on weather conditions. So as the commission was gearing up for the beginning of ceremonies to mark the four years of World War I, the 2.8-millimetre-deep inscriptions on the headstones were already fading away.

This realization sank in sometime in the early 1990s. Within ten years, all the engravings on the World War I headstones would be fading or gone. Yet to replace 1.1 million of them over a handful of years was going to be prohibitively expensive. So the commission decided to re-engrave rather than replace most of them. A staff of sixteen engravers now travels from one cemetery to another to skilfully re-engrave the information on each headstone. In some cases, where regimental insignia or the Canadian maple leaf symbol has totally eroded away, the engravers use a pattern, which they pencil onto the headstone and then re-engrave it. Each engraver does 5.8 headstones a day in order to meet his or her assigned target. Like all good companies, the commission sets performance standards. The team of engravers' goal is to complete fourteen thousand headstones a year in France alone. Re-engraving the headstones from World War I continues in what is expected to be a twenty-five-year project. When that is finished, the engravers will turn to World War II headstones. Basically, they have a job for life.

Not all headstones can be re-engraved. Hence there's a growing need to replace them. Back in 2009, the Beaurains Factory in France, where all the headstones are manufactured, annually produced only 3,500 headstones. By 2013, that number had increased to 19,666, and for 2014, a ceiling of 22,000 was set. This speed of construction was made possible by adopting machinery, particularly lasers, to do all the inscribing. Gone are the days of craftsmen patiently chipping away with hammer and chisel. Even the best machinery is fallible, of course. If an inscription is improperly engraved and repair is impossible, the headstone is deliberately smashed to pieces and sent to the landfill. The commission could easily slice the top off headstones to produce and sell as lovely pavers. But imagine the outcry if someone turned over a paving stone and found the name of a dead soldier on it. The commission's reputation would be damaged. So the headstones are destroyed.

With the passage of time, the commission also found that not all information on existing headstones could be trusted. Names were spelled wrong, incorrect ages given, inscriptions requested by families never engraved on headstones. Now, as all military records are digitized and computerized, a staff member can stand before a headstone and download to his or her tablet every bit of data that the commission has on that fallen soldier. This makes it easier to identify headstone errors. Six hundred rules are also checked electronically before a replacement headstone is manufactured. And even with that degree of oversight, there is sufficient question regarding about 10 per cent of headstones that their archives have to be individually checked to verify all the information.

The commission's work will truly never be done. This is why it has a worldwide staff of about 1,200 people, 120 alone working at the 30,000-square-metre Beaurains Factory. Funding all this costs 66 million pounds per year, of which the British government pays 78.43 per cent. The British pay the lion's share because those who fell in World War I are considered to have done so at the behest of the Empire. So Britain covers all World War I costs and its share of the World War II losses. Canada is next in line, contributing 10.07 per cent. Australia provides 6.05 per cent, New Zealand 2.14 per cent, South Africa 2.11 per cent, and India 1.2 per cent. The British share works out to about a pound a year per taxpayer living in the United Kingdom. It is probably even less for taxpayers in Canada or the other contributing nations. A small bit of change to maintain the graves of two generations who died serving their country.

SOME DAYS DURING Op Husky, we break from our usual routine, and July 19 is definitely one of those days. The night in the sports centre in Raddusa proves dreadful. Frances and I don't fall asleep until long after midnight, and then we are up early—not to get marching before the sun is up, but because there will be no major marching this day. The ceremony is to be held in Valguarnera, a town set on a high mountain accessible only by dangerously winding roads. The Carabinieri have declared there to be no safe approach. Instead, we arrive on the outskirts in vehicles and are met by the town's marching band.

We follow it through serpentine streets. Although every band encountered has been good, Valguarnera's is exceptional. It is large, about an even mix of men and women. They wear stylish dark-blue uniforms with white caps. The male tuba player marches along as if he were carrying no more than a flute and follows no sheet music. Very few of the players do. Yet they work through an extensive selection as we wind toward the square. This is also the only band with a drum majorette, a young woman in wedge heels who flourishes a metre-and-a-half-long mace with great dexterity and skill. When we get to the square, a little girl who seems more likely a sister than daughter falls in behind her, as if in training.

Today's ceremony is particularly impressive. Both Valguarnera's band and our pipe band give spirited performances, each seemingly feeding off the talent of the other. As the bands play, Don Aitchison stands at attention alongside the war memorial holding a large Canadian flag, while on the opposite side an Italian in a suit does the same with the tricolour. Then the *sindaco*, Steve, and other dignitaries lay wreaths before the memorial. To our surprise, however, the *sindaco* makes no speech. Only Sherry Atkinson is asked to say a few words. He wins the crowd over as always, including the TLN camera crew, who have arrived. This Canadian-based Latino network is the only one from Canada to shoot a full-scale documentary.

As part of that, I am whisked away after the ceremony for an interview. We talk about remembrance and the history of the Sicilian campaign. When I mention my respect and admiration for Sherry and particularly for the way he handles himself each day at the ceremonies, Sharon—the interviewer—says she has interviewed many celebrities, athletes, and other famous people, but the session with him is the most moving she has ever done.

After our talk, I rejoin the marchers at a reception in the town hall. Plates of cookies have been set out, but there is no formal lunch—which is entirely welcome. I see some of the Valguarnera band talking with our bandsmen. The reception is short and is followed by a tour of a museum featuring displays on historical life in Valguarnera. Tony and Dora Avola have joined us. Dora says that because she left Valguarnera as a child, she knows little about her hometown. The museum has many artifacts, which Tony explains. One is an aged saddle that he says was strapped on the back of a donkey or mule. It has large earthen jugs, one per side, each held in a leather pouch. These, he says, were filled with olive oil or wine. One display needs no explanation. It consists of World War II ammunition crates with Italian lettering and a couple of Italian army helmets. Tucked into a web-kit belt pocket that looks to be Canadian is a black-and-white photo of several Princess Patricias soldiers lying on their stomachs in a shell-torn field and firing toward the enemy. The shot was taken just outside Valguarnera, which fell to our troops on July 18. We are only a day late in holding the ceremony here.

From the museum, a group of us travel in several cars to the junction of the main highway and the road to Valguarnera, where fifteen markers have been planted. They have been set out in three groups of five. The dozen or so people assembled conduct a short ceremony at each cluster. Approaching one of the clusters, I read the name Major John Henry William Pope and claim it for the roll call. When I call out his name, it is impossible not to tear up. Major Billy Pope was the second-in-command of the Royal Canadian Regiment and a best friend of then captain Strome Galloway. Early on in researching and writing the Canadian Battle Series, I interviewed Strome at his Ottawa home. A friendship was kindled that ended only with his death at eighty-eight years on August 11, 2004. Many times, our conversation came around to Billy Pope and the circumstances of his death.

As an officer, Pope was a bit of a rogue, which made him popular with his compatriots. As Strome described him in his book *Some Died at Ortona*, Pope had a "close-cropped head, round as a cannon ball, with china-white teeth under a Zorro moustache." As the

Canadians sailed from Britain to Sicily, he often pulled the regiment's junior lieutenants aside. "Have you seen much of death in the sun—in the morning?" he would ask. Before the apprehensive young men could answer, Pope flashed a grin that twitched the scar curving down his chin and said, "Well, you will." Pope always claimed the scar resulted from a sabre duel in university. It had really been caused by a motorcycle accident.

On July 18, the Royal Canadian Regiment had its first real brush with death in the morning sun, and Pope should have missed it. With the battalion's commander forward in the thick of the action, Pope was to stay back with the reserve company. Should Lieutenant Colonel Ralph Crowe be killed or wounded, Pope would assume command. Pope lamented his situation as akin to being "always the bridesmaid, never the bride."

Seeing that a section of men from the Hasty Ps off on the flank of his battalion were pinned down by German fire, Pope realized he had an opportunity to get into the action. Gathering a few men, he led them scrambling down a virtual cliff and rescued the embattled soldiers. As the composite group returned to the RCR lines, Pope spotted a German blockhouse three hundred yards distant, on Valguarnera's southern outskirts. Grabbing a PIAT gun and several bombs, Pope and his men crawled to within a hundred yards of the blockhouse. Two bombs killed the Germans inside and severely damaged the structure. As Pope finished this job, three German Mark IV tanks ground up onto a nearby roadway and brought one of the RCR companies under fire with their 75-millimetre guns. Dashing around several houses to get in range and achieve a good firing line, Pope attacked the tanks. He had three PIAT bombs remaining. We will never know whether in his excitement Pope forgot to prime the bombs or they were defective, but none of the bombs detonated. Moments later, the thirty-year-old native of Victoria was hit by a machine-gun burst fired by one of the tanks. He fell dead. Pope was the first RCR officer to die in Sicily. He died under an afternoon sun, at 2:00 p.m.

"It was a very brave and also very foolish thing that Billy did," Strome told me once over a drink in the pub that operated on the

ground floor of his condominium building and was a primary reason he lived where he did. Many days he lunched there and savoured
a scotch or two. "We were all making a lot of mistakes in Sicily. The
kind of mistakes that come from battlefield inexperience." Looking
off across the pub, Strome added softly, "Had he knocked those tanks
out, Billy would probably have won a vc for it. And he probably was
thinking that at the time. I wish I could have told him to be more
careful." Strome laughed wryly. "Of course, he wouldn't have lis-
tened." A Victoria Cross. The highest Commonwealth medal of
honour, an award that only fifteen Canadians received during World
War II. I have researched the circumstances behind almost every
one of those Victoria Cross wins. I found that none of those heroes
was thinking about his chances for a vc when he acted and did
something that extended far beyond normal bravery.

I have stood before Billy Pope's headstone at the Agira cemetery
in the past, and I plan to do so again whenever my path leads to
Agira. I will do it because Billy's story is a sad one and, yes, one that
speaks of bravery—even if there is some foolishness to be found in
it. I will do it also for Strome, because he never forgot Billy Pope.

Standing here before a simple white marker on which Pope's
name and details are inscribed in Italian, I am more moved than
when I've stood before his headstone. Perhaps it is the sheer proxim-
ity to where he died. These markers are close to the southeastern
flank of Valguarnera. I look up at the steep cliffs and sharp cuts in
the ground leading to the town and wonder exactly where Pope was
when those bullets tore into his body and took his life away. Did you
see it coming, Billy? Was there a sudden moment of clarity, the realization of having made an irreparable mistake? Or were you still
bound for glory, fearless? China-white teeth bared in a fierce grin. I
am not religious, but softly I say, "God bless you, Billy. Be safe." And
then I say the same for Strome, nine years gone. It is the same, probably meaningless, prayer I generally offer when I visit my father's
grave.

AFTER THE MARKER ceremony, Don Aitchison, Phil Bury, Andrew
Gregory, and I get into the Colonel's Car, and Bill Rodgers drives us

to another historic spot near Valguarnera. Once again, I have used the coordinate translator to this time fix the precise location where, on July 18, two Hasty P companies ambushed six German trucks passing on a road beneath their position. The Germans were making a getaway from Valguarnera. 'A' and 'C' Companies had dug in on an overlooking hill. Each truck was loaded with twenty to thirty infantrymen. At a range of about a hundred metres, the Hasty Ps opened fire with their rifles and Bren guns. 'A' Company's commander, Captain Alex Campbell, grabbed a Bren gun from one of his men and charged down the hill, firing from the hip. Clenched in his teeth was a spare ammunition magazine around which he shouted incomprehensible demands for the Germans to surrender. Unlike most Canadian soldiers, Campbell despised anything and anybody German. Seeing that the back of one truck was still fully loaded, Campbell raked it with fire and personally slaughtered eighteen of his hated enemy.

As Lieutenant Farley Mowat descended from the hilltop, he was sickened by the carnage. Badly wounded Germans lay around the trucks or hanging out of doors and off the sides. A German medical orderly dazedly wandered from one man to another, but could do little for them as he lacked any first-aid supplies. Neither could the Hasty Ps, for they were equally ill equipped.

For the rest of his days, Mowat was haunted by the sight of a truck driver draped over his steering wheel, coughing up foaming blood from a lung shot that gushed through the splintered cracks in the windshield that his face was pressed against. Each bloody cough was accompanied by a sucking heave and then a hissing expulsion, as the man tried desperately to clear his lungs of the blood drowning him. I have often thought it likely that this incident triggered Mowat's descent into what was known then as battle exhaustion and is today called post-traumatic stress disorder. Following the fighting at Ortona in December 1943, Mowat was transferred quietly out of his infantry company and made the battalion's intelligence officer—a headquarters job. He performed the duty masterfully, writing such compelling versions of the day's events in the battalion war diary that it served as his core source when he went on to write the regiment's acclaimed official World War II history, *The Regiment*. Seldom has a regimental history become an international best seller, but this one did.

One lieutenant suggested that perhaps the kindest thing would be to put the wounded Germans out of their misery. The previously berserk Campbell sharply rebuked the man and forbade any killing of prisoners. "The anomaly of hearing such sentiments voiced by a man who had just butchered twenty or thirty Germans did not strike me at the time. It does now. The line between brutal murder and heroic slaughter flickers and wavers...and becomes invisible," Mowat wrote in his war memoir *And No Birds Sang*.

Gazing at the site of that past carnage, Bill says, "When I stand in places like this, it strikes me how ordinary they are." The road is no wider than an alley, pavement badly cracked and heaving in the centre and along the edges. Knee-high wild grass runs up the slope past a few struggling olive trees. We kick about along the side of the road, searching for some sign of the past—a spent cartridge, a bullet, or a chunk of shrapnel—and turn up nothing. The slope is steep. I can hardly picture Campbell, a large, powerful man, charging down it. All but impossible to imagine the trucks, here where we stand on the road, and the Germans trying frantically to escape before bullets cut them down. We discuss how the ambush was triggered and how it unfolded. The brutal simplicity of it. The Hasty Ps coincidentally being perfectly positioned, the Germans all but defenceless. One Canadian fuming with hatred, the rest just doing their duty. Knowing as well that if roles were reversed, the Germans would serve up the same punishment with equal ferocity. The time for mercy comes when the firing stops and the enemy is clearly vanquished. To show it beforehand is to risk your life and that of your comrades.

Before us, the road winds off through rolling grain fields. Turning my back to the hillside, I see the wide Dittaino valley beyond another line of hills. It is a cloudy, hazy day. Neither Monte Teja, on whose eastern flank the ancient town of Agira clings, nor Etna is visible. With the sun behind cloud, it is not hot even standing on this road. My eyes wander back to the Dittaino valley. Tomorrow we walk through it.

OUR MARCH ON July 20 starts just after dawn, down the road a short distance from Enna. Centuries ago, Enna was confined to the hilltop and entirely protected by a high fortress wall. Today, it spills down from the old quarter to the hill's base and into the valley beyond. Whereas the old quarter attracts tourists, the newer part is a shambles of housing projects, shopping strips, and factories.

On this day seventy years ago, Enna was the finish line for a race by American and Canadian troops. The senior commander of each nation's army was bent on his troops being the first to arrive as liberators. The American 1st Infantry Division made for it in force, with its 18th Infantry Brigade and 70th Light Tank Brigade leading. Imagine hundreds of infantrymen and dozens of Sherman tanks approaching from the southwest. Dashing in from the east was a single troop of 'A' Squadron, Princess Louise Dragoon Guards. Imagine no more than thirty men riding on four Bren carriers.

When the "Plugs," as they were nicknamed, closed in on the badly bomb-damaged town, some civilians opened fire with rifles and threw several grenades their way. Whether these were defiant fascists, or just guys angry about their town being half destroyed by Allied bombing, the Plugs had no idea. Opting for prudence, the troop commander ordered a hurried withdrawal to seek reinforcement by the rest of the squadron. When the squadron's commander learned what was happening, he ordered the troop to reverse course and press on to Enna. There was a race to win. Finding the civilians gone, the troop pushed on until it came to a point where the road up to Enna had been so badly cratered by bomb blasts that the carriers could go no farther. It was decided to send just four men on by foot. The remaining distance was four miles, and after trudging up a road with one hairpin turn after another in the sweltering heat, the men "got browned off and commandeered a donkey to carry them in turns. A pretty sight they were, a patrol led by a man on a donkey to capture Enna for the Canadians," their squadron leader wrote afterwards in an official report. Ninety minutes later, the party reached a junction where they met the lead Americans driving toward Enna in trucks and jeeps. Setting the donkey loose, they crowded onto a jeep, and in this way American and Canadian forces jointly liberated

Enna. Instead of being greeted by disgruntled citizens firing guns, the four Canadians and the American hordes were welcomed by a cheering crowd. After partaking of some "vino par excellence," the four men walked back to their squadron.

The liberation of Enna was of little import to the progress of the campaign, but it sparked a bitter controversy. Learning about the exploit of the Plugs, BBC correspondents broadcast that the Canadians alone had liberated the town. This so incensed the Americans that the Supreme Commander, Allied Expeditionary Force, General Dwight D. Eisenhower wrote an angry letter to Prime Minister Winston Churchill demanding that the record be set straight. Ultimately, credit for liberating Enna was given to the Americans, although several Canadian army reports continued to cheekily attribute the feat to the four Plugs.

So today we at first follow the return journey of the Plugs toward where the rest of 1st Division was deployed in the Dittaino valley in preparation for an advance into the mountains to its north. Our destination is Dittaino Station, which served as a staging point for this advance and also stands alongside a railway that runs from Catania through Enna and on to Palermo. Our marching distance is 20.5 kilometres. None of us is complaining about the fact that the entire route is either downhill or along the dead flat road running through the valley.

Just before we set off, two Carabinieri officers roll up on BMW motorcycles. A broad-shouldered, balding officer introduces himself as Marco. The other, Saverio, has dark hair shaved close at the sides with the slightly longer hair on top gelled to stand straight up. As is always the case with the Carabinieri, their uniforms look freshly pressed, and the white leather shoulder straps that connect to the black belt their pistols are strapped to glisten as if just polished that morning. With one riding ahead and the other following behind, we descend the winding road from Enna and then walk out into the valley. The road is almost as straight as it is flat. As we have traded seemingly endless blind corners for long lines of visibility, the two Carabinieri loiter side by side. Idling the motorcycles along at a walking pace is not easy. So they roll back and forth past us, sometimes looking frustrated. Each day, I have suspected that the Carabinieri assigned to watch over us are only too happy to see their duty shift come to an end. But to our surprise, Marco and Saverio will become our regular escorts for the rest of our marching days. Even on this first day, they quickly integrate into the team. When invited to participate in the marker ceremony, they do so solemnly. At times, in a mix of English and Italian, they explain roadside features or local customs to us. Saverio proves to have a culinary streak and shows us how to harvest, shuck, and eat almonds growing on bushes beside the road. He is also a runner, and says that almonds should only be eaten fresh because they provide a source of both energy and water. When told that most of us have only eaten roasted almonds, he expresses genuine wonderment, as if we'd come from a different planet. Later, he points out caper plants, which we also pick and eat while walking. I find these a bit too bitter, but the almonds are tasty.

At the same time as Marco and Saverio joined us, so too did another stray dog. This one is a nondescript, short-haired mutt of indeterminate parentage with a reddish-brown coat. He's so scrawny his ribs show. After efforts to deter him from following fail, we dub him Husky II. As with the first Husky, he keeps pace with us, drifting back and forth along our line to trot beside one marcher or another or in the middle of the large gap that develops as the faster walkers outpace those who are slower or linger to take photographs.

The valley is a barren place but also beautiful in its own stark way—when we are not passing clusters of buildings in generally failed industrial parks. There are wide, flat stretches of grain fields intermixed with herds of grazing cattle and sheep. On the north side of the road, the Dittaino River is visible only as a line of green marsh grass and bordering trees. The river's headwaters are near Enna, and its course through the valley is almost ruler straight for 105 kilometres, until it joins the larger Simeto River on the Catania Plain, about 30 kilometres short of the sea. Were it not for the Dittaino, this valley would be a desert. Its waters provide the irrigation lifeblood that keeps the agricultural operations thriving. It is also this source of ready water that drew the industrial operations. Why so many of these failed is never clear. But it is a story that we see elsewhere in our Sicilian travels, plain evidence of a deeply troubled economy.

We march under another brilliantly blue sky. No breeze blows. The mountains flanking the valley create a bowl effect. We simmer at the bottom of the bowl. Don's phone shows the temperature as 41 Celsius, but it feels far hotter. At one point, Phil steps into a pothole near the edge of the road and takes a nasty fall. With surprising agility, though, he executes a perfect shoulder roll and quickly recovers. In his army days, Phil took airborne training, and I credit this for what seemed to be an instinctive response. Still, as Phil brushes himself off and gruffly reports that he is fine, I worry that the heat is getting to him. During the next hour, Frances and I both offer him electrolyte tablets, but he declines. Water and fruit alone will suffice, he says. Taking no chances, I dissolve another tablet in a water bottle. Frances and I drink our fill.

It is approaching noon when we reach the motorhome, which is invitingly parked under the shade of a cluster of pine trees. A sizeable group has gathered. All of Max Fraser's film crew have been dogging us from Enna. Rosie Scifo and Tony and Dora Avola are here, along with several other Sicilians I don't recognize. One of the pipers treats us to an impromptu performance that is well received. Soon enough, however, Steve is warning us to get ready to move. It takes about fifteen minutes to pry us from the shade, and then we are back on the road with the Carabinieri out front. Husky 11 pads along, seemingly indifferent to the hot asphalt underfoot. The heat is fearsome. The road surface is like a turned-on stove burner. I can feel a burning sensation coming right through the soles of my shoes.

My favourite wartime photo from Sicily is one of Princess Patricias Bren gunner Private Stephen Wallace, taken near Valguarnera and, I am pretty sure from the background of wide, open, stubbly fields, likely in the Dittaino valley. He is sitting in the stubble. His shorts are rolled up a couple of turns to a point well above the knees. Socks are equally turned down. Shirt sleeves are also rolled about as high as they can go. Instead of a helmet he has a bandana tied around his head. The Bren gun is tossed carelessly down beside him on one side and a web belt with extra magazines on the other. He is hitting hard on a canteen. Private Wallace looks young, tough, and competent.

I think about this photo and how even the youngest of us marchers is probably twice Private Wallace's age. We look like what we are—middle-aged, middle-class Canadians. Yet here we are, doing this thing. This walk of remembrance under a sizzling Sicilian sun. The days are hard, for sure, and, as we climb farther into the mountains, become only more difficult. I think of the harsh climbs into Ispica and then Vizzini during the early days, which were also very tough. I remember straggling past André Durand as he leaned against the side of a car watching us come into Vizzini's square. André served as a trainer with the Canadian Rangers for a good part of his military career. Like a lot of us, he carries a little too much weight now and could do with more workout time. As I passed, André said, "You know, I never really thought you guys would make it this far. You've surprised me. I'm impressed."

And there, I thought but did not reply, is the nub of our problem. Each day, either Richard or André, usually in the company of officer cadet Dave Domagala, is frantically cobbling together the following day's marching route. Yet several times in the two years leading up to the march's start, various members of the logistics team travelled to Sicily. One of their main tasks was supposedly to reconnoitre the march route to determine distance, safe paths, and historical relevance. On their return, spreadsheets were developed that seemed to provide these details. Once we hit the ground and started marching, however, it became clear these routes were largely a fantasy. Many were obviously unsafe or for other reasons not practicable for walking within our time constraints. A route that may have seemed reasonable to somebody clipping along in a car is entirely different for someone on foot.

Of course, on those reconnaissance trips to Sicily, the logistics team did have to juggle a host of planning and organizational tasks. None was more demanding than pinning down the various municipal authorities and arranging the dates and details of the ceremony in each town. There is much upheaval in Sicilian municipal politics, and the *sindaci* and other contacts came and went as the organizing continued. Each time one left, the new one had to be approached and lobbied into consenting anew.

I appreciated these demands and their complexity, but I could never quite dismiss the disquieting image of logistics team personnel spending many an afternoon lounging on the beach at Porto Palo when perhaps they should have been out working on the marching route. Over the last two years, it had become obvious that the marchers were going to be just a few civilians for all but the last day or two. Department of National Defence officials had made it clear that only a small number of armed forces personnel would be sent to participate, and they would not be allowed to march the full distance. So it would be just we few, we happy few, who would do that.

And, as André confessed that day, the logistics team did not think we could do it. They imagined that after a couple of hot, hard days, we would accept the impossibility of people at our age and in our condition completing the task. We would quit. A couple of vans would be rented, and we would motor to the outskirts of the towns and then march in behind our pipers and drummers. There would be a pretence of a march but not the real thing. We would definitely not end up walking through the frying pan of the Dittaino valley on July 21. But here we are, and for now, André and Richard are keeping one day's jump ahead of us and increasingly coming up with better, more suitable routes. I think their admiration for our determination to keep walking is prompting them to try harder. And we appreciate that. People make mistaken judgements, and it takes a certain courage to accept that and work to rectify the situation.

COMING TO AN overpass that accesses another abandoned industrial site, we stand under its shade drinking water and eating nuts. I am aware that Phil is clearly struggling. He seems a bit unsteady and keeps mopping his forehead with a large handkerchief. At any moment, I expect Steve to order him into the motorhome. He has done so before with both Phil and Terry Dolan. Instead, it is Terry who gathers a few of us and says, "Phil's in distress. He's staggering and I think hallucinating. What are we going to do about it? He shouldn't be marching." Later, Bill Rodgers will remind me that Terry served in the army before leaving it and joining the Parliament Hill security force. "That was his army training kicking in," Bill maintains. "Watch out for your buddies, and if one of them is in trouble, deal with it." We all agree with Terry that Phil should pack it in.

But unlike the army, none of us can make Phil go into the motor-home. It quickly becomes evident that Phil would refuse even Steve. I look toward Phil and Bob, who are sitting back to back on a large, flat chunk of concrete. Phil is looking straight ahead, clearly exhausted, open water bottle in one hand and a carton of orange juice at his side. Bob has stripped the boot and sock from his left foot. The ankle is so puffed up there's no delineation between it and the calf above. Bob is probably the most stalwart of us all, but it's easy to see that today is taking a toll.

When Steve calls out that it's time to move, Bob and Phil both rise wearily. Terry goes over and suggests that Phil not walk farther. Phil shrugs off the advice. Instead, he strips off his shirt, slathers on sunscreen, grabs a bottle of water, and starts walking. I took a photo-graph soon after. In it, Steve, Phil, and Don are walking more or less abreast. Don is looking at his phone, possibly researching Phil's con-dition. In the photo, Phil's physical distress is plain to see. Bob Werbiski is visible just behind. Husky II is a few metres ahead of them all, with Oliver Glaser off to one side. Oliver is carrying a World War II–era film camera with which he is shooting black-and-white footage. It's the type powered by a hand-cranked spring. Crank it up, release, and you have about five minutes of shooting time. Duncan Vogel is behind Steve taking footage with a regular camera, and Matt Pancer is alongside Bob recording sound. The three young film-crew members, as usual, are wearing flip-flops, in which they often match our pace. I consider this a testament to youth. They could probably keep up with Private Wallace.

As we continue, Bob is close to Phil, his expression one of concen-trated concern. He asks questions that require Phil to demonstrate mental cognition. What's his age? And the age of his son? What are the two ages added together?

We are all worried about Phil. Another photo I took shows Bill and Terry walking together out ahead of the group with Phil. It is probably Terry that Bill spoke to when he remembers later telling another marcher, "I think Phil is going to go down. We may have a serious medical issue on our hands in a few minutes." But, he recounts, "there was a reluctance to intervene, to assert authority not only over Philip but over Steve." It was Steve, Bill was thinking at the time, who should have ordered Phil into the motorhome and brooked no argument. But Steve had indicated that Phil could do as he liked. Bill did not agree with that decision. "I was walking along and thinking about this," he says. "I thought, what happens if this guy dies? It was an option. What happens if he dies? What will happen to this event? Will we all just go home? Will we be asked to carry on? What will happen?"

Fortunately, Bill's worst fears go unrealized, and after more long, hard slogging in the heat, we come to Dittaino Station. Across from the yellow-painted building stand a large number of markers, fifteen or more. Near the station, the motorhome is parked again in the shade of some trees, and several tables and a bunch of chairs have been rounded up from somewhere and deployed. The motorhome's awning has been extended to shade some of these. It all looks quite inviting, but first there is the ceremony to hold.

As Dittaino Station is virtually just a whistle stop for the railway, there is no *sindaco*, marching band, or citizenry to greet us. I suspect we are all thankful for this, as the prospect of standing in the sun while various dignitaries drone on is less than inviting. Instead, our attention focuses directly on the markers. One, I see, is for Lieutenant Colonel Bruce Sutcliffe, and another for Captain Maurice Herbert Battle Cockin. Today is July 20, the date on which, in 1943, the two men died planning the Hasty Ps' attack on Monte Assoro. They were quite near here when an artillery shell claimed their lives. One of Sutcliffe's children has sponsored his marker and asked that the following be written on the back: "In loving memory of my father, 70 years since you left us but you are forever loved and never forgotten." It was to honour these two men that Steve made his fateful trip to Agira Canadian War Cemetery seven years ago. I look over at him as the piper plays the lament. Tears roll down his cheeks. I brush some away as well.

Standing there in the heat, looking beyond the markers to where both Monte Assoro and Leonforte are visible, I think of the soldiers gathered in this spot seventy years ago. Today, the towns in the distance offer an impressive vista, clinging to the sides of tall mountains. But I think the soldiers, including Sutcliffe and Cockin, would not have seen any beauty there. They saw instead a barrier— two hills strongly defended, with open ground that stretched from Dittaino Station to the foot of each. Little cover from the German artillery, mortars, and machine guns positioned on their summits. The soldiers looked upon a killing field and were now experienced enough to recognize this.

When the ceremony ends, we drift over to the motorhome, where Tony Avola is cutting up melons with a large knife and washing grapes. I am munching on a big slice of melon when I overhear somebody asking the two Carabinieri if it is normal for stray dogs to follow people across the countryside. Emphatically, they say no, this never happens. And then one says, and the other nods in agreement, "This dog is a spirit joining us." Is it that of a dead soldier? Who can know? But they are adamant that it is a spirit. A few minutes later, they say the same thing for the cameras, with Dora providing translation.

I'm digesting this opinion and half accepting it when I notice that Bill and Rod are over on the landing of the station. They are leaning back in fire-red plastic chairs with several bottles of beer arrayed on the matching red-plastic table before them. Until then, I had not noticed that there is a small bar operating in one part of the station. The setting they are in and their lazy, relaxed manner puts me in mind of one of Sergio Leone's 1960s spaghetti westerns. It just needs Clint Eastwood to ride up and fix them with steely eyes. A long pause. Close-up of the eyes of each person twitching back and forth. Then everybody goes for their guns. I begin to think about joining them just as Steve announces it's time for us all to saddle up and head for Sicilia Outlet Village for lunch.

I would be quite content to stay here eating melons and grapes, perhaps washed down by a cold beer from that bar. I suspect others feel the same. But Steve is suddenly in full command mode and not to be denied. So the fruit is left behind. Husky II, we realize, has disappeared, just as Husky before him. The spirit has flown. And if he is not a spirit, what is the fate of a dog that left crowded Enna to take up life in whistle-stop Dittaino Station? I doubt the bar owner is going to take him in. Sicilians are not big on dog adoption.

But Husky II shall have to fend for himself, because our convoy is bound for Sicily's shopping mecca. Built to resemble a modern village, Sicilia Outlet Village stands almost precisely in the island's centre. It is, says the billboard we pass, eighty minutes from Messina, seventy minutes from Palermo, and forty minutes from Catania. We are soon standing in a vast food court. I opt for a tired-looking salad. Rod orders lasagna and regrets it after the first bite. Around us, Sicilians by the hundreds are happily scarfing down pasta, salads, panini, hamburgers, and fries. It's as if they have suspended their culinary senses to fit the expectations of mass consumption.

Since we will be abandoning the shared accommodation at Raddusa today for the hotel near Regalbuto, Bill, Rod, Frances, and I agree we have no interest in joining the others in what Steve announces will be two hours for shopping. Jean and Brittany Blow, though, are particularly pleased by this prospect. They begin to discuss shoes and purses as they head toward one part of this massive complex. I walk over to Steve and tell him we four are leaving and will meet everybody next morning at the march's Dittaino Station start point. Before going to our hotel, we first return to Raddusa and liberate our luggage from the shared accommodation. We then drive for about forty minutes northeastward to Regalbuto. En route, we discuss Phil, Husky II, and the Carabinieri's claim that the dogs are spirits. We all consider ourselves people governed by rationality and logic. Yet not one of us is discounting the idea. We have all wondered if it might be true.

OUR DEPARTURE FROM the hotel at 5:30 a.m. catches the management by surprise. At night, the hotel parking lot is secured by tall steel gates across the two entry points. It takes us several minutes to rouse one of the owner's sons, who unlocks and opens one. Hereafter, they understand what we are doing, and there is not only someone awake and waiting each morning, but they make available coffee, baguettes, packaged croissants, and other pastries for a light breakfast.

The Hotel Castel Miralago is a small three-storey, pinkish-orange structure with twelve rooms. These are simply furnished but comfortable and clean, light years ahead of the shared accommodation. This is not a hotel used to catering to non-Sicilians. Most of its guests are businessmen and tradesmen on the road. They eat dinners in the small pizzeria next to the management desk, where a large television plays continuously. Some stare at its screen inattentively, but most fixate on their cellphones or converse with compatriots while they eat. The room is dark, with a low ceiling. On the other side of the hotel's main floor is a bigger and brighter dining room, with large windows that look out to the north upon the Salso River valley. Lake Pozzillo is directly below, its water a stunning greenish blue. Damming the river in 1959 created what is Sicily's largest artificial lake. Its purpose was to provide a year-round water source to be used largely for irrigating the Catania Plain, which was subject to regular summer droughts. Although the lake is reputedly popular for fishing and various kinds of boating, I never see any signs of human activity on its expansive waters.

Another bank of windows facing west provides a spectacular view of Monte Teja, with Agira clinging to its flank and the ruins of an Arab-Byzantine castle scattered on the summit. Etna is visible from the hotel, too, but not from the dining room. Seeing how nicely appointed the dining room is and the views it offers, we set up there for dinner most evenings. We also use it to do our computer work at the end of the day or just to hang out in. At first, the management is a little resistant to this, but they quickly come around when we prove to have healthy appetites for dinners and appropriate libations that will ensure a substantial profit above the room charges.

We arrive at Dittaino Station on July 21 just as the sun begins to rise directly over Etna. A thin trail of smoke emanates from the crater and drifts ruler-straight southward. The sun is a flaring ball of immense dimensions. It is already hot. This is one of those good starting days, common now, when everybody is present before splitting off in various directions to carry out different tasks. The motorhome is here, with Les Gilles and the five-man band. Having recently rebelled against always wearing their period uniform dress, the four officer cadets are present and looking more comfortable in regular shorts, T-shirts, and sandals. Dave MacLeod, Erik Gregory, and Christopher-Denny Matte of the marker team are here—the back of their car loaded with markers. Chris is probably Erik's best friend and has been for fourteen years. André and Richard are joking with Jean in the big vehicle's shade. She and Richard have taken to teasing each other about who is fitter. They are similar in height—Jean willowy, Richard solid. Both are runners. The only one missing is Husky II. I had half expected to see him emerge from the shade around the station to join us for another march. At least that would get him to Nissoria, where some people actually live. Also present are our two Carabinieri friends, Marco and Saverio. Today, they are in a car rather than on motorcycles, because the road we are to take will be a rough backcountry one, rather than the main road cutting through the heart of the valley.

The moment we got out of the car, I noticed that Bob Werbiski and Phil Bury were missing. We learn that shortly after everyone returned to Raddusa from the shopping mall, Phil collapsed. He was quickly taken to a clinic and then sent on to hospital for admission. The diagnosis was heat exhaustion, and the doctors at the hospital wanted to keep him for a day or two for observation and rehydration by intravenous drip. Bob decided to stay with him. Everyone is relieved that it appears Phil is going to be okay. We will also henceforth keep a more watchful eye on each other to ensure that this kind of thing does not happen again.

Dave digs out his tablet, and everyone gathers in a circle to hear me read the Action of the Day. This briefing is a key one, I realize, for it tells the full story of the event that stirred Steve's imagination in Agira cemetery, setting him on the mission that became Operation Husky 2013.

Since we are not always marching now in direct relation to the soldiers' route, today's report is less about where we are going than about what we can see to the north—which is the hulking presence of Monte Assoro. I explain that seventy years ago, during the night just ended, the Hasty Ps carried out a famous stealthy march cross-country, with Captain Alex Campbell and four officers leading. One of the four was Lieutenant Farley Mowat. At 4:00 a.m., these officers and sixty volunteers began to scale the cliff on the opposite side of the mountain from the one with the road toward which the German defenders on the summit were training their guns. The cliff was sculpted into forty-seven steep and overgrown terraces, on which vineyards had once grown. Today, most of these terraces have collapsed, leaving little trace of their existence. But on that night, each had to be scaled in turn. One man was boosted to the top of the first terrace. He took all the guns of the others, quietly stacked them, and then helped haul up the other men. This process continued up the mountain and happened across a fairly broad front, the Hasty Ps working in five teams. The clatter of a single gun against a rock, the rattle of gear, or any other betraying sound could have alerted the German guards on the summit and resulted in a slaughter. Instead, in what Mowat described as a night of individual "private miracles," the Hasty Ps gained the summit, surprised the guards there, and ambushed the rest of the German defenders from an unexpected direction—literally striking them from the rear. Until late in the day on July 22, the battalion fended off a steady series of counterattacks. As night fell, the Germans abandoned the struggle. This victory enabled the 48th Highlanders to advance west of Leonforte to conduct an eastward hook into Nissoria.

As usual, I am asked a number of questions after the briefing. Some are tactical. Some are about the personalities involved. Often somebody comments on what the soldiers might have been thinking or experiencing. Each day during this time, I am struck by the attentiveness of everybody present. They listen keenly, and in this case, now look at Monte Assoro with a different eye—one less drawn by its beauty than by the tactical challenge it presented to the soldiers. And some are thinking of the challenge to come. For the plan is that in a few days, a small group will recreate that climb up the mountain.

I realize that these Action of the Day briefings have become an important part of the overall remembrance experience in which we are engaged. As Jean says later, they have brought more "meaning and remembrance to our marches, parades, and ceremonies. They allowed us snapshots into the past and, as we walked, time to reflect on those details of actions and feel them in our steps as we marched." For Phil, hearing the briefings "settled it all in our minds each day, set the scene, and helped us understand. Knowing what happened at that place seventy years ago brought it all home."

As the group disperses, the happy foursome of Rod, Bill, Frances, and I split up. When Rod learned that the marker team was planning to install a large number of Seaforth Highlander markers today outside Leonforte, near where those soldiers had died, he announced that he needed to be part of that effort. Bill and Terry Dolan both volunteered to accompany him. I was tempted, but with Phil and Rob off today's marcher roster, it seemed I needed to march, as there would only be five of us.

Because of its poor condition, the road we take has almost no traffic on it, so we enjoy a day of not having to wear safety vests. The country just keeps getting more beautiful. Etna is always there in the distance. Living in Victoria, I am used to the sight of our local volcano, Mount Baker, across the water in Washington State. At times, it is possible to also see Mount Rainier in the very far distance, beyond the Strait of Juan de Fuca. Both, however, seem small compared to Etna. It is not so much her height, which is only a little more than that of Baker and almost a thousand metres less than Rainier. But both these volcanoes are in the Cascade Range and surrounded by lesser mountains. Etna stands alone and seems to reach to the heavens and possess a vast girth.

We are again in big country—vast fields that wrap up, around, and over hills. There are large patches of ploughed brown dirt, straw-coloured expanses of wheat and wild grass, and stark higher hills where there is neither the soil nor irrigation to make farming possible. Soon we begin climbing into those higher hills. Don has an app on his phone that keeps track of the elevation gains. When we reach our destination of Nissoria, he shows it to me. The distance today was again just over twenty kilometres. We started out at an elevation of about 300 metres and climbed to a maximum elevation of 688 metres, with a number of steep descents and ascents in between. Despite this, the march does not seem particularly arduous, and I chalk that up to the beauty of the countryside, which is a good distraction from the physical exertion. Or maybe I am getting fitter.

Arriving in Nissoria, we find that the residents have strung pennants in the pattern of the Italian flag across the street, from one balcony to the other. Max Fraser's film crew is staying in a bed and breakfast here, and Arlin McFarlane tells us that on the previous evening, people simply came out with the pennants and in no time had them all strung into place. It appears that people keep them handy for whenever a parade might happen.

Nissoria is a small town, but there is a marching band and also a *sindaco*, who is short, bearded, and very earnest. Today, Steve calls upon me to read a poem called "Prayer before Battle," which the German-hating Alex Campbell of the Hasty Ps wrote in pencil on a dirty slip of Salvation Army canteen paper and then gave to Farley Mowat. With Dora Avola translating, I read:

> When 'neath the rumble of the guns
> I lead my men against the Huns
> I am alone, and weak, and scared
> And wonder how I ever dared
> Accept the task of leading them.
> I wonder, worry, then I pray:
> Oh God, who takes men's pain away,
> Now, in my spirit's fight with fear,
> Draw near, dear God, draw near, draw near!
> Make me more willing to obey,
> Help me to merit my command.
> And if this be my fatal day,
> Reach out, oh God, thy helping hand.
> These men of mine must never know
> How much afraid I really am!
> Help me to stand against the foe
> So they will say: He was a man!

When I finish reading the poem, I explain that Alexander Railton Campbell of Perth, Ontario, was killed on December 25, 1943, while fighting just outside Ortona. He was thirty-three. As reading the poem, with Dora translating every two or three lines, has taken up a good chunk of time, I do not go into the details of Campbell's death. How on that Christmas morning, one of his platoons was ambushed by three German machine guns that killed or wounded several men and pinned down the rest. Instead of sending another platoon to out-flank the German position, Campbell grabbed a Thompson submachine gun, just as he had the Bren gun in the ambush outside Valguarnera. As Farley Mowat recounts in his memoir, "he then levered his great bulk to its full height, gave an inarticulate bellow, and charged straight at the enemy." This time, Campbell took no more than three or four paces before the machine guns riddled him with bullets. Mowat did not witness Campbell's death; he learned of it instead from a wounded sergeant passing his position. The ser-geant described Campbell's last act as "crazy as hell! But Jesus, what a man!"

Sherry Atkinson now takes the microphone. It was just outside Nissoria that Sherry's war had come to an end. He was in an olive grove and taking cover behind an abandoned German tank, when shrapnel from an artillery shell hit him in the shoulder. He tells the crowd, "My blood has been shed upon your earth, and I consider myself one of you." The crowd gobbles up his words, and later he is mobbed by people wanting to shake his hand and have their picture taken beside him.

After the ceremony, we follow the *sindaco* to a street that is being officially renamed today. The street is to be called Via Giuseppe Rinaldi, after a soldier from Nissoria who, according to the street-name plaque, was killed in fighting at Ragusa. From the *sindaco*'s comments earlier, I sense it is generally believed that Canadians were responsible for his death. In fact, it was more likely Americans of the 45th (Thunderbird) Division. I determine later that Giuseppe Rinaldi served in the 383rd Coastal Battalion and died along with his comrades on July 10 defending a fortified blockhouse alongside SP25, which runs straight from Marina di Ragusa, on the sea, inland to

Ragusa. The blockhouse was positioned close to the hamlet of Camemi, about four kilometres from the sea. This was well inside the American sector.

The renaming of the street was likely pushed along by Rinaldi's son, for on July 10, 2014—at his initiative—a monument to the man's father would also be installed, with much ceremony, next to the remains of the blockhouse. A news article on that event says that Giuseppe Rinaldi did his duty as a soldier and was tragically ripped forever from his family. The article speaks of how he and his comrades kept "fidelity to the military oath sworn." This monument is intended to ensure that the "grandfathers, fathers and brothers, forgotten for too long, finally will be remembered."

In Nissoria, the renamed street is intended to do the same for the town's one soldier who died fighting in Sicily. The question goes unanswered as to whether Giuseppe Rinaldi was a true fascist believer or just a soldier who ended up in a place where he and his comrades put up a fight rather than surrender, and died for doing so. This is the dilemma that surrounds Italian remembrance of its soldiers who fell in World War II. Can all be remembered as one? Or do you sort them into factions—fascists over here, regular folks over there? And if you do that, how is the act of remembrance performed?

Nationally, Italy remembers its military war dead on November 4. This is the day in 1918 when the ceasefire following the signing of the Armistice of Villa Giusti, which ended the country's role in World War I, came into effect. Of course, as with many things in Italy, where the threads of history seldom nicely intertwine, the commemoration of this day has two components. November 4 is known as both Armed Forces Day and National Unity Day. The Armed Forces Day component remembers the soldiers who died defending Italy, with a strong emphasis on World War I losses. National Unity Day (sometimes called Victory Day) recognizes that when the Italian troops wrested Trieste and Trento from the grip of the Austrians, they symbolically concluded the Risorgimento—the unification of Italy that was officially achieved in 1870—by bringing back into the fold the last missing piece of what were seen as the country's true lands. Whereas Remembrance and Armistice Day services in the Commonwealth nations and the United States have expanded their focus over time to include the dead of subsequent wars, comparable services in Italy largely retain their original focus—and thereby side-step the uncomfortable reality of the country's World War II military history.

At times, we have noticed a young man of some apparent promi-nence following us. He has spoken at one conference and at least one remembrance ceremony. Each time, I got the impression—which Steve, whose Italian is fairly good, confirmed—that his comments were rather hostile toward the Canadians and the other Allies. Today, he speaks at some length, and whenever he looks in our direction, his expression is grim. Then the *sindaco* lets loose with a forty-five-minute speech that leaves even most of the Nissorians looking exhausted and uncomfortable. As always, I am astonished not only by the *sindaco*'s stamina but also by his ability to speak for so long without reference to a single note. "Never give an Italian a microphone," I mutter.

Throughout this ceremony, the new street sign has been covered, awaiting its formal unveiling. His speech over, the *sindaco* indicates that Steve should perform the act. But with surprising agility, Steve sweeps the small daughter of the first speaker—the possible pro-fascist—into his arms and volunteers her for the duty. The girl looks to be about four, is wearing a white sunhat and multicoloured dress—an Impressionist splash of white, yellow, pink, and blue. Steve holds her in his arms as the *sindaco* raises the microphone so she can tell everybody her name. With delight, she pulls the covering away, and *soldato* Giuseppe Rinaldi has his street, seventy years after he died defending a doomed position.

After the street renaming, we are guided to an area where local merchants have set up a long table of refreshments and servers cir-culate with large trays of food. As was the case in Licodia Ubea and Vizzini, I sense that more than a few people here think back wist-fully to the time when fascism reigned supreme. Fortunately, if they exist, they are greatly outnumbered. The evidence is plain to see as I chew on bruschetta and sip quite good cider from a plastic glass.

Sherry is sitting in a chair in the middle of everything, obviously holding the place of honour. As his wife, Susan, blogs that evening, "I had a devil of a time getting him away, as everyone wanted to speak, touch, or get a photo. He is their own hero!" To most Nissorians, then, the Canadians were liberators rather than oppressors. The repressors were the fascists, and no amount of modern-day revisionism, either wistful or with malicious intent, can change that.

I HAVE A photo of markers set out by the team in a room off the open area where people slept in the sports centre at Caltagirone. Dozens upon dozens of markers, all painted identically white, all bearing the red maple leaf, the Italian tricolour, and the small brass plaque detailing information about the fallen soldier. Some have inscriptions by the students, others do not. The marker team has grouped together those that are to be planted on a specific day but at different places in the dry Sicilian countryside. The photo is digitally date-stamped July 18. That was the day twenty-five markers were planted, the day seventy years ago that the campaign heated up as the Germans began contesting every defensible bit of ground. Canadian casualties mounted rapidly. And the day's work for the marker team grew ever more demanding, and carried with it not just a physical but an emotional toll.

Having decided only a month before Op Husky began to become part of the marker team, Christopher-Denny Matte admitted later he had little idea what that meant. For the past twelve years, he had attended a school that held a Remembrance Day ceremony on November 11. Like many students, Chris came to think of it more as "a way to avoid class than as something close to me. Every year was the same." And every year, the meaning of it seemed "less and less significant."

Once their boots hit Sicilian ground, Chris and Erik realized the magnitude of the task they had volunteered for. It was two days until the Pachino beach ceremony would formally put everything into motion. Although the markers were mostly made, some were not. Working frantically to get all 562 ready to go, Chris "lost touch with what we were truly there for. But as soon as things started to run a bit more smoothly, I could finally think about what was going on. Planting each marker, choosing an appropriate site for them, and all the while knowing we were doing this not only for the soldiers that had fallen but for the marchers who would honour our work with a brief and touching ceremony, made everything worthwhile."

Perhaps the most memorable day for Chris was the one on which Sherry Atkinson joined the team to plant the marker of a soldier from his platoon. It was an especially moving day for all of us. I had assumed that the soldier who had died was one of the friends that Sherry said an infantryman should never make. And I referred to him that way to Sherry. But later, Sherry told me in an email that the reference had caused him a great deal of reflection. "I had never initially categorized him as anything other than a member of my anti-tank platoon—a person for whom I had a direct and personal responsibility and inwardly liked," Sherry said. "Later, I developed a much different relationship with this fine young soldier. Come to think of it, we were close to the same age."

Private Kenneth John Earnshaw was nicknamed "Squeak." He had a bad stutter and initially drove one of the trucks that pulled an anti-tank gun. Shortly before the unit left for Sicily, Earnshaw had pleaded with Sherry to let him become a gunner. As there was an opening for a shooter on one of the gun crews, Sherry, with some hesitation, gave him the job. Earnshaw "was like a kid with his first toy gun," he recounted. "His enthusiasm was beyond bounds, and he learned his job quicker than most of the other gunners. I felt very comfortable with him." After the landing in Sicily, Sherry promised a bottle of rum to the first gun crew that knocked out a German tank. When he was wounded at Nissoria, the rum was still unclaimed.

The rest of Earnshaw's story Sherry learned from gun-crew members questioned after the war. When the Royal Canadian Regiment attacked Regalbuto on August 1, Earnshaw's anti-tank gun crew set up in a position covering a T-junction through which any approaching German tanks would have to pass. "Shortly afterwards, a German Mark IV turned the corner and faced directly toward the 6-pounder crew. Sadly, the tank fired first, and Squeak was instantly killed. Later, when the town was cleared, one of the crews examined the damaged 6-pounder and was able to open the breech. To their surprise, it contained an empty shell casing. Squeak must have fired a fraction of a second after the German tank.

"So ends the story," Sherry continued. "I have visited his grave site at Agira many times and have always felt some blame for having agreed to transfer him from being a driver to a gunner. I know all the reasons that don't support this feeling, but I will always carry it. Was he a friend or just a soldier in my platoon? I think you know the answer."

Earnshaw's marker is one of several that has presented a complication for Op Husky planners. As the remembrance project is scheduled to wind up on July 30, it is impossible to plant markers on the actual day that soldiers who were killed in the first days of August fell. Instead, the marker team has added them to the rosters for other days but has tried to place them close to where they died. To achieve this, the team sometimes has to drive significant distances to plant markers both for men who fell on the actual day and, in other places, for soldiers who died in August.

Standing on a patch of ground outside Regalbuto, Chris watched in wonder as Sherry, in his RCR association uniform, gamely took up a hammer to pound Private Earnshaw's marker into the hard soil. "Simply being there was enough to make someone cry," he said later. "But the effort and force he put in behind every stroke of the hammer was truly inspirational." This and other experiences during the tour completely turned around his notions about Remembrance Day. "At every ceremony, be it within the town or a smaller one in front of the markers, I was touched and felt the weight of our duty to remember those who fell for us surge through me. I was enlightened and will forever hold all remembrance ceremonies in high respect and importance."

Another special day for the marker team occurs this July 21, when Rod Hoffmeister, accompanied by Bill Rodgers and Terry Dolan, help plant markers for Seaforth Highlanders who died outside Leonforte. It is an event I am sorry to miss, for I know the story behind those fallen troops very well and have related it to Rod in detail. It would have been good to be with him for that moment. Instead, I march, and later learn about the marker planting both from Rod and Bill and also from footage that Max's film crew shoots.

For the Seaforths, July 21 was the costliest day in Sicily. The day got off to a bad start when a patrol of thirty men was sent to check a ravine separating the Canadians from the steep slope leading up to the town, which sat on a shelf near the top of a mountain. As soon as the men reached the bottom of the ravine, Leonforte above them erupted in gunfire that seemed to come from every street and from every window and door of the buildings along the town's overlooking edge. Corporal Johnnie Cromb was shot twice in his thigh. Nearby, his twenty-four-year-old brother, Private Charles Alexander Cromb, lay dead in a ditch. Not far from the body, what remained of their section took cover, until finally, toward sunset, they were able to escape back to the Seaforth lines.

This first attempt having cost the Seaforths dearly, Lieutenant Colonel Bert Hoffmeister and his officers were working out a new plan of attack for 1630 hours. An hour before the scheduled attack, a salvo fired by Canadian artillery fell directly on their own headquarters. The officers were standing on a concrete platform in the middle of a farmyard when the shells struck. Although blown flat and badly dazed, Rod's father was the only officer unhurt. His adjutant, Captain Douglas Haig Strain, died instantly. The life of Lieutenant James Harry Budd, who commanded the regiment's pioneer platoon, bled away even as the medical officer reached his side. Captain Bill Merritt, whose older brother had received a Victoria Cross for his heroism during the Dieppe raid and was in a German prisoner-of-war camp, had one of his legs practically torn off. Two signallers were dead. Many other men of the headquarters were seriously wounded. In all, between the fiasco in the ravine and the disaster at the headquarters, thirty-one Seaforths died.

They were not, of course, alone. Before the day was done, the Loyal Edmonton Regiment had fought its way into Leonforte's streets and taken heavy casualties along the way. As a result, the ridgeline the marker team identified as fitting for the installation of today's markers bristles with white stakes by the time the job is complete.

Sixty-one in all. Placing a rock on top of each Seaforth marker to avoid damaging it with the hammer blows, Rod drives them into the ground. Others dig up the soil to make the hammering somewhat easier. It's a hard job, carried out under a relentless sun. When the job is finished, however, there is no formal ceremony there. The band is bound for Nissoria. Padre Don is with us, marching to the town, so Rod and the others working with the marker team spend some time in silence before loading up the shovels, hammers, and other equipment and driving away.

"Placing the markers," Rod says later, "was really heart-wrenching. Remembrance became personal. I knew some of the names—such as Doug Strain, who was dad's adjutant. Other names rang bells, prominent names in Vancouver. And what struck me was that because these guys had spent three years together in the United Kingdom and had paraded together for years in Vancouver, they would all know each other. They knew their wives and families. When dad started to lose troops, he could visualize their wives, kids. He made one trip to a field hospital and found he couldn't do it anymore. His ties to his men were so close that he had to pull away in order to survive mentally. It never became numbers, but became less personal for him as he went up the ranks. It became very personal for me. It made me question how leadership works when you start having fatalities like that. How do you move on ten minutes later to the next challenge and just put that out of your mind? It just raised all sorts of questions and very much increased my appreciation of the work he did over there.

"I didn't know how I would be affected by visiting and remembering those who died seventy years ago—Seaforths in particular. But I can't think of anywhere else in the world where you could walk in the exact footsteps of the soldiers of World War II. It's a unique experience that I will always remember."

For us marchers and likely everybody else involved in Op Husky, the marker ceremonies promise to be one of the things that we will always carry close to our hearts. Don Aitchison told me later that his liturgical role became attached to the almost daily marker ceremonies. "These were meaningful to me in several ways," he said, "in particular,

because I felt that by walking the roads in Sicily, I was finding commu-
nion with Padre Stuart East—the 48th Highlanders chaplain who
served with the regiment all through Operation Husky and on into
mainland Italy, where he won the Military Cross for bravery in connection with an attempt to rescue wounded soldiers and wherein he was
himself wounded. Standing at the head of a row of markers, I felt like I
was burying them all over again—and could begin to imagine what it
felt like for war-time padres to put to rest so many of their flock. I
found these ceremonies more meaningful than the larger, more pomp-
ous marches into town squares. Although these were exciting, truly
thrilling in the best sense of the word, and important, there was always
a sense of them being co-opted by various agendas of the players—the
remembrance being used to underwrite the legitimacy of those
remembering. In contrast, our quiet, unobserved marker ceremonies
were purer because we had no one to impress."

Those ceremonies, Jean Miso added, "spoke loudly to me, and the
remembrance of each soldier in calling out their names was meaningful. It allowed me time to acknowledge each person as their name
was read. They were no longer lumped into a generic group of dead
soldiers. This act created an intimate connection with each soldier, a
powerful recognition of their ultimate gift in loss of life. It was
brilliant!"

ON JULY 22, we reunite for a twenty-kilometre march from Valguarnera to Raddusa. Once again, the scenery is spectacular. Early
on, I spot a strange tower in the distance and speculate that perhaps
it was built by the Normans as an outpost connected to the large fortress they erected to the west, on the summit of Monte Assoro. The
tower is built on the flank of a rocky outcrop, and from its top a guard
would have enjoyed commanding views over the surrounding countryside. Later, I determine the structure is formally known as
Castello di Pietratagliata, which refers to the fact that some of its
rooms were cut into the very rock against which it was constructed.
And I was right that the Normans built it, although whether there
was any connection to the fortress on Monte Assoro is beyond
determining.

Equally puzzling this day are a series of pillbox-shaped houses scattered across one side of the first valley we enter after leaving Valguarnera and just before coming upon the Norman castle. All are abandoned, with the fields running around them as if they were large boulders the farmers could not clear away. All are built of the same stone and are two storeys high. All have an identical small outbuilding close beside them. In Sicily, where many farmhouses are hundreds of years old, these buildings seem comparatively modern, possibly built sometime before World War II. We speculate that they may be some failed fascist agricultural cooperative effort. All attempts to determine the origin of these structures prove fruitless, however. We soon turn a corner in the road, and they are lost from sight.

The Norman castle is a different story. It remains visible in the distance long after we pass it—proof of its strategic value to the Normans and to those who used it afterwards down through the centuries. Today, it is clearly abandoned.

As on the previous day, we walk a road only lightly trafficked. Occasionally, a large flatbed truck rolls past with a precariously stacked load of hay bales. Across one field, about a dozen horses, including several young colts, trot with long manes flying. In another, a long line of at least a hundred sheep march three abreast in orderly fashion off toward the horizon.

We reach Raddusa and are met by a large children's choir that bursts forth in a fine rendition of "O Canada." With one boy carrying the Italian tricolour and the other our Maple Leaf, the children lead the march through the streets to the square where the war memorial stands. A large number of people join us.

Sherry and Susan Atkinson arrived earlier, having undertaken a cross-country drive that was, Susan says, a "beautiful, if at times terrifying," passage through a national forest, "up and over several small mountains and around more switchbacks than I could count, all on extremely narrow and rough roads." As it was market day in Raddusa, all the streets Susan's GPS directed her to were closed. At last, she happened on a policewoman standing beside the Italian and Canadian flags the children later carried and managed to get permission to drive through to the square and park illegally on a side street. Adjourning to a café for a cold drink, they were soon joined by Steve MacKinnon and Brittany Blow. As they waited for the "troops" to arrive, a man setting up the sound system played the two national anthems repeatedly. "We kept standing up, singing, and sitting down," Susan recounts. "Eventually, we just gave up."

Finally, what has turned into a grand parade arrives. There are the children, a local band, our pipe band, our small group of marchers, and a collection of men wearing purple shirts with crests that identify them as veterans of the Italian army's Bersaglieri, which is a corps of highly mobile light infantry. Their shirts and black pants are overshadowed by the distinctive wide-brimmed black hat from which a large cluster of black feathers dangles dramatically off to the right. I learn later that these feathers are taken from the western capercaillie, a grouse-like bird.

The ceremony rolls out in front of the Chiesa Immacolata Concezione, as the war memorial is attached to one of its walls. The Bersaglieri's bugler plays the last post, and then one of our pipers, the lament. As usual, the local priest gives a sermon, this one painfully long. I look around at the marchers and see that we are a tired-looking bunch, and standing in the hot sun is not helping. Although the walk today was no more arduous than any other, and less so than some, I feel a deep weariness descending. It is all I can do not to plop down on the pavement, lean back against a stone wall, and close my eyes. Instead, we all shuffle around at the directions of police officers and members of the Bersaglieri to clear a wide section of the square and a steep street that passes close by the war memorial. The Bersaglieri form into a rank, with two men in the centre carrying banners that declare them to be members of the National Association Bersaglieri of Catania province. These fellows have come from all over the province to be here today. A signal from their leader and the formation advances—not at a march but at a strange run that falls somewhere between a jog and a sprint—past clapping Raddusans. They run across the square, up the street, and out of sight. Apparently, it is the pace with which these soldiers traditionally run toward the fight. As these mostly middle-aged men disappear over the street's horizon, I am duly impressed by their ability to keep the pace.

During the process of clearing the way for this exit parade, Frances ended up on one side of the street and I on the other. I see her standing now next to the patio of a pizza joint with an elderly couple who both have Canadian flags in chest pockets and Canada pins also attached. I go over, and the three of them pose for a couple of photos. Frances says later that the elderly woman approached her during the ceremony and took hold of her hand and arm gently but firmly. Although Frances had trouble understanding her accent, she determined that the woman was eighteen when Nissoria was liberated and still remembers the day vividly. The rest of her story she is unable to discern. But Frances was deeply moved, and later I jot in my notebook, "It's the moments like these that resonate and touch the heart."

Afterwards, we are approached by a young fellow who looks to be about twenty. He's scrawny and has many piercings. Instead of asking for a handout or something, he gestures for us to follow him in the direction many citizens are headed. Somewhat reluctantly, as we are both feeling quite exhausted, we follow him up a long, steep street. Whenever we flag, he beckons us to follow and gives us a crooked grin. Whatever he says in Italian is lost on us, and he may be speaking a Sicilian dialect. Eventually, we come to the village's Red Cross building and inside find that an extensive lunch has been set out. The young man's delight at having guided us here is evident, and we both shake his hand in thanks. Throughout the ensuing lunch, he is always nearby, watching, ready to step forward at any time to assist. A couple of items we are served are unrecognizable, and his explanations fail to clarify their origins. But it matters little, for everything is delicious and there is no shortage. We are all stuffed when the luncheon finally winds down.

During the lunch, the marker team with Bill, Rod, and Terry had turned up. When it's over, Rod, Bill, Frances, and I, a happy foursome, walk to the Colonel's Car and drive to our hotel. I have always made it a practice never to nap when somebody else is trying to stay alert in order to drive. But I am unable to keep from drifting off, and each time that happens, I awake sharply with a forward head jerk. When we reach the hotel, Frances and I go to our room, undress, climb into bed, and sleep dreamlessly for almost three hours. Tomorrow, the march is to be thirty kilometres from Raddusa to Monte Scalpello.

Still feeling somewhat dazed, I spend an hour or so in the hotel dining room downloading a Google Map screenshot from André that shows the route we are to take and the predicted times when specific junction points will be reached. By the time I get this all worked out, Frances, Bill, and Rod have joined me for dinner. We have a short discussion about the coming day and agree that none of us is up to a thirty-kilometre march. Between his rash and his still-bleeding feet, Rod is not sure he can manage any marching at all tomorrow, and Bill is not keen either. We decide to rendezvous with the others at a midpoint and are relieved to note that the time for arrival there is estimated to be 9:30. No need for the usual 4:00 or 5:00 a.m. departure, because the spot—a hamlet called Castel di Judica—is not more than an hour's drive away. I send André and Steve an email informing them of this decision.

Bill reports that Don Aitchison is thinking of moving out of the shared accommodation. To this point, though not thrilled by the conditions and able to afford the cost of moving, Don has considered it his duty as a minister to remain with the others. He particularly wants to be there for the younger members of the team, when they find the whole experience overwhelming or upsetting, or just need somebody to talk to. This is a role he is familiar with, playing it daily as the chaplain at Trinity College School in Port Hope, Ontario. Jean Miso has also felt a responsibility to stay. As a teacher and mother, she thinks her presence serves a useful function. But now Don has decided the time may have come to look after himself, to ensure that he is able to finish Op Husky properly. So he asks if we could see if a room is available at the hotel. Angelo, the hotel owner, confirms that he has a small room at a reasonable price. Hardly anybody besides us is staying here, so he could take in a lot more of our people.

Bill says he will discuss this with Steve. As far as he is concerned, everyone in the shared accommodation should be moved to better quarters at Op Husky's expense. As an honorary lieutenant colonel, Bill believes his job includes looking out for the welfare of his regiment's soldiers, and he's now getting worried about the welfare of those cadets, bandsmen, marker team members, and other marchers in the shared accommodation. The younger members of the band are clearly weary and seem increasingly demoralized by the day-to-day grind. They spend most of the day crammed inside the motorhome, which, though air-conditioned, is hardly comfortable. Then it is out into the hot sun for a few hours for the marches into towns and the ceremonies. Then to the shared accommodation to get whatever sleep they can on uncomfortable cots in a crowded, hot, stuffy room full of snoring people. Bill says it's time to get them out of that.

"If Rod and I hadn't stayed in a hotel," he says later, "I don't know how we could have functioned, because when we got back after the march and the lunch, we slept solidly four or five hours. We were up at 5:00 each morning, if not earlier. We're not twenty. I thought, going into this, 'Hey, I've slept in ditches.' When I go out with the army, they say, 'Look, sir, we've got a comfortable truck for you to sleep under.' And I'm okay with that for a few nights. But I realize that my hiking and camping experience wasn't as strenuous and draining as the walk we were doing for Op Husky—four hours, some of it uphill, really, really hot. That pace every day. And so we were—at least I was—tired. After the march, back to my hotel room, have a shower, wash my clothes, fall asleep at 2:30 p.m., and wake up at 7:00 for dinner. Be in bed by 9:00 and up at 5:00. Same routine day after day."

By July 22, that routine is clearly taking its toll on everybody. I am more exhausted than ever. And I think the same is true of Steve, for he behaves strangely. Before the march began outside Valguarnera, Terry Dolan came over to us, seemingly on the edge of tears, his voice shaking with anger. "Steve tore a strip off us all," he says. The evening before, a local musical group had put on a classical performance. Steve had it in mind that everybody would put on their Op

Husky shirts and ball caps and sit in the front row of the seats set up for the concert, all of which were right in the middle of the still-hot sunshine. Sensibly, most of the marchers opted for the shade of a bar on the square, just as most of the locals did. Steve's rebuke in the morning goes over well with nobody.

Outside the Red Cross building, Steve acted up again by blasting André for not having attended the ceremony. With half the marchers and several other personnel off planting markers at Leonforte, he considers overall attendance in Raddusa to have been too low. So instead of going off to recce the next marching route, André should have attended the ceremony. Some sharp words are exchanged, and André does a lot of shoulder shrugging. I am sympathetic. Although I'm one of the logistics team's harshest critics, I also recognize they have a difficult job. Like us, they are up extremely early every morning, and judging by the late hour when routing information is emailed to us, I have a pretty good idea that the lights are on at their quarters until close to midnight. And then they do it all over again the next day.

During the walk today, Don tells a couple of us, Steve said he had only four real friends, and that they were all family. Friction is developing, and I agree with Bill. It's time to get people into more comfortable quarters. But I wonder if Bill will have much luck convincing Steve of this.

THERE'S A LOT of yawning as we gather around the hotel bar next morning and watch Angelo whip up cappuccinos for us, despite everybody reporting having slept deeply through the night. Soon we are on the road, headed for Castel di Judica. We drive a familiar route. Head east to Agira, turn due south on the SP21, cross the A19. But then, instead of carrying on south to Raddusa, we divert east on the SS192 and shortly hook southeast on the snaking SP123. The country this side of Raddusa is virtually the same as that we passed through on foot yesterday when approaching from the west—the same expanses of rolling fields. As we pass a trio of mules, Rod orders Bill to stop. This is a moment he has been looking for. It was mules and donkeys like these that the Canadians drafted to carry equipment and sometimes themselves in lieu of the vehicles lost at sea.

Rod hops out of the car. Two of the mules quickly retreat to a safe distance, but the other remains standing placidly by the road as Rod approaches. "Mules are generally stubborn and skittish," he explains later. Having worked on a ranch his father owned or part-owned, Rod is comfortable around horses and has some experience with mules. He says he's surprised that this mule stayed so calmly in place when approached by a stranger. "It was as if he were waiting for us. I sort of made clicking noises and stuff as I approached him, but his ears were forward, and it was like, 'Hey, welcome! Let's talk.'"

The mule is thin, a little swaybacked. Not unhealthy, but not robust either. As we all climb out of the car and start taking photos of Rod standing beside the mule, rubbing his ears and neck, I expect him to bolt. But the mule stands patiently, contentedly. He doesn't even blink an eye when Rod puts a red ball cap on his head. We're in the midst of this communing on the roadside when Max Fraser and Arlin McFarlane arrive. They get out and shoot some footage as the mule stoically submits to his moment of fame. Reluctantly, I remind everybody that the clock is ticking and we need to get to Castel di Judica in time to meet the other marchers. As we drive off, the mule remains on the side of the road, watching us disappear.

"I think after what we were doing so intensely, the mind starts to turn a bit and maybe becomes more receptive to things like that," Rod says later, the things in question being spirits—Husky I, Husky II, and perhaps a mule. "It's like people out in the bush for two weeks, and finally they see a Sasquatch. They come back thoroughly convinced that's what they saw. I won't say the mind plays tricks on you, but it modifies your view of things." But he adds, "How do we reconcile all of the dog stories that have come out of Sicily? How do you reconcile that? Just accept that they could have been spirits?" I decide to set aside my skepticism and do exactly that. Surprisingly, doing otherwise—assuming that the animals behaved dramatically out of character for no logical reason or followed a logic indiscernible to us—seems to strain credulity more than declaring them likely spirits. So that is what I do. It also seems to be what the rest of the marchers do. For Husky I and Husky II continue to be discussed with a certain reverence to this day. I suspect we will discuss them to our dying days, not entirely convinced but not disbelieving either. We will remember them.

CASTEL DI JUDICA proves to be a tiny cluster of mostly old, battered, stone-and-brick houses. Max and Arlin leave for Monte Scalpello. Bill parks in shade cast by a high stone wall. From here, we can see down a steep street to the junction the other marchers must pass through. It is 9:20, and the schedule predicts their arrival at 9:45. It is blazing hot outside and not much better inside the car. After a few minutes, we decide to walk down to a store on the corner of a long multi-unit building on the opposite side of the junction. We could do with some more water. Two elderly women stand behind the counter. An equally elderly man in the coveralls Italian farmers favour sits on a stool at one end. He is smoking a cigarette and staring with what seems regret into the bottom of an empty espresso cup. Possibly thinking of ordering another.

"*Due litri di acqua naturale, per favore,*" I say to the women. They stare back blankly. Trying again gets the same result. Frances gives it a go with far better enunciation, but the expressions remain blank. The old fellow is watching intently, as if we are the best entertainment to come by in a long while. A bell over the door jingles, and a middle-aged man and a young woman enter. Her hair is long and dark, jeans tight and stylishly faded, and she's wearing a black sweater that seems incongruous on such a hot day. Frances is having another shot at ordering the water when the woman says in a prim London accent, "They only speak local dialect." She chatters out something that does not include the word *acqua*, and all three of the elderly people smile happily as one of the women reaches under the counter to produce two litre bottles of water. "Most of the people here have hardly ever been outside the village," the young woman explains. "And the dialect here is different even from normal Sicilian."

The young woman says she has just returned from living and working for a couple of years in London, and the man with her—now chatting with the elderly man—is her father. We explain our purpose here and have her ask if anybody saw others like us come through earlier. It is now past 9:45 and all too probable that we were too late to meet the other marchers. Much head shaking and arm waving. Surely, if another group who looked like us had gone by, they would have noticed.

We return to the car, and I use Rod's cellphone to call André. He says the group left earlier than planned, but the ground was rugged. "No way they could have gone through there already," he assures me. We sit a bit more. Then Rod phones Dave MacLeod. "The marchers are just coming in," he says. "You missed them." No marching for us today, then. Just a scramble to get to Monte Scalpello before the ceremony starts.

Neither Bill nor Rod is particularly sorry about this development, as they had been doubtful about marching today because of the extreme heat and a shared exhaustion. Frances and I are disappointed.

Soon the car turns a corner, and we see a large cluster of parked vehicles, including the motorhome. The marker team and others are installing a long line of markers on a steep, dry adjacent slope with Monte Scalpello towering behind. There are many strangers—people we have known were coming for this last week of Op Husky but have yet to meet. Sherry Atkinson is sitting in a folding camp chair with Susan holding an umbrella protectively over him. The mercury has ascended well above 40 degrees Celsius, but Sherry looks comfortable enough. He is surrounded by a gaggle of film crew personnel—some from Max's team, the TLN crew, and a couple of photographers from local Sicilian media.

Originally, the plan had been to place these markers on Monte Scalpello's summit. But the mountain is now a nature sanctuary and therefore out of bounds. This side of the mountain is actually opposite to the side where the Royal 22e Régiment of Quebec fought its hardest battle of the Sicily campaign and suffered seventy-four casualties, including eighteen killed. But fortunately, the property owners on this side have granted permission to have the markers placed here. They stand in front of a sun-beaten tree a good two hundred metres up a fairly steep slope. Likely, up to a day or two ago, the field was home to some mules or horses. Their "calling cards," as Susan Atkinson puts it, lay scattered about like so many unearthed mines, creating a messy minefield rather than a deadly one.

I am surprised to see Sherry so far up such a steep slope, but Susan explains that a "certain stubborn Irishman was determined that he was going to go up there! With a few stops along the way, and some strong hands to help him, Sherry eventually topped the rise and sat down gratefully into the chair."

Frances and I walk over to Don Aitchison. We talk about the missed rendezvous. Only he, Jean, Bob, and Steve did the full thirty kilometres, and he says it was hard going. Terry hung in for two kilometres and then gave up, as the pace being set was seven kilometres an hour. "We were really smoking," Don says. They were already a good hour past Castel di Judica when we arrived there.

A group of three new people bound up to me. A slender middle-aged man named Chris Vaughan-Jones is followed by his wife, Guylaine Tarte, and their nineteen-year-old daughter, Emilie Vaughan-Jones. Some time ago, Chris had contacted me to say they were planning to participate in the last week of Op Husky in memory of Guylaine's uncle, Ephrem Tarte. He had served with the Royal 22e Régiment, known as the Van Doos, and died on July 28, either on or near Monte Santa Maria, a slightly lower hill adjacent to Monte Scalpello. Both mountains had been the scene of intensive fighting for the Van Doos. Little is known about the circumstances of the twenty-one-year-old's death. Guylaine's father heard from a soldier who served with him that his section had been returning from a patrol when it was caught by mortar fire, and shrapnel sliced into Ephrem's back. "We don't know if he was truly on Santa Maria or in the riverbed below it. But the records say it was on Santa Maria," Guylaine says.

For the family, Op Husky was a godsend. Chris and Guylaine had talked for years about travelling to Sicily to visit Ephrem's grave in Agira cemetery. But life kept intervening, and the journey was repeatedly postponed. Tying in with the Op Husky team meant making a definite commitment. Then it was a matter of determining their role. Chris had originally considered doing at least some of the walking, but since their arrival in Sicily, his thoughts had turned toward the marker team. That idea cinched into place when André suggested Chris help determine where to place the markers for the fallen Van Doos.

Before coming to Sicily, while researching Ephrem's story, the family had established direct links with the present-day Royal 22e Régiment. This led to the regiment holding a special commemoration ceremony in Ephrem's honour on July 28, 2012, to mark the sixty-ninth anniversary of his death. It was held at the war memorial in Saint-Hyacinthe, where Guylaine's father lives. The regiment brought in about a hundred of its soldiers and several Van Doo Sicily veterans, cordoned off the street in front of the memorial, and held a parade, complete with twenty-one-gun salute. Since then, the family has retained close ties with the Van Doos commanders and, on the ground in Sicily, are ensuring through their efforts that the memory of fallen soldiers from this regiment are marked.

This morning, they met up here with the marker team, who were being dogged by the TLN crew. With cameras rolling, the three of them worked alongside Dave MacLeod, Erik Gregory, and Chris-Denny Matte to get about thirty markers in the ground before the marchers arrived. Before leaving for Sicily, Emilie had been wondering what her "place in the whole thing" would be. Meeting the marker team settled that. "Here was Dave, and here's what he was doing, and I got grounded," she tells me later. "It all just clicked, and I said, 'holy shit, this is big'—just being on the ground and doing the physical work. Doing the walk would have been interesting and given us a different perspective. But for us and what we needed to do, I think, planting the markers was the best thing.

"That very first day, there were the six of us plus our film crew. They had us all wired and were running around filming us and yelling, 'Action,' and Julien was slithering through the grass filming different angles. We were trying to get the markers planted before the marchers showed up. And probably one of the most remarkable things was when Guylaine found Ephrem's marker. She started bawling her eyes out. So we planted Ephrem's marker, and Guylaine wrote on it, 'We have never forgotten. With love your family.'"

Instead of the small Maple Leaf flags that we have often placed in front of markers, they placed the blue-and-white Quebec provincial Fleurdelisé and a small rock that Chris had painted before leaving their home in Tsawwassen, south of Vancouver. Having previously visited Commonwealth War Cemeteries in France, he had often seen people leaving rocks before headstones. Because the maintenance crews would not remove these, it was a way to leave a tangible part of Canada beside a person's grave.

Today, as had happened at Dittaino Station, there is no formal Italian delegation present. Gathered here are our Carabinieri friends, Sicilian media, and a good number of the active Op Husky Sicilian participants, such as Tony and Dora Avola. I read the Action of the Day. Then, as there are so many of us here, a single person is placed in front of each marker and reads out the name, regiment, and day of death. Marchers, officer cadets, logistics team personnel, the Vaughan-Jones family, and camera personnel all participate. Don follows this with a prayer in French, one of the pipers plays, and there is a moment of silence.

After the ceremony, most of us adjourn to the Hotel Castel Miralago for lunch, a robust affair that requires four knives to properly tackle the number of courses. I learn later, however, that the Vaughan-Jones family with TLN in tow drove around the other side of the mountain to find the approximate place where Ephrem died. They drove up Monte Santa Maria to where the road stopped. The film crew asked Chris what they were going to do. "We'll just walk a little way toward the summit," he replied. But once they started, everybody just kept going. It was a tough slog, especially for the film crew lugging their heavy equipment. On the summit, the crew insisted on interviewing Guylaine. As the camera started rolling, a thunderstorm closed in. Lightning flashed. "We took it as a sign," Guylaine told me.

The storm followed them to Agira cemetery, where they paid their respects before Ephrem's grave. "It was terribly emotional," Guylaine said. "You see the tombstone for the first time. And this is after seeing the marker and then where he had been killed." Clouds were wrapped around the mountain where Agira stood. Then the sky parted, and "all of a sudden the town had a beam of light coming down, and we all kind of stopped and turned around and looked at it," Chris said. "It looked like a spotlight of sun coming down on the town. Oh my God, it was beautiful. We were all in shock. It seemed like one of those spiritual things happening." "It kind of explained the whole trip," Emilie added.

Something else had happened at the cemetery that felt like a "spiritual thing." They encountered a strange and obviously stray dog. "It was weird," Chris reported. "We show up and the dog shows up—just materializes. The dog runs around a bit, and it has a little rope on it. Em is trying to get the rope off and be a Good Samaritan. And then the dog disappears." Guylaine added, "It was so weird. We arrived, got out of the car, and within minutes the dog was there and stayed with us. We have a picture of him with my uncle's tombstone, and the dog is sitting there." And when the family returned to the cemetery for a final time on July 31, the dog immediately reappeared and stayed with them. As they were walking toward the car, however, it again vanished as mysteriously as it had the first time.

When I tell them about Husky I and Husky II and what the Carabinieri said about them, they become three more people who are not about to discount the idea of there being spirits at play in the heart of Sicily.

WE START OFF on July 24 in darkness, illuminated only by the gentle light of a full moon that seems much higher in the sky than it would have been back in Canada—a little dime shining out of a vast blanket of blackness. It casts sufficient light, though, that the luminescent strips on our safety vests glisten. It is 5:00 a.m. Before us is a relatively short march of fifteen kilometres. We are eight: Phil, Don, Jean, Bob, Rod, Bill, Frances, and me. Terry Dolan and Steve Gregory are absent.

Terry has gone to Catania with some of the logistics team to rent a car. Sick of depending on others to drive him places, he has decided to become self-sufficient. And he's decided to move to the hotel, a decision that Don has made today as well. As for Steve, Don reports that last night, he was carried into the gymnasium at Regalbuto on a stretcher. Vomiting and suffering severe stomach cramps, he weakly explained his condition as the result of food poisoning. Our general consensus is that he went down with heatstroke and is also just exhausted. This morning, he is supposed to be resting. This is a hard thing to picture. I expect that at any moment, a car will pull up from which Steve will pop, full of seemingly boundless energy and determination to lead off at the head of the pack in what he calls his "old man's shuffle."

The pace Steve has maintained since I first met him on July 5 at the Canadian Embassy in Rome is amazing. Not only has he walked most distances every day, but when the marching is over, he has normally flown off by car to visit *sindaci* in communities toward which we are bound. While there, he will sometimes coax, sometimes bully, the marker team to perform their duties more quickly and efficiently. The logistics personnel are afforded the same attention. When the mayor of Agira announces that he wants a series of markers erected in the town to honour the Italian dead, Steve agrees. But how to do that when the ceremony is only a few days away? He proposes adding the names to the markers already made for the Canadian soldiers. Rod and I are present for this meeting, which includes a very tired-looking Dave MacLeod. The three of us insist that this is unacceptable, and we're rather of a mind to let the Agira mayor make the markers himself if it's so important. It is too late in the play to bring this forward now.

A couple of days after this meeting, Steve and Phil are in a car passing a lumberyard. Steve turns in hard. Moving like a whirlwind, he gathers several long lengths of one-by-four lumber, grabs a skill saw and measuring tape, and begins cutting the lumber into marker lengths. When surprised staff intervene, Steve explains the mission. They volunteer to cut the boards to the correct dimensions and sharpen the ends that go into the ground. A man painting a lumberyard wall finds some white paint and whitewashes the boards after Phil or Steve gives them a quick sanding. When the markers are finished, the lumberyard owner refuses any payment. ("I still have a chunk of sandpaper that I found in my kit," Phil tells me long after he is back in Canada.)

It is so easy to imagine this scene. Steve in his white Husky shirt and baggy shorts, sunglasses propped on his forehead, moving feverishly. Then, confronted, explaining with much gesturing. His boyish delight and bonhomie with everyone as the job gets done. The effusive and genuine gratitude displayed when the owner refuses payment. That infectious enthusiasm and vision that accepts no barriers to the realization of a purpose. Steve at his finest.

As I think about this, a pre-dawn light washes the countryside. We are walking another side road, one considered so safe the Carabinieri have taken the day off. Richard Vincent and two officer cadets keep watch in a single car. Behind us, Etna is a greyed-out silhouette, smoke drifting off its summit in a fairly thick, pink plume. As always, the smoke drifts ruler-straight southward. The terrain is mostly level, something for which we are all grateful.

I took a group photo shortly before sunrise when the little dime of moon was still visible high above. It is slightly out of focus. In past photos, everybody tended to be smiling. Today, only the irrepressible Jean and Richard are. Frances stands almost at attention, eyes fixed on the middle distance. Rod is staring at the ground. Phil, hair mussed and shoulders sagging, is squeezing sunscreen into his right palm. Bob is drinking coffee from a mug. Don is adjusting the kerchief he wears around his neck and is also looking away. Bill, hands on hips, stares at the camera with the studied seriousness I have seen in so many group photos of Canadian soldiers in Sicily. Even Jean's smile looks tired. Looking at this photo, even the evening after I took it, I think: "We few, we weary few." But we are mostly all there, still marching.

The dread rash is commonplace. Some suffer from it more than others. Rod's is extensive—a long line of blisters and scabs up the back of both legs—and his feet remain a daily misery. Phil just looks exhausted. In the shared accommodation, it is never lights-out before 10:00 p.m., and the next day begins at 3:00 a.m. That is pretty much the routine for us in the hotel as well. Sleep deprivation is general. As are swollen feet and ankles. Frances has pains shooting through her right foot, particularly the sole and then into her ankle. It started fleetingly around Dittaino Station but now is persistent. My left knee aches chronically, but I suspect not as badly as it would without my walking pole. More alarming is the pain that has started shooting up the length of my shins with each step, particularly the right one—probably because I am shifting more weight to that leg to spare the left knee. Frances and I think that her foot and my shin pains are a result of the many kilometres logged on unforgiving pavement.

And there is always the heat. As the sun rises over Etna, the temperature climb is instantaneous and implacable. Fortunately, we walk through a number of narrow valleys bordered by low hills that shade the road. The pre-dawn start ensures this. A couple of hours more, and the sun will pierce these valleys. By then, however, we have reached our destination. We are back in Regalbuto, for today we walked more or less in a circle.

We assemble in Regalbuto's Piazza Giacomo Matteotti, a small square situated close to the town's western outskirts. The small and derelict Chiesa Madonna del Carmelo stands on one side of the square. Because of our early start, the ceremony is several hours off. Nobody complains. The square is open, and there are lots of shady spots with benches. For a while we occupy these, sometimes chatting, mostly just sitting. Max's film crew drifts about, but none of them seem overly energetic either. Frances, Don, Phil, Arlin McFarlane, and I take a table at a sidewalk café. None of us has an appetite, so we drink cappuccinos. Eventually, we surrender the table and drift over to sit on the derelict church's shaded stone steps. Through a crack in a door, I see an elegantly carved altar. Baroque-style walls are as lavishly decorated as a wedding cake, but the white paint has faded. Arched porticos are buttressed with frameworks of wooden beams to prevent their collapse. A thick coat of dust covers the floor. Chiesa Madonna del Carmelo, I learn, stands on a site where, records say, there has been a Christian church since 400 AD. Originally constructed in 1650, the current structure fell into such disrepair that it was closed in 1760. After extensive rebuilding, it reopened in 1778, but it has since been closed once again. Even as a ruin, the elegance of its interior is striking. There are, of course, hopes for an eventual restoration. But there is also the reality of a small community facing a very high cost.

Shortly before 11:00, Steve appears, looking little the worse for wear, and accompanied by the logistics personnel and pipe band. Then Regalbuto's officials arrive. Soon a large formation sets off from the square in a parade through the streets that ends at the large Piazza Vittorio Veneto. The town's war memorial stands across from Chiesa Santa Maria della Croce, which dominates the square. The church is notably plain, except for a metre-high white Madonna statuette set within an open circle in the centre of its decorated pediment.

The war memorial is more impressive. A tarnished bronze angel, wings spread and clutching a laurel wreath in one hand, stands atop a pillar. At its base, two equally tarnished Italian soldiers in World War I uniforms stand. One holds a bayoneted rifle as if ready to thrust it out from his hip. The man alongside is bareheaded and about to chuck a grenade toward an unseen enemy. A plaque at the memorial's base says that it was a gift from the state of New York. I later learn that in the 1920s, a former Regalbuto citizen named Luigi Sample raised $13,500 among fellow emigrants from the village, who were then living in New York, to fund the memorial's construction.

We marchers circulate through the dense crowd that has filled the square, dispensing Maple Leaf flags and pins. When it is time for the national anthems, we proudly sing not only "O Canada" but also the Italian anthem. During the past week, we have been learning the lyrics under the tutelage of our Carabinieri friends and rehearsing it as we walk. The Carabinieri even provided us with a few printouts of the words. There are enough of us—though not I—sufficiently musically talented to lead us in the melody. So today, with great gusto, we sing along with the Italians, and those nearby seem delighted. Frances and Bob then secure the opposite ends of a large Canadian flag draped over the metal fence surrounding the memorial, as officer cadet Myriam Rochon reads the roll of honour and the Action of the Day, and Gaetano Catalano translates the latter into

Italian. Everyone listens respectfully to the *sindaco* and Steve. As he does each day, Steve presses home the message that we are remembering not only our Canadian sacrifice but also that of the Sicilians. When Sherry speaks, he holds the crowd in his hands, as always.

Everything clicks together so smoothly. It strikes me then that the Op Husky team, we marchers included, have got these ceremonies down to a science. However, the next one will be different. For tomorrow is a day off, and the following day, we are to be reinforced by a contingent of extra civilians, about sixty Canadian Forces personnel, and the Seaforth Highlanders Pipe Band. All of us wonder how we and they will mesh together.

But that is for the future. For now, it is past and present that absorb us. When the ceremony ends, we go to the gymnasium, collect Don's luggage, and then drive to the hotel. Don checks in and stows his gear. Leaving a weary Frances to an envied siesta, I join Bill, Rod, and Don in driving to the Agira cemetery. Max and Arlin follow. We are fulfilling one of Don's missions. As Trinity College School's chaplain, Don wants to visit the headstone of the only alumnus to die in Sicily. Robert Osler entered TCS at age eleven in 1921 and graduated eight years later. He was remembered as an enthusiastic member of the school community, "becoming especially proficient at cricket." Upon graduating, he returned to his birthplace of Toronto and entered the family's brokerage firm. With the outbreak of war, he was commissioned in the 48th Highlanders, going overseas in 1940.

By the time of Operation Husky, Osler was a thirty-three-year-old lieutenant commanding a platoon of the 48th's 'D' Company. On July 25, the 48th were east of Nissoria attempting to gain a foothold on the heavily defended Monte Nissoria. The battalion's plan of attack called for 'D' Company to advance up a narrow defile that appeared to lead to the summit. But as the company emerged on what was thought to be Monte Nissoria's summit, it was raked by fire. In the confusing, multi-folded ground of Sicily's mountainous heart, Osler and his comrades had mistaken a lower ridge for the summit. Monte Nissoria still loomed above them, and from it came a deadly rain of machine-gun fire. 'D' Company vainly tried to fight its way forward. When Osler attempted to set his platoon's Bren gun into a new position, a bullet struck him in the head, killing him instantly.

At the Agira cemetery, we all walk with Don to Osler's headstone. It is on the reverse slope from the entrance. Below, the lake glimmers, and in the far distance Etna soars. Although this is a place of remembrance, it is also stunningly beautiful. While Max films Don paying his respects, I wander off to check on the headstone of Lieutenant Earl Christie of the Loyal Edmonton Regiment. He died on August 5, 1943, during an attack on the 736-metre Hill 736 in the Salso River valley. Two platoons put in the attack, the one led by Christie and another commanded by Lieutenant John Dougan. The two men were close friends, having attended the University of Alberta together and then marching off in step to war. Christie died on that hill, and Dougan was badly wounded. Blood spilling across his face, Dougan led a mad charge with a handful of survivors and took the summit. For his reckless bravery, he was awarded a Military Cross. But Hill 736 haunted Johnny, as I came to know him, in the last years of his life. Against all reason, he always thought that it should have been his life lost there. Earl had planned to study medicine when the war ended. Johnny and the other university friends who went to war with Earl all believed he was the one who would make the most of life—perhaps find a cure for cancer or something equally beneficial to humanity. But there on a barren hill in Sicily, the twenty-six-year-old died, and all those possibilities ended. The inscription etched on the headstone at the request of a surviving parent reads: "In memory of my son/He faced destiny/As he did life/With courage and a smile."

After my first visit to Agira cemetery in 2000, I told Johnny that I had been there and had looked up Earl's headstone. Genuinely pleased, he asked with concern how it was kept. It had been years since his last visit, and there would be no future ones. I assured him the headstone was well maintained. Knowing that I would surely return to Sicily, I pledged that each time, I would stand before Earl's headstone for a few moments and remember his sacrifice. On that first visit, rosemary grew in front of it. Now, a sage-coloured sedum

with small, delicate orange flowers grows there. I notice little rosemary anywhere in the cemetery, where in the years before it was
common. Perhaps even rosemary suffers in the heat of a Sicilian
summer. As there is no irrigation at Agira, plants and grass must
endure months of drought.

As I walk away from Earl's headstone, I see Rod quietly walking
the rows. At each Seaforth headstone, he pauses, reaches out, and
rests a hand on it. "It was very emotional and very satisfying," he
says, "to visit their graves and actually say a little prayer over each of
the Seaforths who died in Sicily. I felt I had represented my dad well,
and we had accomplished something by doing so."

AT THE COMMONWEALTH War Graves Beaurains Factory, each time a new
headstone is prepared, a laser first slowly and meticulously passes
over the entire stone surface to create a map. This is necessary
because there is no such thing as a perfectly flat piece of stone. There
are always some imperfections, such as minute rippling. The laser
basically memorizes the surface as it truly is and then cuts into it so
that at every point the inscription will be a precise 2.8 millimetres deep.
This was the depth the stone carvers who engraved the original headstones worked toward as well.

There is a purpose to this extreme precision. At the very beginning,
when the commission's architects—Lutyens, Blomfield, and Baker—
were designing the headstones and their placement, they thought
carefully about that first time a family member would walk into the
cemetery and approach the grave of a loved one. How could they make
that moment as emotionally resonant as possible? That was when they
agreed to make the depth of the inscriptions uniform. The result was
that when a person stands at a 45-degree angle to the headstone, the
shadows fall away and the engravings on the headstone are clearly
visible.

I have seen this many times. I am walking along a row of headstones, counting down toward the one of interest, and there, suddenly
from the side and still a metre or two distant, the name of the soldier
comes into focus—sharp and crisp. This is truly a better view of the
headstone details than you get standing directly in front. That was the

idea. The architects wanted the family members approaching the headstone to be struck by recognition before they were standing in front of the headstone and consequently on the grave itself.

Nothing in these cemeteries was left to chance. Even how the grave would be approached and found was carefully choreographed. A phenomenal level of detail was put into play so that even that first encounter would occur in a certain way and have the desired emotional and commemorative response.

One can walk into any of the 2,500 Commonwealth cemeteries found around the world and see that while each is uniquely designed to fit into its surrounding environment, there is also a common pattern at work—a pattern that rests on magnificent design. Blomfield, Lutyens, and Baker set the main parameters for the World War I cemeteries, and these were applied again to those of World War II. But in the aftermath of that first war's slaughter—with more than a million dead to be buried or commemorated on memorials—three men could not possibly do all the work. So a pattern of cemetery features was agreed to. Then, working under their supervision, other architects—mostly men who had served on the Western Front and saw their job as tending to their friends who had fallen—could produce the smaller cemeteries.

Memorial design followed an entirely different course. With so many soldiers having disappeared without a trace, the memorials were considered of seminal importance. At first, only one was envisioned— the Menin Gate at Ypres. In considering its design, Blomfield wrote, he recognized that this "was a man's war far too terrible for any fripperies, and I hoped to get within range of the infinite in this symbol." When completed and unveiled on July 24, 1927, the soaring gate, standing astride a road along which thousands of Commonwealth troops had for four years marched toward the Ypres Salient, bore 54,400 engraved names. But however vast, the gate's walls could not accommodate the names of the many, many more missing dead. So more memorials were commissioned, including the ones at Tyne Cot and Thiepval, which matched the scale of Menin Gate, and other, smaller ones. Utterly distinct is the Vimy Ridge Memorial, which was commissioned by the Canadian government. Engraved on its outside enclosing walls are the names of 11,285 Canadians killed in France whose final resting place is unknown. This memorial was designed by Canadian sculptor Walter Allward. As with the memorials designed by the British architects, the intent was to attain a unique artistic vision.

By contrast, the cemeteries are works of conformity. Each features restful landscaping that incorporates many details of traditional British garden design. The surrounding hedges and walls create an enclosed, dedicated space that feels well separated from the world beyond. Small stands of trees or clusters of flowering shrubs, such as roses and rhododendrons, sometimes contribute to this air of seclusion, while expanses of open ground, usually grassed, prevent the enclosure from feeling cramped. In the midst of this enclosure run the orderly ranks of identically shaped white headstones. Usually these are bordered by flowers, herbs, or other plantings that provide a soft touch of colour. Standing in every cemetery of more than forty graves is the Cross of Sacrifice. Those with a thousand burials or more also include the Stone of Remembrance. Smaller cemeteries in which most of the graves are of non-Christian soldiers may also include both the cross and the stone. Entrance to each cemetery is usually via a black wrought-iron gate bordered by a brick shelter building, which houses the cemetery's register and visitor book. The atmosphere in these cemeteries is one of serenity rather than sorrow. Their ultimate purpose is to leave visitors with the feeling that the dead lying within are souls at peace, not tormented by the horrors of war or the suffering they experienced at the moment of death.

Even the Commonwealth's largest cemetery, Tyne Cot, emanates this sense of peace. Nine kilometres northeast of Ypres, it holds the graves of 11,956 soldiers and lists 35,000 names on the Tyne Cot Memorial standing on the cemetery's northern flank. The memorial is one of two hundred worldwide that bear the names of soldiers whose bodies were never recovered from the battlefields of both world wars. At Tyne Cot, even the buried dead are mostly unknown—8,369 of them. When you walk through the cemetery's visitor centre, a woman's voice, lacking both accent and emotion, slowly and measuredly and barely above a whisper, recites the name of one soldier after another. It is an unending litany of sacrifice and loss. Being the largest, Tyne Cot is also the most visited Commonwealth cemetery. In 2013, 359,000 people funnelled through, and that number jumped a staggering 80 per cent the following year as hundredth anniversary commemorations of World War I began. As Tyne Cot is considered the iconic cemetery, most people making remembrance pilgrimages to France and Belgium visit it.

But Tyne Cot is just a matter of scale. I find it no more emotionally powerful to visit than the small ones, some containing no more than thirty graves and situated in the middle of a farm field. This is why Agira Canadian War Cemetery has emotionally resonated with me since I first walked among its headstones in 2000. The isolation that makes it little visited, its relative smallness, and its location, surrounded by the hard Sicilian landscape, render the cemetery's serenity all the more evocative.

ON OUR WAY out of the cemetery, Rod, Don, Max, and I pause to sign the visitor book and note that already, even though it is only July 24 and nearly a week before the main ceremony on July 30, the number of signatures for 2013 far surpasses that of 2012. As we get into the car, Don notes that his phone is reporting a temperature of 44 Celsius in the cemetery. We are all sweating profusely. The heat is so intense it is almost dizzying. "If it's this hot for the ceremony, it's going to be hellish. People will be dropping like flies," somebody says.

With air conditioner blasting away to little effect, we drive to Nissoria and find a cluster of markers on the edge of the village. We climb over a wall to reach them and perform a short ceremony, mostly just Don saying a prayer after we read out the names. Don does the honours for Robert Osler, and I do so for Royal Canadian Regiment commander Lieutenant Colonel Ralph Marston Crowe, who was killed near Nissoria on July 24, seventy years ago today. He died charging a machine-gun position that had ambushed his headquarters section.

From where the markers stand, we look up at a small, reddish two-storey building on a hill with Monte Nissoria rising above it. The Canadians dubbed that building "the Schoolhouse" because its red paint reminded them of the schools scattered across the prairies. In fact, it was where a road maintenance crew lived, such buildings commonly found alongside roads throughout Sicily. It's been abandoned now for decades. Several Canadian battalions came to grief attacking that building. We know that Robert Osler died in the ground behind it.

We drive up to the Schoolhouse, then manage to bump along a rough track that gets us in behind the building. A short walk through tall grass brings us to a spot offering a view into the defile. We are probably standing on the false summit where Osler met his death, but we may be on the opposite side of the defile. There are no surviving signs of the furious fighting that raged here seventy years ago. Don takes some photos. Max and Arlin ask him a few questions on camera. Then we trudge back to the cars.

Our plan had been to circle around from Nissoria to find another battlefield site at Catenanuova that is important to Bill. But the heat is so extreme that we abandon this mission and drive to the hotel to rest until it's time to return to Regalbuto for the scheduled late afternoon and evening activities. Quietly, I enter our room. Frances is sleeping. It's tempting. But if I lie down, there will be no getting back up until the morning. So I pick up my laptop and notebook. I have developed the habit of recording the day's impressions by hand in the notebook rather than keyboarding. But I also download each day's photos to the computer for backup. Then I post a few to Facebook sites to keep a growing number of Canadians at home informed about what is happening with Op Husky 2013.

As I walk past the main desk and bar downstairs, Angelo smiles and sets out a frost-covered glass and equally frosty bottle of Birra Moretti. At first we had to pay for each drink up front, but within a couple of days, Angelo was keeping a tab. It is likely inaccurate, for we have been invited to just help ourselves if no staff are around. Frances and I try and keep a record of our own. But it's hopeless— we're far too tired for that. I figure the balance will be horrendous at the end of our stay. But the beer is deliciously cold. I sit in the dining room looking out over the lake below and Agira off to the west. Write in the journal, load photos to the computer, and post them to the rest of the world via Facebook and Twitter. It's a strange world, Alice. Back in Canada, hundreds of people are following this and responding to it with likes, Facebook comments, and Twitter favouriting. All this remembrance feedback is heartening and reminds us that our mission here is not just important to us personally, but has meaning for many others across the country.

WE RECOGNIZE THAT we are also unofficial envoys representing Canada to the Sicilians. An important part of that duty is to attend the various events to which each community invites us. Regalbuto rolls out the welcome mat. When we return in the late afternoon, it is to take a tour through the town, which will be followed by a special mass at Chiesa Madre San Basilio. Completed in 1764, this is but one of Regalbuto's sixteen Catholic churches.

Our guide for the tour is Regalbuto's vice-mayor. A group of us follow him up a long winding path from Piazza Vittorio Veneto into what he says is the very heart of the old Christian quarter. The highlight of the tour is a close inspection of the interior of Chiesa di Santa Maria delle Grazie, which stands on the highest spot of ground in Regalbuto. The church itself is not that large, but the attached and now abandoned convent is. Together, they dominate the town's skyline and are visible from many kilometres away. I look at the church's tower and imagine the dominating view it afforded the Germans as the Canadian troops closed on Regalbuto from the west. I remember reports of how the soldiers came under deadly accurate artillery and mortar fire that was likely directed by spotters set up there. Architecturally, the exterior is quite bland, but inside, the church explodes with Baroque grandeur. Ornate pillars, gilt walls, extensive frescoes, harp-wielding cherubs, and soaring domes. Every single centimetre of wall or window is in some manner lavishly adorned.

Leaving the church, we embark on what battlefield historians like me call "Then and now." The guide points to a narrow street. At the far end, the square turret of a small church stands on an overlooking hill. He opens a binder and shows us a photo taken on this very spot in 1943. A couple of Sherman tanks are grinding along the street, passing several buildings that have been reduced to piles of rubble. Another has had an exterior wall cleanly severed so that its interior is exposed. Two Sicilian men wearing only shorts and boots stand by the rubble pile watching the tanks pass. One man holds a shovel, the other a pick. I imagine the tanks turning the corner at the end of the street and disappearing, then the two Sicilians returning to the seemingly endless task of digging through the rubble for bodies or precious possessions.

The vice-mayor tells us that in 1943, Regalbuto had a population of just 1,200. Because the Germans made a stand here on August 2, Canadian artillery pounded the town mercilessly, as fighter bombers swooped down to unleash their ordnance on it. In the late afternoon, a patrol of Hasty Ps crept into the town and found that the Germans had abandoned it. Of its 1,200 citizens, the vice-mayor says, 300 were dead—most killed by the August 2 bombardment. This information, he says, was only unearthed last year when some archival documents were uncovered.

Today, the town has a population of about 7,300, down from about 8,000 a decade ago. Each year sees an average decline of 0.19 per cent, the result of a stagnant local economy. It is a common Sicilian story.

Our tour ends at the Piazza della Repubblica, where Chiesa Madre San Basilio stands. The vice-mayor turns to another photo in his binder. It shows the church looking remarkably undamaged, but rubble is strewn across the square and an army bulldozer has been deployed to clear it away. On the wall of an old building, he points out a faded red Maltese cross—a bit of graffiti left behind by the British 231st (Malta) Brigade when it briefly occupied the town after its liberation.

Tour over, we enter the church for mass. Until now, the fact that Don is an ordained minister has gone largely ignored by the Sicilian clergy. At the beginning of Op Husky, Don had thought it would be one of his jobs to represent the marchers at the daily civic ceremonies by saying a prayer. He knew they would have liked that by the comments they made on the road. But he had never been acknowledged. "Once or twice I tried to muscle my way up to the front," he tells me, "only to be cut off by an even more aggressive and verbose Sicilian monsignor!"

Not the case this evening, however. After the ceremony in the square this morning, the priest had sought Don out and invited him to celebrate the mass with him. Suspecting that the priest assumed he was Catholic, Don explained in French—which both spoke fluently—that he was Anglican. But, Don says, the priest "shrugged it off and intimated that we were all on the same side in any way that was important, and encouraged me to read the lesson and lead the Psalm." Humbled by the priest's "great generosity and hospitality," Don readily agreed.

The church is large, with dozens of pews and a massive, ornate altar. Above it is a gleaming, intricately carved, bronze-plated balcony for a choir. As we white-shirted marchers and other personnel occupy a few rows at the front, the rest of the church fills to capacity.

Don had told me earlier how preparation for this trip had presented a packing nightmare, as it included four or five different components. He was to be away seven weeks. In addition to the weeks spent on Op Husky, he was going to visit friends in the United Kingdom and then travel from London to New York via the *Queen Mary II*. Different clothes were required for each phase. And for Op Husky, he needed clothes and boots for walking, his 48th Highlanders of Canada's dress uniform and shoes, and in case any clerical commitments came up, appropriate dress for that. As a result, Don's dress for this evening mass is a clever assemblage. He is wearing hiking boots and pants, black clerical shirt with white collar, and a powder-blue blazer that will also serve in London and at dinners aboard the ocean liner.

We marchers are all like proud parents when he ascends to the pulpit to lead the Psalm and lesson. I am not surprised that the lesson is a reading from Exodus with much emphasis on wandering journeys. For what else are we about here? Wandering across Sicily in, ultimately, what is both an act of remembrance and a quest to understand fully what that means.

Before and after the lesson, the priest and his assistant lead the parishioners in singing hymns. Both men have beautiful voices, as does the man playing the organ. And it's as if the hundred or more parishioners are members of a well-trained choir. They even seem to sit so there's a section of tenors, altos, and basses. The acoustics in the church are excellent, and the song washes around us. It is less a mass than an utterly glorious concert.

Frances and I, neither of us particularly religious, emerge from the church exhilarated. The sun is only just setting and casts a gentle, yellow light on the fronts of some of the buildings in the square. Like the Piazza Vittorio Veneto, the Piazza della Repubblica has a large tiled pedestrian area that extends outward from the municipal building in a wide semicircle. On its outer edge, a dozen or more elderly men sit on white plastic outdoor chairs arranged in a row. The rest of the pedestrian area is given over to a small *passeggiata*, the traditional end-of-the-day sociable stroll before dinner that is still commonly practised in many Italian communities. This is the first time we have encountered it in Sicily. The young women are all fashionably attired, and there is more than one young man trying to catch their eye. After all, *la passeggiata*, as Giovanna Delnegro observed in her book of the same title, is "a socially sanctioned opportunity for flirting and courting." It is in the square or street during these orchestrated strolls that young people learn "the rhetorical skills" that "become useful in the marriage market, the work place and the complex politics of the town." Mothers and fathers maintain a watchful eye, and nothing escapes the notice of the row of elderly men. Several men walk over to shake the hand of one or another of these elders, after which words and pleasantries are exchanged. Frances and I love this tradition and have often joined it in Italian towns large and small. The trick to it is the stroll. This is no time for brisk, purposeful walking. It is not about the arriving but the doing. We are tempted to join in tonight, but none of us has much energy left. Ultimately, the appeal of returning to the hotel for an early dinner and early bed wins out. My dreams that night spool out to a soundtrack sung by an angelic choir.

WE SLEEP IN next morning and breakfast late. Rod and Bill had left earlier for Catania to greet the Seaforth Highlanders of Canada pipe band. Rod will also rendezvous with his wife, Pat, and sister, Margo. Don is moving in with Bill, and Phil Bury is taking the single room the padre occupied the night before.

Last night, Bill had the conversation with Steve suggesting that it was time to move people out of shared accommodation. Steve, still feeling ill, quickly agreed. He recognized that morale was flagging. A small number, including Steve and Phil, will bunk at the hotel. Most of the others are to be relocated to a bed and breakfast in the lower part of Agira. For several days, the logistics personnel have been based in a B & B close to Agira's summit that is far more luxurious and boasts a swimming pool. A number of Op Husky participants have noted rather wryly that the logistics team has enjoyed a high level of comfort from the beginning.

Bumping into Don over breakfast, the three of us decide to take a local transit bus from Regalbuto to Agira and play tourist. When we ask the hotel owner if he has a bus schedule, Angelo offers to drive us to the Regalbuto bus stop. As we walk toward his car, Angelo points to the hillside across the road and says that several Canadian soldiers were killed on its slopes. When he was a little boy, his family had a small farm close to where the hotel stands today. On winter days, when it was too cold for Angelo and his siblings to play outside, his mother used to sit them by the fire and tell stories. She often described seeing the bodies of Canadians lying on that hillside, he says, and how sad the sight made her.

As we approach Regalbuto's outskirts, Angelo points out Chiesa Santa Maria della Croce dead ahead of us in the Piazza Vittorio Veneto. He explains that the Germans defending the town on August 1, 1943, mounted a machine gun on its roof so they could fire past the white Madonna statuette I had noticed yesterday as we marched into the square for the ceremony. The Canadian soldiers— likely Hasty Ps—leading the advance up the dead-straight street we drive along were caught by a burst of fire from this hidden gun. Angelo says that four soldiers died instantly and were initially buried in a field alongside the road, which today is bordered by buildings. Until the bodies were exhumed and moved to Agira cemetery, his mother and other local women tended the graves and regularly placed flowers on them. She did the same for the temporary graves of the men who died on the hillside across from the hotel. During those story sessions, Angelo says, "she spoke all the time about the poor Canadians who were killed when they came to liberate us."

Angelo drops us in the square next to the church. From side on, I can see the back of the hole in the decorated pediment through which the machine gun fired. A steel ladder is anchored to one side of the opening. The roof behind is tiled and almost level. Simple enough for the Germans to create a platform for gun and crew. Made of stone blocks, the pediment is a good metre thick. From its heights, the gun would have completely dominated the street before it, which would become a perfect killing ground.

Later, Angelo mentions that his mother and her family had fled Regalbuto to escape the bombardment that killed a quarter of the town's people. When the family returned, they discovered that their home had been destroyed. "That's how it is in war," Angelo says with an accepting shrug. And yet it was not the loss of home or the deaths of many people she knew that dominated her remembrance of the war years. Instead, she dwelt on the deaths of Canadians who had come from so far away to liberate her.

PART TWO

The Final Push

ABOUT AN HOUR after sunrise, we gather on the side of the road to begin a twenty-kilometre march ending in Piazza Armerina. Although it is July 26, we are retracing the footsteps our soldiers took on July 16. This is necessary because of complications in arranging a date for the ceremony in Piazza Armerina. I find this step backwards in time disquieting, as not only is the chronology confusing but we've also driven out of the mountains and are now back on the coastal plain close to Ragusa. This way, though, we are at least advancing along the line of march the army took, rather than retreating toward Piazza Armerina from the mountains.

Adding to my disquiet is the fact that five new marchers have joined the team. Steve is still unwell, so is not marching. Neither is Phil. The new people were all involved in helping Steve get Op Husky off the ground. There is the seventy-six-year-old Honourable Consiglio Di Nino, who sat in the Senate for twenty-one years before retiring in 2012. He goes by "Con," displays a politician's brash confidence, and tends to expound on many matters. The retired senator looks fit for his age. Travelling with him is Beverly Topping, a slender middle-aged woman who is also in good physical shape. Beverly's mother was a British Nursing Sister in the war, and her father served in a Royal Canadian Air Force bomber squadron, logging fifty-three missions over enemy territory. After a short hiatus, her father rejoined the military when she was four. "So seventeen schools and five different countries later, all by the time I finished high school, the military was pretty much in my DNA," she tells us. "My friend Con Di Nino knew I was a 'military brat' and proud of it, so when he told me about Operation Husky, he was not surprised when I said I wanted to make the trip."

There is also seventy-year-old Brigadier General Ernest Beno, or Ernie. He is short and serious, and, as I would expect of somebody who served in the military for thirty-seven years, also looks fit. He says later that he spent the five weeks before travelling to Sicily walking six to ten kilometres every second day.

Until he retired just before coming to Sicily, Mark Clearihue had been supporting Op Husky 2013 with sponsorships through his position as vice-president of TD Canada Trust's real estate secured lending division in Toronto. His friend Drew Davis came along because his father-in-law had taken part in the invasion, landing at Pachino and losing an eye at Ortona. Both look fairly fit. When he decided to participate, Drew realized that as a sixty-six-year-old retired business executive with "no real fitness regimen," he needed to get in better shape. "On Boxing Day, 2012, I started a disciplined program of diet and daily exercise," he told us. "I cut out three main vices—bread, beer, and chocolate—and started to take advantage of the many hiking trails at our home in midtown Toronto and at our cottage in the Kawartha Lakes. By early July 2013, I had dropped twenty-five pounds and was walking seventy-five to one hundred kilometres weekly."

Soon after we start marching, it becomes clear that the new people are fit enough. The pace is brisk, averaging the six kilometres per hour that has become our unofficial norm. We walk along roads unusually heavy with traffic—those at the rear of the column regularly shouting "Car!" or, with more alarm, "Truck!" to warn the rest of us that a vehicle, small or large, is about to rush by. In the past, most motorists have eased off the pedal a bit and pulled over if possible when passing us. Not today. Of all days, this is the one when we have no Carabinieri or other police escort. The motorhome with its protective bulk and large Canadian flag on the back is also absent. It seems the logistics team has completely fumbled both the route plan and their normal practice of being up ahead to resupply us with water and snacks.

When a member of the logistics team does appear in a car, I note Ernie glowering at him intently. "I expected things to be better organized," the retired general says later, "in terms of clarity in daily instructions, guidance, and such." He quickly accepts the need to lower his standards. Despite the fact that the logistics team members all have a military background, this is a civilian operation, and one that is beginning to fray around the edges as the days pile one upon the other. Setting aside his initial disgruntlement, Ernie seizes upon the "memorable experience" of "marching through the country" as "an opportunity to reflect on what our soldiers faced in 1943."

As we close in on Piazza Armerina, the traffic thickens. We leave the farm fields behind and pass long stretches of tract housing, industrial parks, and commercial centres. All are modern, look poorly constructed, and are uniformly unattractive. It is hard to reconcile the outskirts of this town with what I know of its older centre. This is one of Sicily's most frequented tourist sites. But it is not the town that draws people. They come instead for the Villa Romana del Casale, a Roman hunting lodge built in the fourth century A D. The lodge is home to some of the world's finest, best preserved, and most extensive collections of Roman mosaics. Undoubtedly, the mosaics survive today because the villa was buried under a landslide in the twelfth century and not rediscovered for seven hundred years. Most of the archaeological excavation here was conducted after 1929 and only completed in the early 1960s. It is now a UNESCO World Heritage Site.

The old town centre dates back to the fourteenth century and was established during the Norman conquest of Sicily. Through marriage, ties were built between the Norman rulers and families from the Lombardy region of Italy. This led to a wave of migration from Lombardy to Sicily, with many settling in Piazza Armerina and its adjacent farmlands. Many of its 22,000 citizens reportedly still speak a Norman-related dialect that is a blend of Gallic and Italian. In the eighteenth century, the imposing Duomo was constructed close to the summit of the 721-metre hill upon which the old city stands.

A short distance past the outskirts and still within the modern quarter, we come upon a large roundabout where a tall, brown concrete cross is mounted on a matching stone-and-brick base. Three marker clusters, each numbering six or seven, stand near the cross. Our band and many other Op Husky personnel are here. Also present is Piazza Armerina's *sindaco* and a small group of citizens, who join us in our remembrance ceremony.

From here we walk to a square, still in the new part of the town, where the sixty Canadian Forces personnel are formed up. Prominent among them are fifteen members of the Seaforth Highlanders Regimental Pipes and Drums. Getting the Department of National Defence to buy into participating in Op Husky 2013 was no easy matter, and the fact that this small group is here at all says much for Steve's unflagging tenacity and diplomatic skill. Every step of the way and at virtually every command level, obstacles were thrown up to ensure that participation would never happen. One of the more bizarre obstructive efforts was an attempt to impose on the Seaforth pipe band a requirement that they demonstrate the same fitness level as any soldier deploying to Afghanistan. With a number of the band members set to retire soon, passing this test was not viable. After much argument, this requirement was lifted. And as each barrier erected was slowly pulled down, a plan for Canadian military involvement fell into place. The sixty personnel were drawn from all branches of the service. The military's initiative was organized to run parallel to Op Husky and code-named Operation Sicily. This was done not only to ensure military control of its personnel, but also to recognize that ours was a civilian enterprise.

Heading up the contingent is Major General Jim Ferron, commander of the 1st Canadian Division. In a briefing at Canadian Forces Base (CFB) Kingston prior to the deployment to Sicily, Lorne Scots Regiment Corporal Devon Schorr-Bigg wrote in the regiment's newsletter, *The Primrose Hackle*, that Ferron "explained with excitement his expectations for the Operation and made very clear his devotion to the message we would be sending, not only to the people of Sicily but to Canadians as well, that Canada had played a significant role in the liberation of Sicily and should not be forgotten."

For simplicity, I will refer to all the military personnel as soldiers. They are wearing forest-green camouflage fatigues rather than the desert camouflage of Afghanistan, and the brighter colour makes the soldiers stand out vividly in a crowd. We form up and start marching up a cobblestone street that leads to a square in the heart of the town's old quarter, where the memorial stands. We follow our pipe band, which is out front playing their hearts out. Directly behind us marches the Seaforth band, also playing with determined gusto, and behind them come the remaining soldiers. It's a formidable formation, with townsfolk all mixed in alongside.

Our band plays one tune, the Seaforths another. Both loudly. It is quickly evident that each is determined to outdo the other. But our smaller group competes in vain. They simply don't have enough bagpipes or drums and especially lack the booming bass drum that the Seaforths deploy.

This is the first experience the soldiers have had of Sicilian heat. A few fall out and are tended to by the contingent's medic. It is, of course, another searing hot day at the end of July, so the effect is hardly surprising. By the time we reach the square, everybody is flagging a bit.

As the ceremony plays out, a number of us marchers take refuge under umbrellas, but the soldiers stand in three orderly lines at parade rest. Many are sweating profusely, and some are obviously close to collapse, but they all endure as the speeches drone on. When the ceremony ends, the relief on the faces of both marchers and soldiers is plain. The Sicilian crowd attending this ceremony was quite small today, likely because of the heat, for the square offered not a lick of shade.

After the ceremony ends, a few of us wander over to the soldiers but find it virtually impossible to strike up a conversation. Most of them seem cold, distant, and insular. Whether their reserve results from a discomfort with dealing with civilians, a lack of understanding of what we are doing and who we are, or something else, I am unable to determine. We have only just met, though, so I'm willing to see whether the guardedness drops over the next few days.

Rod Hoffmeister and Bill Rodgers, as honorary colonels, mix more easily with the soldiers. For Rod, the thrill of the day has been having his regiment's pipe band march into Piazza Armerina. But he is less pleased with the discordant musical competition that evolved. Rod brings our pipe major, Bob Stewart, over to meet the Seaforth's Pipe Major Mike Bain. "You guys have got to get together," he tells them. Then he takes Bain aside. "Mike, I know I'm an honorary colonel, but this is an order that you might want to consider obeying. Get together, play together, and appreciate what these guys have done for the walkers." Bain is soon talking with Stewart, two grizzled old Scottish soldiers who appear to immediately hit it off. Henceforth, the two bands, while not merging, will no longer be playing at odds during our marches into towns.

So used to starting each morning before dawn, we find it strange on July 27 to rise at about 7:00 and linger over breakfast at the hotel. It's an opportunity for us veteran marchers and the new recruits to mingle. I hardly expect the strong bond that has developed between those who started from Bark West on July 10 to now extend outward to include the new folks, but the relationship quickly becomes amiable enough.

There is no marching today, hence the lateness of the start. The day's agenda was considered too extensive to include a march. Some of the veterans are grumbling about this, but nevertheless, today's itinerary will include two community ceremonies as well as an extensive one on the summit of Monte Assoro. As the whole genesis of Op Husky traces back to the historical events on that summit, I'm willing to accept the constraints of the day's agenda. Sure, I would rather be walking under the hard sun than standing under it for long stretches while the speeches roll on. But this is the plan, so nothing to do but go with it.

In a small convoy, the hotel group drives to Leonforte and meets the rest of the contingent in a square not far from the outskirts. Parked there are a lot of vehicles and buses in which the soldiers and

Seaforth band have arrived. They are sleeping in barracks at the U.S. Naval Air Station Sigonella. This is a massive, sprawling facility where security is tight. The soldiers have been warned to take no photographs inside the complex, though they are free to use the gyms and swimming pools and eat at any of the restaurants scattered about the place. I overhear one soldier lamenting that there probably won't be time to enjoy any of this, especially the swimming pools. Instead, they form up and march behind us through the streets of Leonforte to the war memorial in the main square.

Up front, the number of Canadians wearing white shirts and red ball caps has grown significantly. We are joined today not only by the few more people who are marching, but by many more who have come primarily for the July 30 ceremony at Agira cemetery and now participate in the town ceremonies. Several of these newcomers have a relative who served in Sicily. For George Gervais and his family, it was his father, Bombardier Vic Gervais of the Royal Canadian Artillery. The family has had t-shirts made with an image of Vic as he was in 1943 and as he is now, standing side by side and superimposed over a black-and-white photo of Canadian soldiers advancing across the plateau not far from Bark West.

The ceremony is well attended by the local people, and their band, mostly composed of middle-aged men, performs. They wear short-sleeved dress shirts, grey pants, and purple ties—creating the impression of a group of bureaucrats and office workers who perhaps rehearse during coffee and lunch breaks. As has always been true of these Sicilian bands, small or large, they are talented musicians.

During the speeches, we meet a new World War II veteran, Bob Wigmore. The ninety-two-year-old was a corporal in the Hasty Ps in 1943 and participated in the historic Monte Assoro climb. I snap a photo of Bob standing below the ceremony's raised stage. Above him, Sherry Atkinson is leaning over the railing, which is draped with a huge Canadian flag. The two men's right hands are just beginning to touch for a handshake, aged and weathered fingers coming together. Later, they stand together on the stage, hands raised in a salute below their berets—Sherry's blue, Bob's red—as the Canadian and Italian anthems are sung.

Of what the mayor said, what Steve said, what Major General Ferron said, or even what Sherry said I have no memory. We have perhaps been at this too long. A certain ennui at the repetitiveness of these events has descended on us that even the surge in Canadian personnel cannot dispel. As the ceremonies are something new to him, Ernie Beno is more attentive. He notes that "the Sicilian local politicians seem to use the ceremonies as a platform for pushing their own issues—not always welcomed by their constituency!" But he finds the ceremonies "touching and appropriate from a Canadian perspective."

When the ceremony ends, everybody mills about for a bit. Then Steve introduces a few of us to Pierre-Paul Pharand. Although I have been involved in numerous teleconference calls that have included him, this is our first face-to-face meeting. It is Pierre-Paul who has been in overall charge of the logistics for Op Husky. He has a politician's carefully sculpted good looks and manner of dress. Nary a bead of sweat on his forehead. Not at all like us marchers. By now, our white shirts are grubby. Jean's brown leather pack has left a stain up the back of her shirt and across the front where the shoulder straps sit. The neck of my shirt is grimy, and no amount of washing with shampoo in the hotel-room sink makes a difference. Backs of legs are covered in rash, ankles puffed up like those of many of the older Italian women we see on the streets.

We have one question, though, for Pierre-Paul, and somebody asks it before I can: "Where and when are we marching tomorrow?" Pierre-Paul shrugs in theatrical dismissal. "There will be no march. The marching is over." We exchange looks of consternation, and eyes turn to Steve—who is surprisingly noncommittal about whether there should be more marching or not. I weigh in, most vocally joined by Jean. "There has to be more marching, at least one more. We need that for closure," I say. "We can't end on this note." There is general agreement. Seeing that Pierre-Paul is considering digging his heels in, I say that if the logistics team will not organize another march and preferably two more, some of us will go it alone, following routes of our own determining. Grudgingly, Pierre-Paul consents to having André and Richard map out two more routes and making the necessary contacts with the Carabinieri to put the plan into effect.

This little contretemps is witnessed by only a few of us. But I view the outcome as a victory for the marching team and affirmation of how seriously we have come to see our purpose over these past weeks. The marching is a keystone of our remembrance. One way or the other, we shall keep going until the very end.

Shortly after this incident, the entire contingent adjourns to a large restaurant for a prepared lunch. We marchers scatter amongst the soldiers. Frances and I end up sitting with about ten soldiers at a table. We are politely ignored, although they do respond to questions when asked. A couple say they are pushing for permission to march, but it is uncertain whether this will be allowed. There seems to be much concern among the top brass that somebody might suffer extreme heatstroke or something equally dire. Of course, such a risk exists. But I look around at these soldiers. Most are young and fit as hell. They are still acclimatizing, but so were we back on July 10. I suspect they could out-walk us easily, and that the risk is slight that any would fall seriously ill.

I also think—eighteen days. That's how long it has been since that first march. Yet it seems so long ago. We have been living this experience with such intensity that it is hard to think of any other time. We are here in this moment, in this act of extreme remembrance. There is nothing else and will not be anything else until we reach the last act and the curtain falls announcing that Op Husky 2013 is at an end.

I am thinking this as a general commotion ripples through the restaurant. I see Jean, Bob Werbiski, Don Aitchison, the Vaughan-Jones family, and other people gathering gear and heading for the door. The three young members of Max Fraser's film crew exit as well. It takes a few minutes to determine what is happening. It seems a group are going to re-enact the Monte Assoro climb. There is a bus leaving right now. I am torn. This is something Steve and I had talked of often in the planning and had both been determined to be on. But somewhere along the way, any formal plan has been lost. This impromptu act has caught me off guard. Already I have

committed to an interview with Max and Arlin on Assoro's summit.
There is also word that the ascent will be gruelling. Am I really up to
it? Frances says I should do what I like, but she is not going. The way
her ankles and feet are feeling, it's not worth the risk of an injury. I
dither, and then realize the opportunity is lost. The group has gone.

CONSEQUENTLY, MY KNOWLEDGE of the climb comes second-hand.
What those I speak with about it remember most, they say, is standing at the base of the mountain and listening to Bob Wigmore
describe the ascent by the Hasty Ps that night seventy years before.
"Bob made the pages of history jump out of the book and into our
hearts," Jean Miso says. "As he spoke, I was in awe of his detailed
account and the thoughtful advice given for success in climbing
Monte Assoro." That advice, adds Guylaine Tarte, focused on "helping each other." This is how, Wigmore told them, the Hasty Ps
succeeded.

A newcomer to Op Husky, having arrived just this day, is Colin
Robinson. After twenty years in the army, Colin retired in 2009 with
a colonel's rank from command of the Royal Montreal Regiment.
Since then, he has been the regiment's honorary lieutenant colonel.
He is also Farley Mowat's cousin. "On my first day on the ground
here," he says, "I was approached to see if I wanted to climb Assoro—
did I ever! I was absolutely thrilled to be able to follow my cousin's
footsteps, and I even carried my mother's copy of his book up with
me in my pack. It was a pleasant little hike, great weather, nice company—and being briefed before we set off by Bob Wigmore was just
the icing on an already perfect cake!"

Although now retired, Colin—"I've done a couple of route
marches in my day"—still has a career infantryman's fitness. So his
"pleasant little hike" was a bit more of a struggle for some others.
The Honourable Con, Don Aitchison reports, lost his balance and
nearly went rolling off down the steep slope. Emilie Vaughan-Jones
was dragging her father, Chris, along in her wake when they
approached the top.

As the climbing party is making its ascent, the rest of us drive
from Leonforte to the summit of Monte Assoro. A variety of events

begin to unfold. Canadian Forces artillery regiment personnel use today's events to unveil a new plaque commemorating the participation of gunners in the Sicily campaign. The plaque has a short description of gunner history rendered in English, Italian, and French, with the unit serial numbers of the three artillery, one anti-tank, and one light anti-aircraft regiments involved running along the bottom. It is a handsome plaque, and I am intrigued to see the emphasis on the fact that from this summit on July 24, 1943, the headquarters of 1st Division "supervised one of the largest bombardments of the campaign as the fight for Nissoria and Agira began."

Quite true. The bombardment was massive, involving 150 guns of not only the three Canadian artillery regiments but also two British field regiments and two British medium regiments—a huge weight of steel fired in support of a single Canadian infantry battalion, the Royal Canadian Regiment. Major General Guy Simonds was a gunner by training, and the "allure of the guns," as his general staff officer, Lieutenant Colonel George Kitching, put it, tended to "unduly influence some of his tactical decisions." A gunner's dream shoot in World War II was virtually the same "creeping barrage" that had prevailed as the essential artillery support tactic during World War I.

The July 24 shoot was a classic example of this methodical orchestration. Many of the guns would fire smoke shells to create a screen one thousand yards ahead of the infantry and across a two-thousand-yard-wide front. Every twenty minutes, these guns would lift their fire another thousand yards to keep the screen advancing precisely ahead of the infantry. At the same time, the majority of the guns would be dropping high-explosive shells about a hundred yards in front of the advancing RCR, with the guns lifting every two minutes. Out beyond the smokescreen, meanwhile, Kittyhawk bombers of the Desert Air Force would strafe and bomb suspected German positions, and six squadrons of medium bombers were to attack Agira and its immediate vicinity. All together, guns and aircraft were to throw down an eight-mile-long and three-mile-wide carpet of fire.

This was a plan the gunnery officers around Simonds loved and of which the infantry officers despaired. The 1st Brigade's Brigadier

Howard Graham admitted in his memoir thinking, "My God! The man must be crazy."

But Simonds was determined. It was a confident divisional head-quarters, accompanied by a gaggle of correspondents, who took their places on Assoro's summit that morning to witness this feat of gun-nery. Instead, they watched an infantry regiment and a squadron of supporting Three Rivers Regiment tanks die. To begin the attack, the RCR was expected to first march two miles just to reach its start line. When the guns started firing at 1300 hours, the battalion was then to march behind the barrage across six miles of plateau and then up the mountain into Agira—a total distance during the attack of about eight miles—while maintaining a steady pace of one hundred yards every two minutes.

Perhaps such a pace could be realistically maintained by tired, heavily burdened soldiers marching through temperatures exceed-ing 40 degrees Celsius if they had crossed ground resembling the surface of a billiard table. But officers like Lieutenant Strome Galloway led their platoons through orchards heavy with ripe fruit hanging from the branches and rotting underfoot, into vineyards whose vines clutched at clothing and weapons, and into and out of deep ditches. There were fences that had to be pushed through or climbed over. Knowing that behind the barrage infantry must be advancing, the Germans attempted to intercept them with mortar and artillery fire. In short order, the great barrage marched on, and the infantrymen and tanks fell far behind.

With the barrage having passed over, Germans slipped unhurt from protective holes and returned to their machine guns and anti-tank guns. The RCR reached Nissoria, and there the attack stalled. Having lost contact with his companies, Lieutenant Colonel Ralph Crowe ran forward, with his wireless operators close behind. He was screaming "R-C-R" to identify himself when a German machine gun sliced into the group. Crowe fell wounded, stumbled to his feet, grabbed a rifle from a signaller, and charged the gun, only to be shot dead.

The survivors stumbled back to Nissoria. Seventeen RCR soldiers died that day and another thirty were wounded. 'A' Squadron lost ten of its Shermans, with four men killed and another thirteen wounded.

An attempt to renew the advance by throwing the Hasty Ps in just added to the casualty list, as five officers and seventy-five other ranks were killed, wounded, or lost as missing and likely taken prisoner. This gave the Hasty Ps the sad distinction of being the Canadian battalion that suffered the highest casualty count on a single day during the Sicily campaign.

The only silver lining in the events of July 24 was the failure of the medium bombers to show up. Somehow, the orders involving them were never received. Had they turned up, Agira may well have been reduced to ruins. Instead, it suffered no serious damage prior to its liberation four days later.

Thinking about this, I look at Bob Wigmore and imagine that some of the Hasty Ps killed or grievously wounded that day were likely his friends. He stands next to the plaque that describes the battalion's heroic July 22 climb of Assoro and is telling those gathered around him that it was precisely where the plaque stands that the first Hasty Ps climbed up onto the summit.

The cliff here falls away precipitously, and it is hard to imagine heavily burdened soldiers climbing it. A few minutes later, today's ascenders come into view. Their route was up a less steep and treacherous one than the Hasty Ps took, and it brought them out on the road that today hooks around that eastern flank to gain the summit. A few minutes later, they reach us. About fifteen have made the climb, followed by Max Fraser's three-man film crew. Oliver, Matt, and Duncan typically made the climb with their cameras and sound gear while wearing flip-flops—a remarkable achievement in its own right.

Emilie is one of the first to arrive and declares that "the best part of the climb" was "seeing the people there, and Steve was there and gave a hand to every person who came over the hill. And everybody was clapping. We just climbed a mountain, not that big of a deal. To have a response like that was pretty moving."

Eight Hasty Ps died or were mortally wounded during the fight for the summit, and markers for six of them are erected here. Standing behind the markers, Don offers a prayer, and then six soldiers from the regiment who are facing them call out each fallen soldier's name, one by one.

We descend to the village of Assoro, where another ceremony unfolds in a large square that offers expansive views over the surrounding countryside. The sun is setting as the ceremony concludes. Both on the summit and again here in the square there is a noticeable divide between the military personnel and the marchers. The sense during the luncheon that the walls the soldiers had erected were coming down is lost. I decide the problem is that they really have no clue as to who we are or what we are doing. This is something that needs resolving before the journey ends at Agira cemetery, where everybody must mesh together if this act of remembrance is to be considered a success.

It is already 10:30 when our group returns to the Hotel Castel Miralago. I check my email and find a message from André with an attached map showing tomorrow's marching route. Back into the Dittaino valley with a departure from Raddusa-Agira Station. Twenty-six kilometres from there to the town of Catenanuova. Rally time such that we must leave the hotel at 3:30 a.m. to be on time. I imagine Pierre-Paul with a smile that does not reach his eyes: "You want a march, so here it is."

I knock lightly on the doors of the marchers. Tell those who answer the details. Standing outside Phil's door, I hear him snoring softly. Quickly jot a note on a good-sized piece of paper and slip it under the door. Frances and I decide to get up at 2:45. While she showers, I'll check with everybody to make sure they are awake and getting ready. We will make this work.

WE GATHER AROUND a small group of markers alongside the road at the Raddusa-Agira train station and hold the day's first ceremony. Two more marchers join us, bringing our group to fifteen. Rod Hoffmeister, the Honourable Con, and Beverly Topping are missing. So we lose some and gain others. Colin Robinson, who climbed Monte Assoro yesterday, is one of the new ones. The other is a short, slight man named Lee Harrison. He is a stalwart supporter of Canada Company and the president of Montreal-based Walker Glass. In a T-shirt, shorts, and sneakers, Lee looks no more like a business executive than Steve or Mark Clearihue. Of course, Ernie Beno looks little like a retired general. Hiking clothes and the heat of Sicily are great social-status levellers. We are also joined today by our Carabinieri friends, Marco and Saverio.

Don offers a prayer over the markers, and we recite the names of the fallen soldiers. As the last name is called out, Colin recites loudly and clearly the famous fourth stanza from Robert Laurence Binyon's poem "For the Fallen."

> They shall not grow old, as we that are left grow old:
> Age shall not weary them, nor the years condemn.
> At the going down of the sun and in the morning
> We will remember them.

"We will remember them," the rest of us respond.

"As a veteran and Legion member," Colin says afterwards, "I felt it was appropriate." When Colin adds that he hopes nobody minds him butting in with this, he is assured it is welcome, something we had not thought of but obviously fitting.

From the junction, we walk another country road, which runs along one flank of the Dittaino valley toward Catenanuova. Sun up, the temperature rises rapidly. I think about Laurence Binyon, the British poet and art critic. When the men we just honoured landed in Sicily on July 10, 1943, Binyon was precisely four months dead— having died that March 10 at age seventy-three. Unlike John McRae's "In Flanders Fields," Binyon's "For the Fallen" is hauntingly prescient. Binyon wrote the poem while sitting on the edge of a cliff looking out to sea from the north Cornish countryside in mid-September of 1914. World War I was barely six weeks on, and he sought to honour the small number reported to have died in those first days of fighting. Did he anticipate the carnage that would follow?

In 1939, Binyon said he had written the fourth stanza first and shaped the rest of the poem around it. That stanza has, of course, become a central part of Remembrance Day ceremonies throughout the Commonwealth. In Britain, it is called "The Exhortation" and in Canada, the "Act of Remembrance." Like so many of us, I have heard those lines recited over a lifetime of November 11 mornings, standing before a cenotaph in one community or another. And I have duly and unhesitatingly answered at the end, "We will remember them."

Today is filled even more than usual with acts of remembrance. The route closely mirrors that taken by 3rd Canadian Infantry Brigade as it advanced along this valley to seize Catenanuova—a major Sicilian interior junction town close to the western flank of Mount Etna. We walk close by Monte Santa Maria and only later learn that the Vaughan-Jones family and a group of soldiers from the Royal 22e Régiment were on its summit about then, conducting a private remembrance ceremony honouring Ephrem Tarte and the others from the regiment who died on or near its slopes. We marchers, meanwhile, come across three different plots of markers and hold a brief ceremony at each. One of these sites is on land owned by a farmer who encountered the marker team as they were installing the markers. He has promised to take care of them after we Canadians have all gone. Considering it likely that some of his grazing stock might damage the markers, the farmer has said he will build a protective fence and keep it maintained. If needed, he will relocate them to a safer spot. One way or another, though, he made it clear these markers are his responsibility now and will be duly cared for.

As we had anticipated, since we moved into the mountainous interior to retrace the days when fighting was hardest, the number of markers grows at each plot we encounter. The one the farmer has adopted holds twenty-five.

Although this is the longest march that most of us have undertaken, we veterans agree that it's far from the hardest, because the terrain covered is largely flat or gently rolling. The Dittaino valley lives up to its former reputation as a frying pan, of course, and takes its greatest toll on the new recruits. But they have the advantage of being relatively fresh. As Drew Davis notes, that means the marches are at once "exhausting and exhilarating" for him and the other new people. Ernie Beno declares that the marches pose "a physical and mental challenge—which makes the experience more meaningful."

The ceremony in Catenanuova rolls out pretty much in accordance with the script now set by the involvement of forces personnel and the Seaforth pipe band. When it ends, the entire Canadian contingent adjourns to a large restaurant for lunch. As we are going in, I pull Steve aside. "The CF people don't understand us marchers and what we're doing," I tell him. "It's the same for the other people who have joined us. You need to tell them about us, so they understand."

Steve quickly agrees. Throughout the day, I have been heartened to see Steve closely engaged in events again. The torpor that seemed to weigh on him the past few days and was probably the product of exhaustion has entirely lifted. He is once again irrepressible.

Before the food arrives, Steve introduces the marchers and describes what we have been doing since July 10. As the soldiers hear about the distances we have walked, one day following the other, they start to look impressed. Once again, we marchers are scattered among them, but this time the conversation is easier, more relaxed. Several of them tell us they are excited that permission has been granted for those who want to do so to join us for the last march tomorrow.

FOLLOWING LUNCH, BILL, Don, Frances, and I set off to find a particular wall connected to a Lieutenant Ross Guy. This was the special mission of Bill's that we abandoned on July 24 because of the searing heat. Today, we feel fresher, and the heat is not as intense. We are also right in the neighbourhood and agree that it's now or never. One of Guy's sons, Stanton, is a friend of Bill's. Upon learning that Bill was going to Sicily for Op Husky, Stanton told him a well-hewn family tale about the wall.

The story was true to the facts. On July 30, 'A' Company of the West Nova Scotia Highlanders was closing on Catenanuova when its commanding officer was wounded. Guy took over, leading the men into a confusing battleground in a rail-marshalling yard on the town's western outskirts. As the battle progressed, the company became ever more hard pressed, and casualties mounted alarmingly. Finding cover behind a low stone wall, Guy used his wireless to call in artillery fire, despite having no training in how to do that. His battalion commander took personal charge of the wireless on the other end and walked the young man through the procedures. So accurate was the fire that the German counterattacks were broken, and Guy earned a Military Cross for—as his medal citation states—his "leadership, courage, and tenacity of the highest order." What the citation fails to say is that Guy was terrified the entire time and considered the low stone wall as providing only "dubious" protection. He was so impressed by that factor that he described the barrier in a later report as a "dubious wall." When his family heard the story, they thought it hilarious that somebody would make such a statement in an official report. Thereafter, everything from ice cream cones to great achievements could be declared as being of dubious quality or value.

Finding the wall proves to be a dubious undertaking. The problem being that Lieutenant Guy provided no map reference in his after-action report. What we are left to work with is a map reference cited as the position of the company on his right flank. But I have convinced Bill this might suffice. We just need to project from that position across to the other side of the rail tracks, where the train station was situated. For the wall is supposed to be close to the station.

At first, however, the coordinates are clearly too far away from the station. But then I realize the station we are focusing on is new. Off across a distant field stands the now derelict earlier station. Around it is a fence made of intermixed sections of high wire and equally high stone. Circling around the wall via a series of increasingly rough tracks, we come to a spot where a dry creek bed is bordered by an even narrower track. The creek bed looks much like the one Guy described in his report as being close to the wall. Bill creeps the car along the track until we come to a small widening. There across the creek is a low, badly deteriorated stone wall. Is it the one? Walking around, we are unable to see any trace of other walls. We walk over to the wall through a tangle of weeds and shrubs, keeping a wary eye out for vipers, as this kind of brushy vegetation is an ideal spot for one to lurk. The wall seems a perfect candidate for the one Guy and his signaller hunkered behind. It is constructed out of hundreds of small stones piled together in the drystone manner we have seen elsewhere. The western side is about three metres high and exposed, and the eastern flank is lower. I can easily imagine Guy using the western side for cover, as it was from that direction the West Novas were advancing. Peeking judiciously over the wall would have enabled him to locate German targets and direct the artillery fire on them. Bill takes a series of photos for Stanton, and we declare the mission of finding the dubious wall a success.

JULY 29, OUR last day of hiking, is unique. Not in the details, although the distance to cover is surprisingly short, just eleven kilometres. The uniqueness factor is the size of the contingent that has gathered on the outskirts of Catenanuova at 5:30 a.m. Most of the veteran marchers are present, along with the new people who have joined us over the past few days. In addition, there are about thirty-five forces personnel in what they call their PT kit—basically, shorts, T-shirts, and running shoes. Also joining us in this last march are a few other Canadians, some of whom have followed us through Sicily over the past weeks. Arlin McFarlane has set aside her camera to walk. Colonel Tony Battista, recently arrived from Rome, is here. Although he is winding up a nearly forty-year military career, Tony could easily pass for a man in his early fifties. At fifty-seven, Major General Jim Ferron is here to lead his troops. A few of these new people are women, but most are male—likely pretty much the standard percentage breakdown within the forces.

Before we set out, everybody gathers round, and I give them the Action of the Day report. Our destination today is the hilltop village of Centuripe, toward which the West Nova Scotia Regiment advanced along a route west of the one we will follow today. I tell them about how the battalion walked into an ambush sprung by German paratroops at Monte Criscina, which had been reported by intelligence staff as likely abandoned. The West Novas suffered their heaviest losses in Sicily that second day in August—nineteen killed and twenty-seven wounded. Centuripe actually fell to the British 38th (Irish) Brigade, which advanced to it along the route we will march. After describing the actions aimed at Centuripe, I describe Canadian operations on August 6 at Adrano. It is at this town that the day's remembrance ceremony is to be held, so it seems fitting to describe that advance as well. All of this makes for a fairly long briefing, made more complicated by the fact that the logistics team has again been unable to provide my earlier written script. Fortunately, I can remember the primary details.

I tell them how Major General Guy Simonds—seeming to have learned from the costly advance on Nissoria and Agira—avoided a drive up the main road from Regalbuto to Adrano, which would surely have been hotly contested. Instead, he slipped 2nd Brigade north into the barren Salso River valley, catching the Germans by surprise. Several stiff actions followed, including the one at Hill 736 where John Dougan was wounded and his friend Earl Christie died, but the Germans were unable to stem the advance. August 6 saw 3rd Brigade taking the lead, with the Van Doos at the head. 'C' Company's Lieutenant Yves Dubé, unaware that orders had been issued for the Canadians to leave Adrano for the British 79th Division to clear, led a strong fighting patrol into its streets. They found that Adrano had been reduced to ruin by relentless artillery and aerial bombardment. Dubé's platoon remained in the town well into the night, expecting the rest of the regiment to join it. Finally, realizing this would not happen, Dubé led the men back to the battalion lines. His patrol proved that Adrano had been abandoned by the Germans. Not a shot had been fired. This was 1st Canadian Division's last combat action in Sicily.

After the briefing ends, a small number of soldiers hang back to ask me questions about what it would have been like to fight in these hills with World War II equipment and tactics. As we ascend a rapidly steepening incline, I point out various positions that the Germans would have used to site their machine guns and mortars onto the road and its verges to create an ambush similar to the one they sprung on the West Novas. The road switchbacks radically up a narrow valley that ends at a saddle in which Centuripe stands. I say it is fortunate our troops did not have to fight a pitched battle to gain the village. Virtually every inch of the road would have fallen into one killing zone or another.

By the time the soldiers run out of questions and march briskly off ahead of me, I'm finding breathing difficult. Talking while ascending the side of a steep valley was obviously a bad idea. I am soon lagging close to the rear of the column and depending more on the support of my walking pole than normal. Sweat courses down my face, and my breath comes in ragged gasps. Undoubtedly, the smart thing would be to sit down by the roadside and rest for a half hour or so. But that would lead to André or Richard in the support vehicle insisting I ride with them to the village. This is something I have not done before and am damn well not going to do today. So I try to strike a measured pace. I remember what Phil Bury commented to me at one point. He said that what he found difficult with the marching was not the actual physical effort entailed—he could set a pace and manage that. But in the heat and with the increasing altitude and steep inclines, he would lose his wind. And once that went, it was almost impossible to regain. So I pant, gasp, and keep pushing on while trying to maintain the illusion that this short walk up these switchbacks is just another day in the paradise of Sicily.

Terry Dolan is a short distance behind. Hills have always been his downfall before, but today one of the women soldiers is matching his pace. Terry seems to be finding it possible to walk and talk at the same time. Two middle-aged civilians on their first march walk alongside me for most of the ascent. I never do catch their names. One carries a small Canadian flag, and Terry's new soldier friend has woven a flag into her hair.

As we approach a sharp bend in the road, Matt Pancer comes racing around the corner going downhill on a skateboard while filming the marchers with a small camera. A sharp turn as he passes the support cars, and Matt's running back up the hill past us with skateboard under one arm and camera cradled in the other. The boundless energy of the three young members of Max Fraser's film crew leaves me feeling old and busted today rather than inspired.

Before we set out this morning, Steve told Bill Rodgers that we might show these young soldiers a thing or two during the ascent. Bill says later, "I said to Steve, 'You have no idea! We were walking with Jim Ferron, the general, and he said, "You know, they're holding back. They wanted to run it. I told them, 'No, you can't run it.' And they said, 'At least we can wear our packs.'" And Ferron said, 'Yeah, okay.'" Soon after that, Bill heard a whisper coming up behind him. "And all of a sudden these soldiers just blow by us. We're going our usual five or six kilometres, and they just ran by us. That was their fitness level. Like nothing we could even dream of matching."

Looking down a steep bank alongside the road, I see a rusty steel box amid a pile of rubbish at the back of a farmyard. Zooming in with my camera, I see German lettering on the side. The box has eight round indentions on the top, equally spaced, with four to a side. Given the height of the box, I figure it held eight light mortar rounds. This type of debris of war is found in many a farmer's junk pile, hung on to in case some use presents itself.

For most of the ascent, Frances has been up close to the front of the marchers, walking with Arlin. At times, she takes photos of me at the back of the group when she is up front on the exact opposite end of one of the switchbacks. We are separated by only twenty or so metres, and these photos later have a surreal quality for both of us because we know just how tightly this road wound. Frances drifts down the line as we close on the summit, and we walk the last kilometre side by side. I tell her about the lack of wind problem. Our pace is slow and measured, and most companionable. We have not held hands before on these marches, but we do so as we enter the village. "The last one," I say. I realize with a pang of sadness that, despite the early mornings, the confusion of logistics, and the sheer challenge of facing each new day with another long march ahead, to be followed by more days of the same, I already miss the sense of fulfilment I had on finishing one hard day while anticipating the day ahead.

This sense of having reached an ending sticks close as we join a group of soldiers and marchers at a large outdoor café. Frances fetches us a couple of bottles of beer, and we chat with the army contingent's medic, who is seated on a public bench just outside the café perimeter. He is methodically inspecting the backpack containing his medical supplies. We learn he has done two tours in Afghanistan. And that each medic organizes his kit differently and includes various supplies according to personal preference.

After a short rest period, the vehicles arrive. The soldiers load into buses and we spread out among our cars. A long convoy snakes up the narrow ss121 that brings us to Adrano, which is just 17.5

kilometres to the northeast. With a population of about 55,000, Adrano is bigger than most of the towns in which we've held ceremonies. Large crowds line the street as we march in behind the pipe band, which today is a fully amalgamated unit of Seaforths and our white-shirted pipers and drummers. The musicians have been practising, and they play well together.

In the wide central square, the town's marching band greets us. It is large, composed of children and adults of all ages. The *sindaco* is the first woman we have seen in this position. She gives a thoughtful speech whose theme is that an event of remembrance such as we are holding today is about joy replacing the sorrow of losses caused by war.

When the ceremony draws to a close, we marchers disperse into the crowd. A lunch is to be served under the shade trees of a nearby park. On the edge of this park, the marker team has installed just over eighty markers in two long rows that run the length of a paved walking path. There is a photo that shows Frances holding her hip belt in one tired hand as she walks slowly along the length of that sobering row of markers, which honour the majority of the Canadians who fell in those first days of August before 1st Division's last shot was fired. Earl Christie's marker is among those planted here, and I spend a longer moment with it than I do with the others.

We hold a last marker ceremony here, and yet its details do not stay in my mind. Instead, I notice how, during the lunch under the shade trees, people drift off from the tables and chairs set up there. How their footsteps carry them out into the sunshine where the long rows of markers stand. How some of the soldiers in uniform walk their length. Sometimes a person walks there alone. Other times, small groups gather and walk slowly along them. Most of the people are Canadian. But I see also a number of Sicilians walking the line and pausing to examine each name plate. Joy to replace the sorrow of losses caused by war, the *sindaco* said. The sorrow seems closer.

I think of Steve. Without his vision, these markers and the ceremonies of remembrance that have become so integral to this whole experience would never have happened. And tomorrow, the final act in his vision will unfold at the Agira Canadian War Cemetery.

PART THREE

Finale

WE ARE AMONG the first to arrive at the cemetery on the morning of July 30. Although I had worried that we would face furnace-like conditions, no sooner do we walk into the cemetery than a stiff breeze comes off Mount Etna and moderates the temperature to the high thirties. As Italian and Canadian military personnel set up canopies to shade the expected dignitaries, Frances and I walk among the rows of headstones. Others are doing the same. As a steady flow of buses and other vehicles disgorge ever-greater numbers, the cemetery begins to fill. I still wonder if there will be enough to make Steve's planned roll call possible, but as each bus comes up the narrow lane and more Canadians disembark, the situation seems promising. Looking back along the lane to where the highway climbs up to the town of Agira, I see dozens upon dozens of parked cars and trucks. Long lines of Sicilians walk from them toward the cemetery.

I think back to when Frances and I first visited here, the long gaps without signatures in the visitor book. Today, a line has already formed before the small building where the book is kept, the people patiently waiting to add their names, addresses, and perhaps thoughts of remembrance. Kept beside the visitor book in a cupboard protected by a brass door is the cemetery register. Several people are using the register to try to locate specific headstones. I spend a few minutes helping a few get oriented, and guide one woman to the headstone of her father, who died in Sicily just months after she was born.

Steve today wears a sports jacket, slacks, white shirt, and red tie. So, too, does his son, Erik. The other civilian dignitaries are similarly dressed. Some of the Op Husky participants have also dressed up for the event. Guylaine Tarte and her daughter, Emilie Vaughan-Jones, are wearing dresses. Our various honorary colonels are all in uniform, Don Aitchison is wearing his 48th Highlanders chaplain uniform. The officer cadets are almost unrecognizable in their Royal Military College Saint-Jean scarlet dress uniforms. All the Canadians wear a poppy. Jean Miso has gone one step further and is wearing a dress with a pattern of large poppies over a white background. As part of the ceremony, Jean is to sing a song she wrote that inspired her book *We'll Never Forget* and bears the same title. She has asked some of us to join her as backup for the chorus.

I walk over to where Steve and Erik huddle below the podium set up for speeches. They are flipping through a thin stack of papers. Sometime during the last few days, they have come to the cemetery and developed a precise list of all those buried here. The names are listed in the same order as the gravestones. As Steve calls out a name, the person standing before that headstone will answer for that soldier, and the next name will be of the soldier buried immediately adjacent, and so on. This way the roll call should unfold seamlessly. Agira cemetery is divided into four alphabetically identified quadrants, which helped with the planning. To further ensure that as a name is read out the person in front of the headstone can answer for him, four linesmen have been appointed. Each will walk along the rows, and as each name is called will point to the person before that headstone. I am one of the linesmen. The others are Phil Bury (helped by Chris Vaughan-Jones), Colin Robinson, and Ernie Beno. Steve says that Erik will stand beside him as he reads out the names. Steve worries that he might break down while reading the names. If he does, Erik will take over.

The plan seems solid. Now all we have to do is ensure that when the time comes, people understand the task and at least one person is standing before each headstone. Fortunately, the numbers of military personnel and Italian police officers, firefighters, and paramedic personnel are substantial. The commanders of each contingent brief its members. Meanwhile, most of us Op Husky participants walk through the civilian crowds and explain to various people how the roll call will work. They in turn are soon informing others, and so word spreads.

I notice that several dozen people, both civilians and forces personnel, have sought out specific headstones relevant to them. Lorne Scot Regiment Corporal Devon Schorr-Bigg, for example, has located the headstone of Corporal Wilbert Alexander Coxe, of Milton, Ontario. The Lorne Scots role in the Sicilian campaign is little known, for they were not a line battalion. They instead provided a platoon responsible for defending 1st Division's headquarters. On July 22, Coxe and fellow Lorne Scot twenty-one-year-old Private Bernard Nancis Barrett, of Paris, Ontario, were killed when the divisional headquarters was strafed by a German fighter plane. Barrett was the eldest of a family of ten. Coxe died at twenty-three, and before enlisting in early 1940, had been one of Milton's star junior hockey and baseball players. His parents, Kenneth and Mary B. Coxe, were to suffer further grief when a second of four sons, Private Kenneth Albert Coxe, was killed on December 6, 1944, while serving in the Royal Regiment of Canada. Kenneth was thirty at the time and left behind a wife and two children in Oakville. The other two brothers also served overseas as drivers with the Royal Canadian Army Service Corps and survived. Schorr-Bigg places a Canadian flag next to Coxe's headstone and arranges his regimental beret on one corner before taking a photo. Upon returning to Canada, he is able to track down some of Coxe's family and provide them with headstone photos. He receives repeated emails of gratitude for this because otherwise the family would never have seen it. Schorr-Bigg is just one of many taking time to collect photos of headstones that resonate for them in one way or another.

PEOPLE ARE STILL flowing into the cemetery as the military personnel and dignitaries form up for the ceremony. There are two formations of Carabinieri. One group wears darker blue shirts than the others. Those in the dark uniforms are armed with what look like World War II–era carbines, and the ones in pale blue carry modern automatic rifles braced at waist height. Next to them stands a small contingent of U.S. Navy personnel in formal whites. Adjacent to the sailors are ranks of Italian soldiers, and then our sixty Canadian Forces personnel complete the military line. Behind them, at least five large Maple Leaf flags snap in what is now a brisk wind.

The speeches by such luminaries as Canada's national defence minister and the ambassador to Italy are mercifully brief. Don, who has avoided being overshadowed by local priests by reminding people that this is a Canadian cemetery, leads us in a prayer. At Bark West beach on July 10, Don says later, watching the Canadian flag rise with the sea behind it, he had felt "so proud of those who had landed and headed into truly unknown danger." But here at the cemetery, that pride is tempered by a sense of mourning. Steve's speech is short but provides a good summary of what we have done over the past twenty days, and how Operation Husky 2013 is culminating in this cemetery with an unprecedented crowd that, he hopes, will carry on the remembrance of Canada's involvement in the Sicilian campaign.

Nobody will ever determine precisely how many people have gathered, but estimates range from seven hundred to a thousand. On the day, I figure eight hundred. And they are roughly half Canadians and half Sicilians. I am surprised at how many of the Sicilians I recognize from ceremonies in towns and villages along our route of march. Many had said they would be here, but to see that they took the time to drive here on a Tuesday morning—many with their entire families in tow—is heartening.

When Jean mounts the podium to perform her song of remembrance, Frances, Terry Dolan, and I join her, while the other marchers join in on the chorus, for we have rehearsed this during our long marches. The chorus goes: "Poppies remember those at war who died./Poppies remember those at war who died." The song honours soldiers who died in past wars, as well as those who continue to serve today in foreign lands. "I was honoured beyond words to be able to sing," Jean says. "And I love that the marchers collectively helped me lead the song. For me, this action synthesized the spirit of camaraderie that was felt by all soldiers seventy years ago as they fought through this campaign. When the marchers joined me in the chorus, I felt that deep in my heart."

Standing on the podium, looking out at a veritable sea of people gathered there among the rows of white marble headstones with the tall Cross of Sacrifice looming above us on its broad base, tears start. There are dozens of red ball caps, hundreds of small Maple Leafs being waved, poppies everywhere I look. My tears are of gratitude for all who have come today to honour these soldiers.

Throughout the ceremony, a Canadian bugler and Seaforth Pipe Major Mike Bain have stood on either side of the Cross of Sacrifice. The bugler now plays the last post while we stand in reflective silence. Pipe Major Bain follows this with the lament. Wreaths are then laid, the ceremony replicating almost precisely that of a Remembrance Day Ceremony back in Canada. Each wreath layer walks from the entrance steps up to the base of the cross where the wreath is set in place. With a soldier on either side and a third carrying the wreath, Sherry Atkinson makes that long walk. He is to lay a wreath on behalf of the Royal Canadian Regiment. An amazing array of cameras record his ascent. And when he suddenly stops halfway up, you can almost hear several hundred people take in their breath. But Sherry pauses only a moment before slowly, determinedly, carrying on to the cross's base to place the wreath.

Soon thereafter, Steve calls to the crowd to disperse through the cemetery and asks people to find a place before a headstone of their choice. Having walked twice past every headstone in the cemetery, Emilie Vaughan-Jones stands before the headstone of an unknown soldier who is identified as a Van Doo—same as her great uncle. "It just stood out for me that here was this unknown soldier who was a part of this family that we now associate with," she says later, for that is how the Vaughan-Joneses now think of the Van Doo regiment. "It was very moving to be able to represent him in the name call. The whole experience—to be there and see these fallen soldiers, people we didn't know, and to know that we were there for them—was very moving." Her mother is, of course, standing before Uncle Ephrem's grave.

Don Aitchison faces Robert Osler's grave. Sherry has taken his place at Private Kenneth John Earnshaw's. I have made sure that someone is there for Earl Christie, so that I can serve as a linesman.

Steve starts calling the names. Last names only, one after another. Overhead, a helicopter circles, dropping lower and lower. The wind is howling louder, blasting cooling air through the cemetery. Steve names fallen soldier after fallen soldier. I see Steve MacKinnon virtually running behind Phil Bury and Chris Vaughan-Jones, filming the roll call with his iPad. As each name is called, the person before the headstone calls out. Most Canadian civilians shout, "Here." I hear Emilie's voice ringing clearly through the air when Steve shouts, "Unknown soldier." Our soldiers bark, "Here, Sir!" Italian civilians call out more softly, "*Presente*," whereas their soldiers and Carabinieri bellow the word. When it is my turn to signal the responders, I have to almost run to keep up with Steve's calls, thrusting my hand toward each person as the preceding name is called. It is hard to take much in, but I see tears streaming down the faces of many as they answer on behalf of *their* soldier. Lee Harrison is one of those, weeping freely as he thinks "of the lives and futures that were saved by the sacrifice of those devoted Canadian soldiers on foreign soil." Don says that thinking of Robert Osler and "knowing what I did about his family and his childhood—all that he had given up to serve and how bravely he died trying to save his men—this moved me with sorrow for the waste of war."

And suddenly, it is over. Steve's voice falls silent. The wind continues to blow. The helicopter thrums overhead (we learn later that it was manned by Carabinieri who were filming the event). With Gianni Blasi translating, Steve says, "Thank you for your presence today. I think our men would be very happy that we are all here." There is a spattering of applause, and the ceremony is ended. But people continue to wander among the headstones, looking at them, talking with each other, often embracing. There is a communal reluctance to leave. I meet people who point out the headstone of an uncle or father. Others had fathers who fought in Sicily and came home but mentioned a friend who was among the fallen. They came for that person. Others just came because they felt it was something that needed to be done. This is particularly true for the many Sicilians present.

Phil Bury meets a woman who never met her father, but now has stood before his headstone. He is deeply touched by the Italians who "came forward to ensure that each grave was attended and each name answered." Several of us had noted particularly a young mother who seemed to have come on her own with two small children in tow. They stood together at one headstone and she called out the man's name clearly and sweetly. What brought her?

Bill Rodgers is struck by the sight of civilians and soldiers remembering side by side. "Usually at these things, the soldiers are over there, and the civilians over at another place. There's no interaction. At the end here, the soldiers and civilians were shaking hands and embracing. The tears were mutual. That was different and significant."

Bob Werbiski was thinking about the day he had spoken at Caltagirone about his father and 4th Field Ambulance helping the civilians there. Thinking, too, about how he had never thanked his father for his service, and had carried that guilt inside. Bob had mentioned that regret to Sherry Atkinson back in Caltagirone. After the roll call, Sherry approached him. "He asked me if I had found what I had come looking for. I told him that, in fact, I had. At that moment, we shook hands. It felt like I had been talking to my father."

Slowly, the cemetery empties. Most of the marchers go down to the edge of the cemetery, where there is some grass under the shade of a couple of pine trees. The wind still blows. Maple Leafs snap hard in the wind. Buses are loading and departing. Carabinieri are directing traffic. We agree to let the crowds disperse before going to our cars. There is no need to rush. Except for the Seaforth Highlanders concert this evening in Agira, we have finished this mission. So we lie on the grass and talk or just sit in companionable silence. Later, I will not be able to recall who was there and who wasn't. I just remember voices, intermixed with silence, and the ever-constant wind. The gentle warmth of the day that was so unlike any other we had experienced. A sense of completion, and a sense of loss. For "we few, we happy few" had come to the end of an always-to-be-remembered journey.

LATE THAT AFTERNOON, we assemble in Agira for a remembrance ceremony at the town's war memorial, which is in a square near the mountain community's summit. The square is bursting with people, and the crowd spills down the steep streets leading to it. At the base of the memorial stand all the markers that Steve had hastily cobbled together at the lumberyard a few days before to fulfill the wishes of the Agira *sindaco* that a set of markers memorialize the Sicilian citizens killed during the war. As the short ceremony there draws to an end, the sun sets.

We descend in a mass parade, led by the *sindaco*, to Agira's main square, which is dominated at one end by the towering and ornately decorated front of the Chiesa Sant'Antonio di Padova. The church was built in 1505, expanded in 1567, and added to again in 1680 with the raising of the impressive belfry that stands to the right. The belfry's pinnacle is elaborately adorned with a mosaic of coloured tiles. Normally, this square is choked with parked cars, but tonight they've all been cleared out, and the square fills with more than a thousand people. A large spotlighted stage has been erected before the church. Every balcony overlooking the square is clogged with people. On one, I see Max Fraser standing behind a camera on a tripod. The rest of his team are scattered about, with Arlin and Oliver onstage. Several camera crews from Italian and Sicilian news agencies are there, and the TLN team is also shooting footage.

This evening, history is to be relived, as the fifteen-strong Seaforth Highlanders pipe band performs precisely the same music in the same place and at the same time as its predecessors did on July 30, 1943. Bill Rodgers, Terry Dolan, Frances, and I snag a table outside at one of the square's copious bars and cafés. It promises to be a long evening, so we are happy to rest weary legs rather than be stuck standing.

Previously, our town ceremonies have been held roughly at 11:00 a.m. to adhere to the tradition of Remembrance Day, but tonight's is

a greatly expanded program, which begins with the local band playing the Italian and Canadian national anthems. We stand for both
and are pleased to be able to sing the verses of the Italian anthem
with fair competence. Then the speeches begin, and the list is long. I
pay little attention to the Canadian and Sicilian politicians. Neither
do most of the Sicilians in the crowd, preferring instead to greet and
chat with friends and relatives. When Steve takes the microphone,
the crowd's attention sharpens. Throughout the speeches, Gianni
Blasi, a major Italian supporter of Op Husky, acts as master of ceremonies and provides the necessary translations. He is dressed like
us in white shirt and red ball cap rather than something formal.
When the politicians are done and before he introduces Steve, Gianni
looks back at him and then turns to the crowd: "I must say this
before I introduce you. Today, I saw the completion of this incredible
adventure, and for one moment I saw tears coming down from your
eyes, Mr. Steve Gregory."

"I have to tell you why we undertook this project called Operation
Husky 2013," Steve begins. As he describes Erik's history project, a
single bell in the church's belfry tolls loudly. Steve tells them there
was little information on the Canadian role in the Sicilian campaign,
that in most books on World War II, it was a footnote. "But the truth
is, 25,000 Canadian soldiers fought here. In total, 100,000 fought
here and in Italy. Five hundred and sixty-two dead, 2,310 wounded
here in Sicily," he says, thrusting a finger toward the ground. "In all
of Italy, nearly 6,000 dead. Men like many of you—farmers, fishermen, doctors, lawyers, shoemakers—many of them had never heard
of Sicily before they stepped foot on your shores. But they fought for
something that is precious to all of us. They fought for peace and liberty. Their blood is in your fields. Despite this effort and sacrifice,
most Canadians today—my *paysans*—don't know anything about
our role in your country. So our project was grand."

Steve holds up one of the markers. "Throughout Sicily where our
men fell, we left markers like this, one for each of the fallen soldiers."
He touches the Italian flag that adorns each marker and explains
that it's there because "we believe that our soldiers, just like the men
and women in front of you here, would be of two minds. They'd be

very happy they won your freedom and liberty, but deeply saddened by the loss of civilian life they witnessed. Our project believes it is our responsibility as citizens to remember those people, those other casualties of the tragic circumstances of that war. At the memorial at the end of this street, you'll notice dozens of these markers for the citizens of Agira who perished during that horrible time.

"No one can speak better of that time than someone who was there," he finishes, as he introduces "Lieutenant Sheridan Atkinson, ninety-one years of age, who fought for your freedom."

The applause is rapturous as Sherry takes the microphone. "Wow," he says while extending his hands to acknowledge the large crowd. "No speech," Sherry declares. "This morning I had a heavy heart. This day our dead soldiers spoke to me, and they spoke to me because I have bled on your earth. Their message was: 'No more war.'" He leads the crowd in a chant of "No more war!"

After more than an hour, the speeches are over. Steve steps to the microphone and calls out, "Pipe Major, let's bring on the concert."

Immediately, black-and-white footage of the 1943 Seaforth concert shot by a Canadian army photographer floods across the entire church wall. On the opposite side of the square comes the beat of drums and skirl of bagpipes from the live band, as Peter Stursberg's voice in the film carries across the square from the onstage speakers. When his report ends, the Seaforths come forward and take the stage for their concert. For the band members, this is a long-anticipated moment finally arrived, but for nobody more so than Pipe Major Mike Bain. As a young cadet, Bain had been taught to play the pipes by Pipe Major Ed Esson, who had led the band through World War II. Even then, Bain "had a dream to take a band back to Agira to recreate that piece of history." After the concert, Bain says that "it was a great honour to march the pipes and drums into that square just like Ed Esson did seventy years ago. We were able to share the experience with older citizens who remembered that first concert. To march on the same street playing the same version of 'Caber Feidh' from 1943, with the bells from the Church of Sant'Antonio ringing, and the voice of Peter Stursberg again announcing the Seaforth Pipes and Drums, was an honour that will not be forgotten."

Peter Stursberg was a CBC war correspondent who had carefully scripted the original performance in order to record it. Having rushed in a jeep to Agira from another part of the front lines, Stursberg and his sound assistant, Paul Johnson, brought with them only the most basic recording equipment, a single vinyl turntable—which meant no second takes were possible, and the recording could not be edited later. So Esson had to ensure that the band played on cue. And so, too, must the priests "in their shabby black robes," as Stursberg later wrote in his memoir *The Sound of War*, ring the church bells only when signalled to do so.

And as he readied to give the signals, Stursberg launched into a broadcast that was the first to come out of Sicily or any other part of Hitler's Fortress Europe. "I am standing on the steps of the ancient church in the main square of Agira. Directly in front of me is the pipe band of the Seaforth Highlanders, which is going to give a concert. Besides hundreds of townspeople there are scores of Canadian soldiers perched on the top of carriers and trucks parked near the church. At the end of the street, over there, you can look across the yellow, sunburned valley and see the hills where the Germans are. You can see the smoke of battle as well, and hear the rumble of the guns. The bells of the old church are going to ring out before the pipers begin playing. And there they are ringing now, the church bells of Agira. And now the band under Pipe Major Edmund Esson of Vancouver," and the band began playing.

Correspondents in World War II embellished sometimes. From where Stursberg stood, it is impossible to see the countryside beyond Agira, and it was also dusk. But others who were there confirm that artillery could be heard firing in the distance, and everybody knew that out toward Regalbuto, Canadian troops were fighting and dying even as this concert of victory unfolded.

Tonight, as the Seaforth Pipes and Drums march toward the stage, there is also a sense of victory in the air. "What mattered to me," Phil Bury says, "was the notion that the original was done within the sounds of the guns and was an act at once of sorrow, triumph, and defiance. We were depicting that, and perhaps reliving it. I was touched again by the number of Canadians and by the size and enthusiasm of the Italian crowd." Pipe Sergeant Vern Kennedy leads the band onto the stage for the rest of the performance. "I brought Ed Esson's pipes back to Sicily and played in that same square he played in seventy years ago. The feeling is unbelievable," he recounts later. The concert is stunning, and throughout most of it, the black-and-white film of the original is also running. The effect is hauntingly beautiful.

"It still lifts up the hair on my arms," Arlin McFarlane wrote months afterward. She was onstage, practically under the feet of the band, videotaping them. "Whenever time folds back on itself, and events are held on top of other previous events, I am engaged more deeply. The re-creation of the past is not just occurring in my imagination, it is occurring in public, and lots of other people are there and it has weight and significance. I loved that the original film of the Seaforths was projected onto the church wall. It was ghostly and moving. And then when the bagpipes started in the dark, it was like the past walking into the present."

And it is like that. Mixed up in the middle of the great teeming crowd of Canadians and Sicilians, soldiers and civilians, marchers and watchers, I find it impossible not to look around and imagine ghosts of those soldiers and civilians past, even as glimpses of them appear on the church wall. I think of the Seaforth's regimental history. The pipers and drummers did not fight on the front lines, but they had spent much of the past weeks acting as "mule skinners," leading cantankerous animals drafted into service in carrying supplies up to the leading troops. Sometime on that July 30, one of the Seaforth's senior officers, perhaps Lieutenant Colonel Bert Hoffmeister himself, had commented to Esson that it was "too bad you don't have your instruments with you." Esson replied, "We do. We put them on the boat with us!" And so the performance was ordered.

The band had not rehearsed in weeks. Sicily's dry heat had wreaked havoc with the pipe and drum settings and tensions. But when they began to play, the Seaforth regimental historian later wrote, "the shrill cry of those Scots tunes never sounded sweeter than in that ancient town. There was pride in every piece, and defiance in every note. There would be times, later, when the pipes would again sound their tunes of glory, but there was something about that 'Retreat' played in Agira which could be remembered with particular poignancy by all who were there to hear it."

It is, I decide, the same this evening seventy years on. And I can think of no more fitting finale to Operation Husky 2013 then this triumphant moment.

IN THE AFTERMATH, Agira cemetery calls some of us back to walk singly or in small groups among the headstones. Although the spectacle of the cemetery filled with people remains vivid in my memory, the memories of the times I have been here either alone or with Frances at my side seem more natural. These are times for reflection. Some people say that all this remembrance—even the ceremonies on Remembrance Day—glorifies war and denies its brutal consequences. I do not believe this. We who choose to perform acts of remembrance fully recognize the costs of war, and are less likely to beat the drum for war when governments urge their people toward entering into one. The costs of war—the losses of civilian and military lives—are foremost in our thoughts and hearts. For those of us who walked more than three hundred kilometres in the footsteps of our Canadian soldiers during that July in 2013, every Remembrance Day thereafter will be enriched for doing so. As Steve said before the pipes and drums began to play, we did something "grand." Like old soldiers, those of us who were there and shared that experience will always cherish the memory. We band of brothers.

Acknowledgements

O PERATION HUSKY 2013 was a one-of-a-kind event that needed the involvement of far too many people than I can possibly thank here. They know who they are. Without them, the venture, and consequently this book, would never have come to be. There are, of course, some people who require specific mention. Steve Gregory, Op Husky was your baby, and from the beginning, you also supported the idea of my writing a book about our adventure. "Viva il Gregory!" as somebody shouted during one ceremony. My fellow marchers, without you, there would have been no story worth telling, and I value our lasting collective friendship. Thanks also to the good number of participants in Op Husky who took the time to respond to my after-action questionnaires with their memories of events and thoughts on the meaning of remembrance. Your responses greatly enriched the narrative.

While I was writing this book, Sherry and Susan Atkinson were always quick to answer questions and share memories and photos. Sherry, you really were our "veteran star." Having veteran Bob Wigmore join us in the latter stage of the journey was also a great boon. Sadly, Bob passed away on June 4, 2015, as this book was nearly going to press. He was ninety-three.

Also sharing photos for use in the book were Don Aitchison, Bill Rodgers, Rod Hoffmeister, Terry Dolan, Steven MacKinnnon, and the Vaughan-Jones family. The last named also took time to spend a couple of hours one afternoon in Tsawwassen sharing their stories of Op Husky with me, because they had often been in one place and I in another.

There are, again, too many Italians and Sicilians who were involved to name them all. But Rosalba and Enza Scifo, Gaetano Catalano, Gianni Blasi, and Paolo Sbarbada deserve special mention. Rosie and Enza, you were always there just when we needed you.

A special thanks to Max Fraser and Arlin McFarlane for providing rides and being such good company. We'll do that Yukon River canoe trip one of these years.

Much of the material relating to Commonwealth War Graves Commission cemetery and memorial design, its operations, and history came from face-to-face interviews I conducted in 2014 with Ian Hussein, CWGC director of the Western Europe Area in Ypres, Belgium, and with headstone production manager Alan Jarvis and horticultural sector supervisor Julian Blake at the Beaurains Factory outside Arras. From the CWGC Mediterranean office in Cyprus, Eleni Photi provided much specific information on the history and design of the Agira Canadian War Cemetery.

The writing of this book was made possible by grants from the British Columbia Arts Council and the Access Copyright Foundation.

I was again fortunate to have Kathy Vanderlinden step in as my editor. This was a challenging book to write, and her deft editorial touch and understanding of what I was about were invaluable. The same can be said for copyeditor Merrie-Ellen Wilcox. The three of us make a good team. Speaking of reliable team members, Stuart Daniel was again on hand to provide the maps showing the routes the soldiers took in 1943 and our route seventy years later. Don Aitchison, without your screen shots of the smartphone app mapping our path, Stuart would have had little to work from, so thank you for being so technologically savvy.

On another once-again note, I am grateful to my agent, Carolyn Swayze, for helping to shepherd these books through contract negotiations and other business essentials, so that I can focus on the creative tasks.

One marcher deserves special mention. For me, the experience of Op Husky 2013 would have been notably less remarkable and pleasurable had my partner in life, Frances Backhouse, not set aside some misgivings to join me in this wild plan to walk across Sicily under a blazing sun.

THE CANADIAN BATTLE SERIES*

Forgotten Victory: First Canadian Army and the Cruel Winter of 1944–45

Tragedy at Dieppe: Operation Jubilee, August 19, 1942

Breakout from Juno: First Canadian Army and the Normandy Campaign, July 4–August 21, 1944

On to Victory: The Canadian Liberation of the Netherlands, March 23–May 5, 1945

Operation Husky: The Canadian Invasion of Sicily, July 10–August 7, 1943

Terrible Victory: First Canadian Army and the Scheldt Estuary Campaign, September 13–November 6, 1944

Holding Juno: Canada's Heroic Defence of the D-Day Beaches, June 7–12, 1944

Juno Beach: Canada's D-Day Victory, June 6, 1944

The Gothic Line: Canada's Month of Hell in World War II Italy

The Liri Valley: Canada's World War II Breakthrough to Rome

Ortona: Canada's Epic World War II Battle

OTHER MILITARY HISTORY BOOKS BY MARK ZUEHLKE

---

*The Canadian Military Atlas: Four Centuries of Conflict from New France to Kosovo (with C. Stuart Daniel)**

Brave Battalion: The Remarkable Saga of the 16th Battalion (Canadian Scottish) in the First World War

The Gallant Cause: Canadians in the Spanish Civil War, 1936–1939

For Honour's Sake: The War of 1812 and the Brokering of an Uneasy Peace

Ortona Street Fight

Assault on Juno

*Available from Douglas & McIntyre

INDEX

PLACES, UNITS, BIOGRAPHICAL NAMES, AND SELECTED TERMS

Due to the nature of this book, many historical figures, places, and units important to the World War II invasion of Sicily are not mentioned. Readers seeking the definitive history of Canada's involvement in the invasion should additionally turn to my *Operation Husky: The Canadian Invasion of Sicily, July 10–August 7, 1943.*

MARK ZUEHLKE IS the award-winning author of the critically acclaimed Canadian Battle Series—the most extensive published account of the battle experiences of Canada's Army in World War II. The series is also the most exhaustive recounting of the battles and campaigns fought by any nation during that war to have been written by a single author. In 2014, he won the Governor General's Award for Popular History, called the Pierre Berton Award, in recognition of his work on this series and in other ways to popularize Canadian history. In 2006, the Canadian Battle Series title *Holding Juno: Canada's Heroic Defence of the D-Day Beaches* won the City of Victoria Butler Book Prize. Of his other six historical works, *For Honour's Sake: The War of 1812 and the Brokering of an Uneasy Peace* won the 2007 Canadian Author's Association Lela Common Award for Canadian History.

Recently, Zuehlke has turned his hand to graphic novels, working with Renegade Arts on a number of projects based on Canadian history. In 2012, he was the co-author of *The Loxleys and the War of 1812* and also wrote the script for the sequel, *The Loxleys and Confederation.* Also a novelist, he is the author of the popular Elias McCann series, the first of which, *Hands Like Clouds,* won the 2000 Crime Writers of Canada Arthur Ellis Award for Best First Novel.

Zuehlke has always been a keen walker, a practice that proved useful when he joined Operation Husky 2013 both to march in the footsteps taken by 1st Canadian Infantry Division soldiers in 1943 and to chronicle the experience in this book. He lives in Victoria with his partner Frances Backhouse, who is also a prize-winning author and was a fellow Op Husky marcher. Currently, he is working on the next Canadian Battle Series book, which will detail First Canadian Army's advance out of Normandy and through the Channel Ports Campaign. On the Internet, Zuehlke can be found at www.zuehlke.ca and www.facebook.com/Canadian Battle Series.